HALICARNASSIAN STUDIES V

General Editor: Poul Pedersen

HALICARNASSIAN STUDIES V

Edited by
Poul Pedersen

University Press of Southern Denmark
2008

© The authors and University Press of Southern Denmark 2008
Printed by Narayana Press
ISBN 978-87-7674-293-5
Cover Illustration: The Torba Monastery 1977 (Photo: Poul Pedersen)

Published with support from:
The Danish Research Council for the Humanities
The New Carlsberg Foundation
The Novo Nordisk Foundation
The Faculty of Humanities at the University of Southern Denmark

Address: Halicarnassian Studies, Department of Greek and Roman Studies,
University of Southern Denmark, Campusvej 55, DK-5230 Odense M, Denmark,

Distribution:
University Press of Southern Denmark
Campusvej 55
DK-5230 Odense M
Phone: +45 6615 7999
Fax: +45 6615 8126
Press@forlag.sdu.dk
www.universitypress.dk

Distribution in the United States and Canada:
International Specialized Book Services
920 NE 58th Ave. Suite 300
Portland, OR 97213
www.isbs.com

Table of contents

Preface 7

Aykut Özet
Excavations in the Torba Monastery 9

Bahadir Berkaya and Poul Pedersen
Bozdağ – an ancient town and
marble quarry near Myndos on
the Halikarnassos Peninsula 43

Anne Marie Carstens
Tombs of the Halikarnassos Peninsula
– The Late Bronze and Early Iron Age 52

Sisse Stine Hansen
Hellenistic Totenmahl reliefs from
the Halikarnassos Peninsula 119

Bahadir Berkaya, Signe Isager and Poul Pedersen
The Stadion of Ancient Halikarnassos 137

Preface

Halicarnassian Studies vol. V is not devoted to one specific theme, as was the case with the previous volumes. Following another aim of this series, the content of this volume is composed of a number of very different contributions on excavations, archaeological research and archaeological studies in the Halikarnassos region – studies that are not directly connected to the research programmes of the Danish Halikarnassos Project.

The book begins with a report by former General Director of Antiquities and Second director of Bodrum Museum of Underwater Archaeology, dr. Aykut Özet on the excavations carried out on behalf of Bodrum Museum at the fascinating early Byzantine site at Torba on the northern shore of the Halikarnassos Peninsula. It is a unique building complex consisting of a mausoleum or chapel, a large basilica, a bath, a "bishop's house" and a large, strange cistern, which surprisingly has remains of floor mosaics. The small Byzantine centre had its own little harbour with a quay running in front of the buildings, and visitors and pilgrims coming by ship would be landed directly in the centre of the site. The Byzantine complex at Torba was excavated under the direction of Dr. Aykut Özet in 2000.

Next follows a brief report of some observations concerning the site of "Bozdağ" on the westernmost part of the Halikarnassos Peninsula south of the important ancient city of Myndos. At this site archaeologist Bahadir Berkaya, along with other members of the staff of Bodrum Museum of Underwater Archaeology, discovered remains of an ancient marble quarry about 10 years ago, and short visits to the site were made again in 1999 and 2004 with members of the Danish team. Earlier travellers have visited Bozdağ and reported on the small, fortified settlement on the summit of the hill and speculated on its possible identification as "Old Myndos". Surprisingly, the marble quarry does not seem to have been noticed before – or perhaps it was believed to be an open mine for silver ore, since the Bozdağ mountain is known to have delivered ore for the silver production, which once gave Myndos its modern name "Gümüşlük".

Dr. Anne Marie Carstens (University of Copenhagen) has worked extensively on the tombs on the Halikarnassos Peninsula, and they were also the subject of her Ph.d. dissertation from 1999 called "Death matters. Funerary Architecture on the Halikarnassos Peninsula". She has already published several articles related to the subject. Her study of the tombs from the late Bronze Age and early Iron Age is published here as the third article of the volume. It is based both on her extensive field studies and on the results of her dissertation.

The so-called "Totenmahl reliefs" are one of the most widespread types of tomb reliefs from the Hellenistic era, although they are not as numerous in Central and South-Western Asia Minor as on the islands and in the cities along the Marmara Sea and the Bosporus strait. Five reliefs of this type are known from the Halikarnassos Peninsula. Sisse Hansen (University of Southern Denmark) has taken a close look on these and analysed the iconographic details in an attempt to determine whether they represent a particular local workshop or are more likely to have been produced at one of the more well-known production centres.

Like other large Hellenistic-Roman cities, Halikarnassos had its gymnasion, theatre and stadion. The stadion of Halikarnassos was discovered during a rescue excavation carried out by Bodrum Museum of Underwater Archaeology in 1987, but unfortunately it had to be covered up again immediately after the excavation. The excavation was carried out under the direction of Bahadir Berkaya, who publishes a brief report of the discovery in cooperation with Poul Pedersen and Signe Isager from the University of Southern Denmark.

The editor of this volume owes great gratitude to a number of persons and institutions who made this volume possible. First among these, the authors must be thanked for their contributions and for their patience, as it has taken quite a long time from the first contributions for this volume were received until the last articles were ready for print. Furthermore, I am extremely grateful to the succeeding directors of Bodrum Museum, Oğuz Alpözen and Yaşar Yildiz for their permission and generous support and to the staff at Bodrum Museum in general for their never-failing help and assistance. Work carried out by Bodrum Museum alone or in cooperation with members of the Danish team constitutes the basis of a large part of the work published in this volume. Thanks are also due to Associate Professor Birte Poulsen for good advice and to Kirsten Dige Larsen, Thorleif Christiansen, Patricia Lunddahl and Elisabeth Hedegaard Kristiansen for valuable help and assistance.

The production of this volume was made possible by the financial support of the Danish Research Council for the Humanities, the Novo Nordisk Foundation, the New Carlsberg Foundation and the Faculty of Humanities at the University of Southern Denmark. To all of these I would like to express my special thanks.

Poul Pedersen
University of Southern Denmark

Excavations in the Torba Monastery

Aykut Özet

At the beginning of April 2000 excavations began at the east end of Torba village, located in the northeast of the Bodrum peninsula, on the site known by local people as Manastır (Monastery) (fig. 1). The excavation team under my direction consisted of archaeologists Aynur Özet, Gürşans Uzala and Kudret Ata.[1] Architect Şule Atukeren and interior architect Mustafa Betin, who made the fastidious plans of the excavated areas and buildings, and technician Yasin Tekin, who drew the mosaics, joined our team for short periods. Dilek Gogo, student of archaeology, and Gamze Örgev and Meriç Coşkun, students at the Ceramic Department at Mimar Sinan University, made the drawings of the small objects.

All excavation expenses were covered by the landowner, Erdal Kesici, who is planning to build villas around the historical buildings. Mr. Kesici has declared that he will also support the restoration and

Fig. 1. *The ruins at Torba from the west before the excavations of 2000. The silted-up harbour can be seen in the foreground (1995).*

Fig. 2. Plan of the ruins at Torba (1:1000).

conservation of the monuments, so that this important historical site can be protected together with its surroundings.

The complex of early Byzantine structures at Torba consists of a small harbour and five buildings (fig. 2): a mausoleum, a large house (Structure B), which had more than one storey, and may have been the home of the bishop, a bath-building (Structure C), a large basilica (Structure D) and a large cistern (Structure E). The walls of the bishop's house and the basilica in particular are very poorly preserved, but all five structures have remains of mosaic floors.

The monastery Port

A ruined breakwater running east-west is visible approximately 7-8 m from the shore in front of the structures of the Torba Monastery. Its connection to the shore to the east is clearly determined, and it is also possible to see where the line of the other breakwater meets the shore; here it consists of large stones. This small port presumably served to protect the ships of the first Christians from the waves and the sea during the 4th-6th centuries AD (fig. 3).

Fig. 4. The Mausoleum (1977).

is a large apse at the back of this rectangular structure, and the only entrance is situated on the front side of the building, facing towards the northwest (figs. 4, 5, 6, 7).

Fig. 3. The breakwater (2000).

Chapel-Mausoleum (Structure A)

Of the buildings of the Torba monastery, the chapel is the one closest to the sea, and the first building one meets when arriving at the little harbour by ship.

The chapel is orientated northwest-southeast and placed north of the other monastery structures, and it is 12.81 m long, 6.88 m wide and 8.24 m high. There

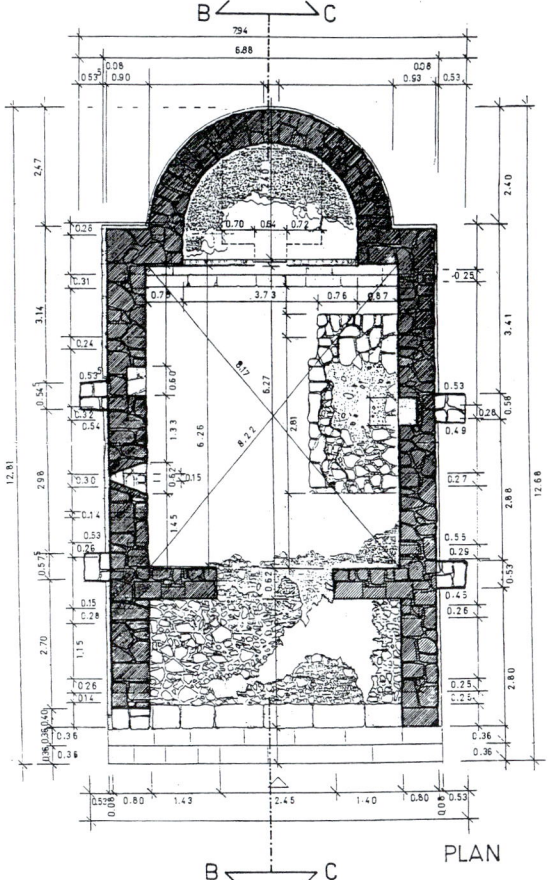

Fig. 5. The Mausoleum. Plan.

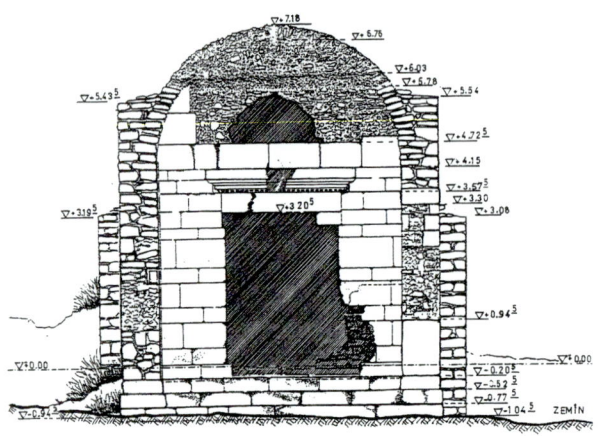

Fig. 6. The Mausoleum. Front.

Fig. 8. The Mausoleum. Re-used ashlar in the northern anta. The underside has cutting for a dovetail clamp from its earlier use (2005).

The chapel's plan can be described as a *templum in antis*. It is accessible by three crepis steps on the front side. Originally there must have been two columns between the anta walls, but neither of these is preserved. However, a large part of a marble column is found in front of the building, and it may have belonged to the chapel. The main part of the structure is built of rubble and mortar, but the front side of the chapel and the two antae were originally faced with rectangular, bluish ashlars of marble (or limestone) arranged as isodomic ashlar masonry. A large number of these blocks are still in their original position. A few clamp-holes on the front and underside of some of these blocks indicate that they were probably re-utilized from some earlier structure (fig. 8). The chapel is entered through a door about 2.45 m in width.

Above the doorway there is a large lintel of marble, like an architrave with two fasciae, carrying a very mutilated cornice (fig. 9). The lintel is broken near its left side, and only one of the two trapezoidal blocks that originally supported this large beam of marble is preserved in place. Above the lintel of the door there is a

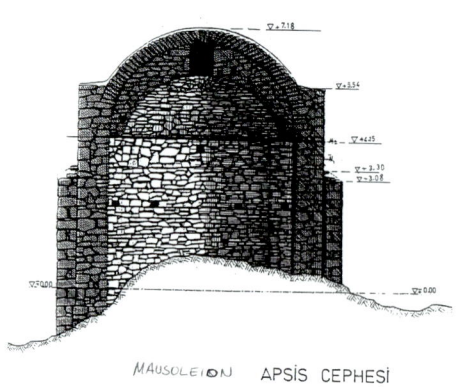

Fig. 7. The Mausoleum. Back side with apse.

Fig. 9. The Mausoleum. Lintel and cornice above the entrance (2005).

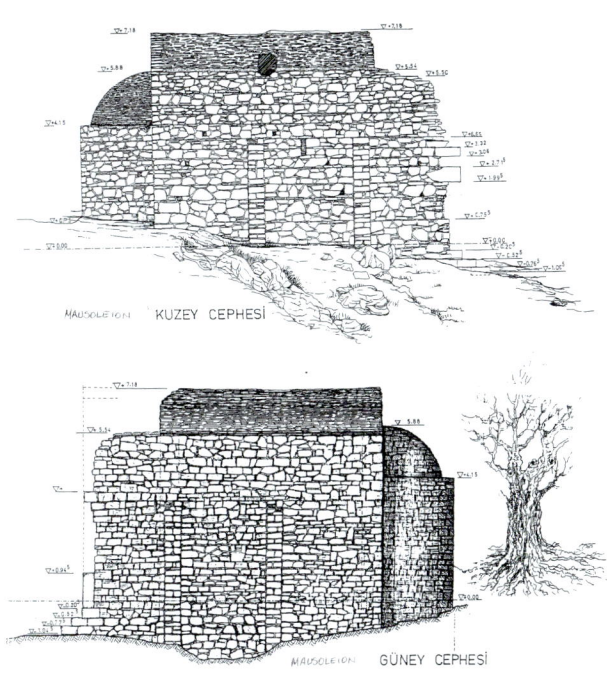

Fig. 10. The Mausoleum. The south side and the north side.

Fig. 11. The Mausoleum. The south side (2005).

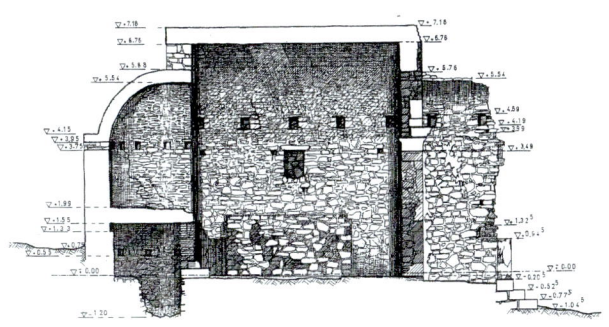

Fig. 12. The Mausoleum. Longitudinal section showing south side of the structure.

slightly longer piece of cornice, which is also carefully placed on the axis of the door. This cornice is quite heavily damaged, but clearly the upper part is a geison, which is supported from below by a row of dentils. The central part of the cornice-block is missing and it may originally have been made up of two sections. The ashlar facing is missing on the uppermost part of the wall, but an opening in the rubble mortar wall behind suggests that there was a semicircular window opening here. The façade of this chapel as well as its plan suggests inspiration from small temples and grave structures of more ancient times.

The roof of the chapel consists of a vault, severely damaged but still in place, and constructed of rubble and lime mortar like the rest of the building. The two longer walls of the chapel were strengthened on the outside by two large buttresses (figs. 10, 11).

The interior of the main room of the chapel is 8.5 m long including the apse, and 5.25 m wide (fig. 12). Along the south side of the room there is a podium constructed of fieldstones. It measures 3.60 m in length, 1.75 m in width and 1.75 in height and is evidently not part of the original layout, as it rests on the mosaic floor of the main room. There are five sockets for crossbeams on each of the long inner walls of the structure. Just below these there is one blind window or niche in the south wall, and in the north wall there are two windows, one of which is blind. Two sockets for crossbeams are seen on the inside of each of the side walls of the "pronaos", and in the apse there are eight sockets of different sizes for crossbeams, and one small central window. The height of the apse is 5.88 m on the outside including the roof, while the inside is 4 m high and 4 m wide. The apse has a crypt with a centrally placed door leading to the main room (figs. 13, 14). The floor of the crypt is below the floor level of the main room of the chapel and is

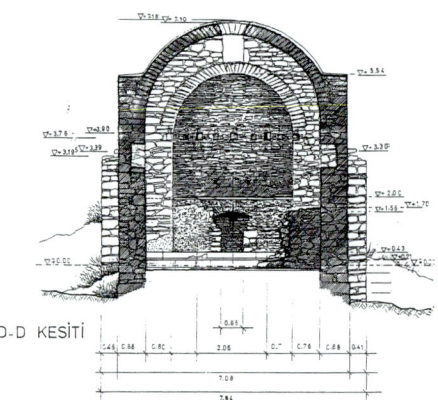

Fig. 13. The Mausoleum. Section. View towards the apse and the crypt.

Fig. 15. The Mausoleum. Marble steps in front of the apse. In the background to the right can be seen the platform which was constructed on the existing mosaic floor (2005).

Fig. 14. The Mausoleum. Photo showing the apse and the crypt from the main hall (2005)

Fig. 16. The Mausoleum. Coarse mosaic on top of the crypt (2005).

reached by two marble steps (fig. 15). Three different floor levels could be determined inside the crypt. The roof of the crypt consists of a vaulting, which reaches a height of 1.57 m above the floor of the chapel. The horizontal upper surface of this vaulting constitutes the floor of the apse. It is approximately 2 m above the floor of the chapel, and it has some remains of a mosaic of rather coarse technique (fig. 16).

Fig. 17. The Mausoleum. Mosaic with floral tendrils. The entrance is to the right (1977).

Fig. 18. The Mausoleum. Corner of the outer border of the mosaic showing floral tendrils growing out of a cantharos (1977).

Most of the mosaic floor of the chapel is destroyed, and in the southernmost part of the room it is hidden under the great podium constructed here at some unknown period. However, part of the outer borders has been preserved. The mosaic is surrounded by a band consisting of white tesserae decorated with rosettes and limited by a dark line. Inside of this follows a border decorated with vine tendrils (figs. 17, 18, Pl. I, A). The tendrils come out of cantharoi depicted in the corners of the room, and there are bunches of grapes, ivy leaves and vine tendrils. This border is followed by a wave crest border (or "stepped pyramid"), inside of which there are remains of a band decorated with a meander motive. According to people who saw this building many years ago, there was once a picture of a dolphin on the floor. The floor mosaic consists of white, black, red and brown tesserae.

As Vincenzo Ruggieri suggested after his research in the region, the structure is possibly a mausoleum. The architectural members inside the building and above the door indicate that the date of the original structure might be as early as the 2nd century AD.[2] It is clear, however, that at a later date the function of the structure changed, and from then on it was used as a chapel, serving religious purposes. The architectural character of the building and the mosaic floors inside show that the secondary usage should be dated to the late-Antique period (the 4th-5th centuries AD).

Unfortunately, most of the marble blocks from the buildings of the Torba monastery have been transformed to lime in a lime-kiln situated close to the south wall of the chapel. The excavations at Torba first started with the cleaning of this lime-kiln on April 11, 2000. The lime-kiln has an almost circular plan, and the outer diameter is between 4.20 and 3.10 m, while the inner diameter is unknown. The height is nearly 2 m. The outer face of the kiln was constructed in dry wall technique, and some remains of plaster are preserved on the inner face. The kiln has an opening facing southwest. The interior of the kiln was cleared to its bottom, where some burned fragments of marble pieces were found.

Fig. 19. Structure B, "The Bishop's House", from the north before excavation (1995).

Fig. 20. "The Bishop's House" after excavation (2000).

Bishop's House (Structure B)

The first building to be excavated in the Torba monastery complex was Structure B (figs. 19, 20). The northwest wall of this structure is almost 20 m long and 3.4 m high, and it has a large window- opening in the middle. The excavation mainly consisted of cleaning and removing debris from the ruined walls and the ceiling of the building, and when this was done, it could be established that Structure B is 22.26 m long and 16.42 m wide. The back wall of the central part of Structure B towards the southeast was reinforced by buttresses.

The building was originally a two-storey rectangular structure, placed in a northeast-southwest direction, with one long side facing the sea and the harbour in front of it. It could be determined that there are 13 rooms in the lower storey (fig. 21).

Entrance space
A doorstep, which was found in situ, proves that the main entrance to the building was from the short, poorly preserved southwest side. After passing over the 1 m long and 0.62 m wide stone doorstep, one enters a rectangular hall.

Room B II
The rectangular hall is 12 m long and 4 m wide. It is entered from the north by an intermediary door to the room at the northern side. On the west side of the structure there is a door and a high, wide window facing the small harbour. Some doorsteps that were uncovered in the debris probably fell from the upper storey as this collapsed, probably due to an earthquake. Two round kilns have been revealed in this area. Some sherds and ashes were uncovered inside the kilns, the sides of which were covered by terracotta plaques. This type of kiln has also been found in earlier houses, and may have served purposes of heating. The floor of the hall is covered with terracotta plaques and its walls show remains of plaster. Some mosaic fragments found in the hall must have fallen from the upper storey. A large number of roof tiles, rubble, and a long terracotta spout with grooves on

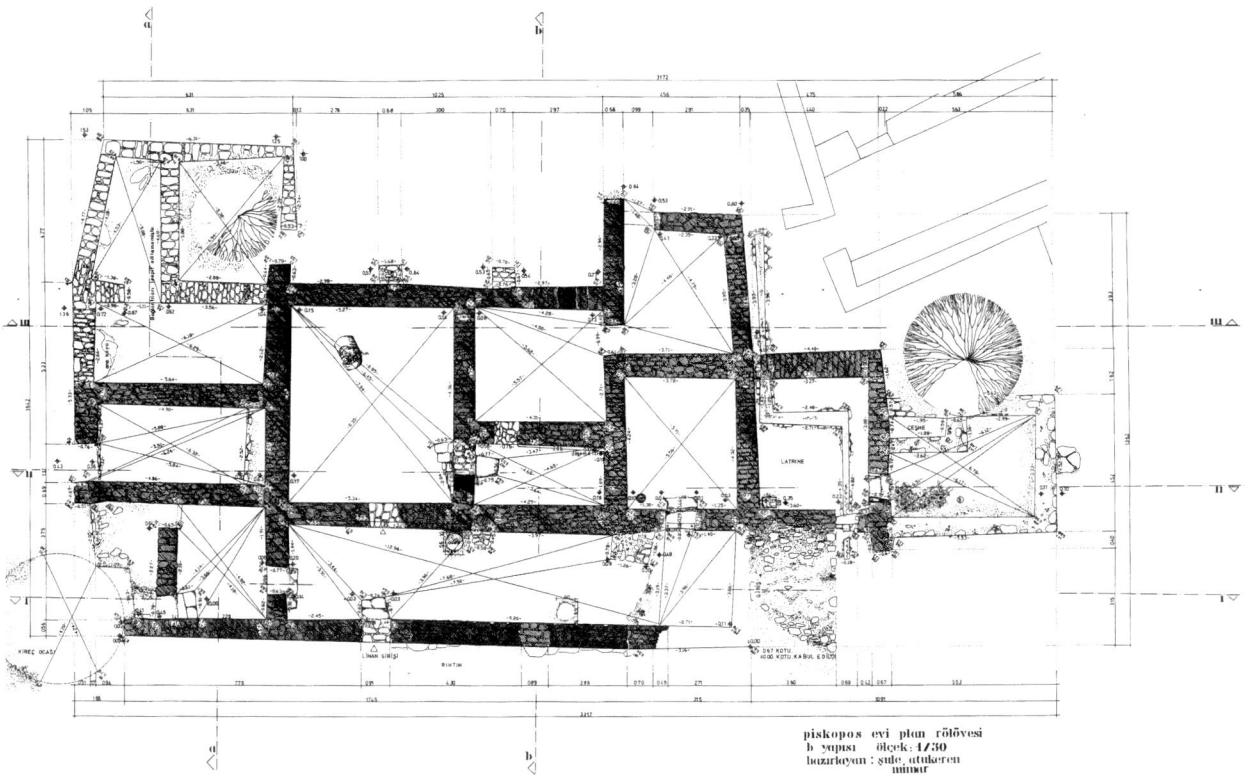

Fig. 21. Plan of the "Bishop's House".

18 *Excavations in the Torba Monastery*

Fig. 22. "The Bishop's House". Spout from a roof tile (2000).

Fig. 23. "The Bishop's House". Lamps from Room I (2000).

its exterior face have been uncovered during the excavations[3] (fig. 22). Next to the large window in the middle of the hall there are remains of a stairway that led to the upper storey.

Room B I
Through a 0.86 m wide doorway there is passage from the hall to the room B I to the north. The north wall of room B I has two openings facing the chapel. The room has an almost square plan measuring 3.70 x 3 m. Numerous fragments of mosaics and roof tiles were uncovered during the excavations. The positions of the mosaics show that the ceiling must have collapsed, and the tesserae of the broken mosaics subsequently spread over the room. The mosaics are polychrome and some fragments have vine tendrils and ivy leaves. Small pieces of plaster indicate that the walls were plastered and coloured.

A large amount of coarse pottery and kitchenware was found at the floor level. Among the finds there are one fragment of an oil lamp that has two fish in relief on the discus[4] and another fragment which has a rosette or flower on the discus (fig. 23 and Pl. III, A, B). A terracotta tile carries a stamped inscription (fig. 24). A few red terra sigillata fish-plates of Late Roman date[5] were also unearthed (Pl. III, C, D, E).

Rooms B III and IV
As the excavations in Structure B were extended towards the east, two more rooms, B III and B IV, were uncovered. The two rooms are of almost identical size, and the floor level of both was reached at a depth of 1.1 m. A great number of roof tiles, some sherds, metal nails and coins were found during the excavation of these rooms. One of the four coins that were found here apparently belongs to very early in the 2nd century BC. On the obverse it has the head of a warrior god (Ares?) with the face turned right and wearing a helmet with protecting cheek-piece, while on the reverse there is a wreath and below this the letters KT. This is most probably a coin minted by one of the Carian cities. The other bronze coin has a diameter of 2.5 mm. On the obverse it has two facing figures, and although the surface of the coin is much worn, the persons should probably be identified as Marcus Aurelius and Commodus, and accordingly the coin should be dated to 177-180 AD[6]. One coin of the Byzantine period was also uncovered in this area. It has on one side the head of the emperor and around the head the inscription THEODOSIUS I (only partly visible). On the reverse there is a cross inside a frame, and it should be dated to sometime in the period 408-450 AD.

Fig. 24. "The Bishop's House". Room I. Terracotta tile with stamped inscription (2000).

Room B V
The large room east of the oblong hall has the dimensions 6.63 x 5.50 m. Just above the floor level of this room there was a great quantity of roof tiles, fragments of coarse kitchenware and bases from broken glass goblets. Two coins were found on the floor. In the middle of the room there were two fragments of a broken column. Many oxidised nails were found in the earth. Remains of mortar and plaster could be seen on the east wall.

One of the coins found here has a right-turned emperor head surrounded by the inscription DN ANASTASIUS PP AUG on the obverse. On the reverse there is the letter M in the middle, a cross at the top, and the writing CONS (Constantinopolis coinage) flanked by floral motives on both sides. It can be dated to 491-518 AD. The second coin has a right-turned emperor head with an inscription on the obverse, and the legend VOT-MULT-MTI (?) in a wreath on the reverse. This coin may belong to the emperor Anastasius II, in which case it should be dated to 713-716 AD.

Room B VI
Room B VI is about 4.18 x 4.31 m and has a door opening to the south. The walls still have remains of plaster, and roof tiles, fragments of polychrome mosaic, some pieces of glass, a few pottery sherds, rubble and stones were found in the room. A large number of oxidised nails were uncovered during the excavation, which is clear evidence of some kind of woodwork in the room.

Room B VI a
To the west of room B VI there is a narrow, rectangular room measuring 1.89 x 4.29 m. This room, B VI a, has communicating doors to both room B VI and room B V.

Room B VIII
From room B VI there is access to the room furthest back to the east, room B VIII. It measures 4.40 x 3.50 m and opens through a door in the east wall to the area east of the building. No roof tiles were found in this room, but finds included some rough stones, pottery sherds and a coin, which can be dated to 450-457 AD[7].

Room B VII
The dimensions of the room between B VIII and the main hall are 3.72 x 4.32 m. It has a door that opens to the long hall, and it is entered by one step. There are remains of plaster on the walls, and the floor consists of beaten earth. In the lower levels above the floor there were fragments of mosaic, sherds of coarse pottery and many fragments of roof tiles. The higher levels contained rough stones and rubble.

Room B IX
An irregular room with trapezoid plan was excavated at the rear northeast corner of Structure B. It is about 4.2 m long and one short side is 1.78 m wide, while the other is 2.1 m wide. The floor slopes upwards towards the rear side of the room. As the floor is partly made up of large stones, the room may have served as an open-air court.

Room B XI
The room B XI adjacent to room B IX has the dimensions 3.46 x 3.88 m, and was probably also an open courtyard. It could only be reached through a door in the southwest wall leading to the open area east of building B. Room B XI may have been a later addition to the structure.

Room B X (latrine)
Room B X is an independent structure built against the walls of structure B. It has a water channel, which enters the room through its southeast wall, and a round evacuation is visible in the northwest side of the room. These installations identify the room as a "latrine". The room has a door in the western side, and opens to the harbour-pier and to the stairway leading to the next room, B XII to the southwest.

A copper pitcher with handle was found in room B X (fig. 25 and Pl. IV, A). It has a tall neck, and the handle is attached to the neck with a flat band hoop. The handle consists of two parts, and a piece of chain is attached to the upper part. A copper jug similar to the one from room B X was found in the "Yassiada" Roman shipwreck excavation and is dated to the 4th century AD. The upper part of the Yassiada pitcher is broken, but the form and dimensions of the lower part of the body are similar to our example.[8]

Fig. 25. "The Bishop's House". Copper pitcher from Room X (2000).

Fig. 26. "The Bishop's House". Mosaic in Room XII (2000).

Room B XII
Room B XII is 4.90 x 3.32 m and is located just opposite the northern corner of the great church. There is a fountain in the eastern corner of the room, and along the north wall there are some remains of a polychrome mosaic floor, which can be reached by a few steps. A large olive tree has destroyed a large part of the mosaic. The decoration of the mosaic consisted of a regular pattern of lotus flowers (fig. 26 and Pl. I, B).[9] Similar mosaic floors have been found in Halikarnassos and Iasos.

Fig. 27. Structure C, the Baths, from south-west (2005).

The purpose of Structure B
Structure B was probably used as the Bishop's home, and it may also have served as a meeting place for the priests and as accommodation for important visitors to the sacred buildings at Torba. The building is conveniently situated close to the side entrance of the narthex of the great church, thus giving the priests and the bishop easy access to the great church when the divine services were taking place there. The front

Fig. 28. The Baths. Plan of the building. 28 a – f: sections.

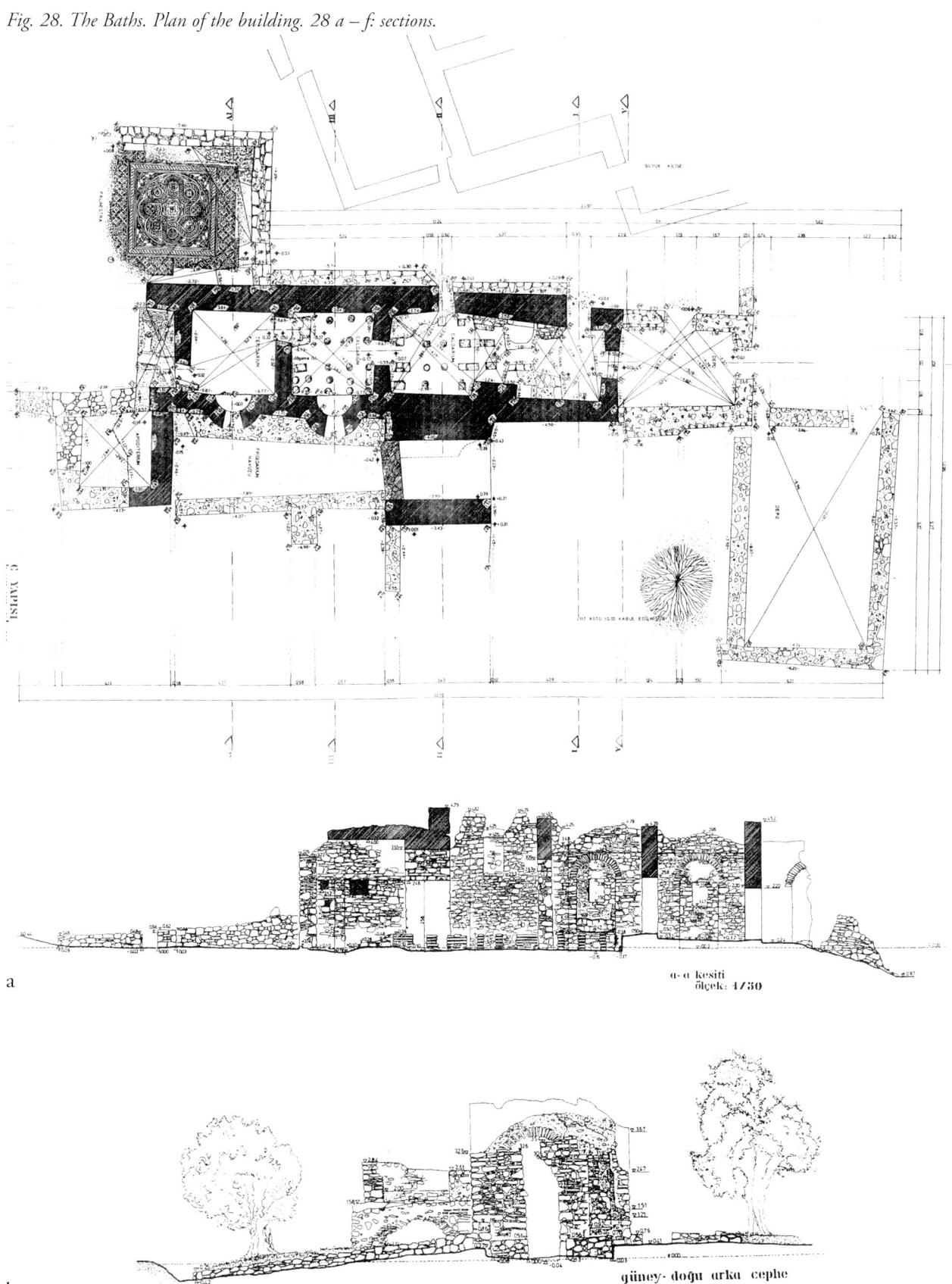

22   *Excavations in the Torba Monastery*

c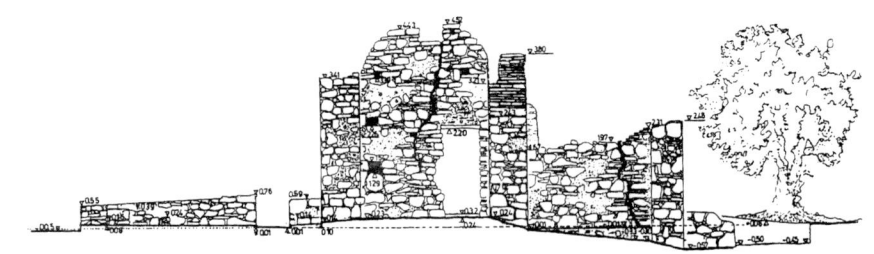
kuzey- batı ön cephe

d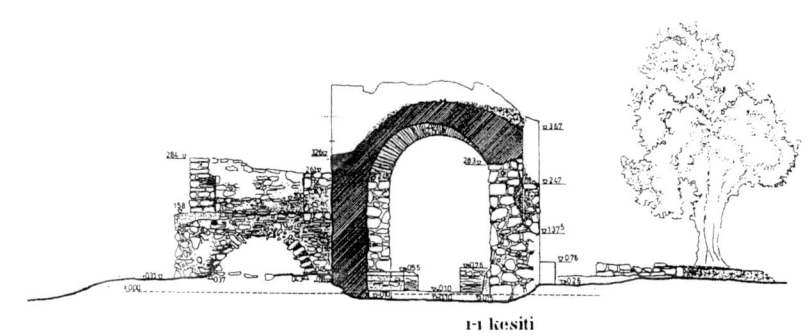
ı-ı kesiti

e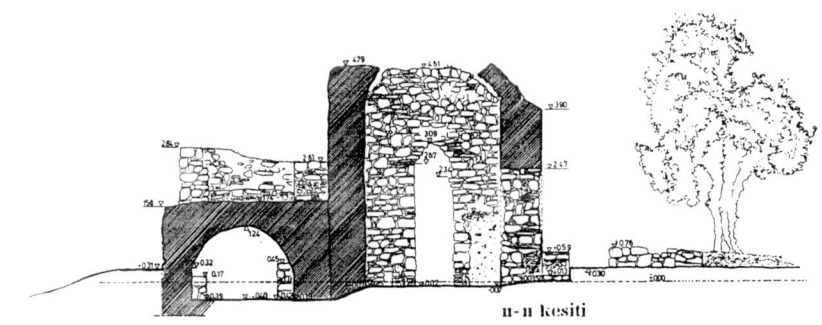
ıı-ıı kesiti

f
ııı-ııı kesiti

Palaestra?

A separate room was erected against the north-eastern corner of Structure C. This room has a well-preserved mosaic floor, which is surrounded on one side by the wall of the bath-structure and on two others by separate walls, while the north-western wall has completely disappeared

The only entrance that has been preserved is a door-opening leading from the area east of the structure through the south-east wall of the room. The door is 0.80 m wide, and on one side of the doorstep a cutting for a wooden dovetail can be seen. Traces of plaster are preserved on some parts of the wall next to the Baths. This room could perhaps be the court of the baths, the *palaestra*.

The mosaic floor, which is made of coloured tesserae, was found in a very good condition (fig. 29 and Pl. I, C). The composition consists of a central circular motive inscribed in a square frame. The very centre is like an emblema with a geometrical decoration. The medallion in the centre contains an inscribed square with lateral loops. This medallion is surrounded by eight smaller medallions, which are interlaced with a two-strand twist and a rainbow-shaded strand. Each contains simple geometrical or floral ornaments. In each of the four triangular fields between the central circular motive and the square frame there is a crater, out of which tendrils of vine or ivy grow (fig. 30). The square surrounding the central circle motive consists of a two-strand twist border, some black bands, and a border with a floral pattern consisting of intersecting circles in white and yellow.[10]

The mosaic in this room is made of white, blue, red, black and yellow tesserae.[11]

Both the north-western side of this room as well as the northern half of the two adjoining front rooms of the main building of the bath structure are completely destroyed.

Apodyterium

The heavily damaged northern part of the bath structure has a total width of about 8.41 m and consists of two rooms. The westernmost room has a simple mosaic of white tesserae and is believed to be the apodyterium of the bath. Remains of marble are preserved on the walls just above the floor and indicate

Fig. 29. The Baths. Mosaic floor in the so-called palaestra (2000).

of the building faced the little harbour and people arriving here from the sea.

Judging from the mosaics and the coins found in the building, it seems that the Bishop's House was most regularly in use from the end of the 4th century AD to the end of the 5th century AD.

Baths (Structure C)

The building consists of a range of rooms placed back-to-back and oriented southeast–northwest, with a narrow rectangular plan. The total length is 33.16 m including the outbuildings, and the northern part of the central building is 8.41 m wide (figs. 27, 28 and 28, a, b, c, d, e, f).

Fig. 30. The Baths. Detail of the mosaic floor showing a corner with tendrils issuing from a cantharos (2000).

Fig. 31. The Baths. Marble floor and mosaics (2000).

Fig. 32. The Baths. Red glazed sherd with impressed figure of a lion (2000).

that the walls of the room were originally covered with marble plaques. The mosaic floor is probably from a secondary phase. The location of the entrance to this room is not known.

Only the southern part of the room to the east of this is known; it has remains of a mosaic floor with a border decorated with a plait- or guilloche motive, and there is a marble floor under the mosaic (fig. 31). From this room it is possible to pass into the next room to the south, the *tepidarium*, through a 0.8 m-wide door. The walls of this room and several others in this part of the building are severely damaged and in danger of collapsing.

Pieces of plaster and fragments of a marble floor were found in the lower levels close to the floor, as were some pottery sherds[12] (fig. 32 and Pl. IV, B, C, D, E).

Tepidarium

The central part of the bath is entered through a square room with the dimensions 3 x 3 m. The floor of the room is made of mortar containing particles and dust from crushed pottery. Some remaining traces show that part of the walls as well as the floor were originally covered with marble. In the middle of the south-western wall there is a semicircular niche with a marble basin. The bottom of the basin is 0.2 m below floor level, and is covered with marble. The sides and upper part of the basin consist of mortar with crushed pottery, but may originally also have been covered with thin slabs of marble. In the middle

Fig. 33. The Baths. The caldarium with hypocaust floor (2005).

Fig. 34. The Baths. Pilae in the caldarium (2000).

of the marble basin there is an orifice, and further up in the outer wall of the niche there is a window, beginning about 1.15 m above the floor level of the room and approximately 0.8 m in height. On the outside of the building this window has an arch at the top. The vaulted roof of the room has collapsed.

Caldarium

From the tepidarium one enters the next room, the *caldarium*, by means of a door with a doorstep 0.2 m in height. The dimensions of the room are 3 x 3 m and thus similar to those of the previous room. The floor of this room was of the hypocaust type, and there are 20 small pillars of circular terracotta tiles, *pilae,* still in place (figs. 33, 34). Each pillar consists of 6 tiles placed on top of each other. The room has also openings for water channels, and holes that would allow the escape of smoke and the passage of hot air inside the walls.

Like the tepidarium, this room also has a semicircular niche in its south-western wall, with a marble basin and a window. Partly due to the hypocaust system, the floor of the caldarium is at a level of about 0.2 m above the floor level of the tepidarium. The window has a height of ca. 0.85 m beginning ca. 1 m above the floor of the room. This window too, appears on the outside of the building (fig. 35) with an arched opening, which is somewhat larger than the actual

Fig. 35. The Baths seen from the west with the water pool in front of the building (2005).

window, thus allowing more light to enter the room than otherwise permitted by the massive wall. The marble basin is of semicircular shape, and its floor is covered with marble. The sides of the basin presently appear as plastered with mortar containing crushed particles of pottery, but may originally have had a marble veneering.

This room is separated from the next one to the southeast by a wall, which was not part of the original layout, and this room too, should be considered to be part of the caldarium. It is entered from the first room of the caldarium by means of a 0.8m wide door. The remains of 13 pillars from the hypocaust system of this room have been cleared, and a great amount of ash was found on the floor among the tile pillars. Terracotta plaques were used both on the floor and on the walls. The vaulted roof has collapsed. In this area the north wall of the structure has an opening (fig. 28), and although it is heavily damaged it is clear that water was lead into the bath at this point. In the southern part of the room there are two stone bases placed so as to leave openings free for the passage of hot air coming from the furnace in the stokery south of the caldarium.[13] In this part of the caldarium many of the pillars of the hypocaust system consist of square terracotta tiles.

Stokery or praefurnium.
The last room of the sequence still has its vaulted roof in place, and although little is preserved of the installations, this must be the stokery of the bath structure, where the furnace, *praefurnium*, was placed. From here hot air was directed into the hypocaust system of the caldarium. At present the stokery is directly connected to the caldarium through a large arched opening, and it is not clear how this opening could be closed when the bath was in use. In addition to the large opening to the caldarium, the stokery has doors leading to the area in front of the great church to the east and to an enclosure south of the room, to which the doorstep is still in place.

This last-mentioned room is rectangular and has three doors leading north, east and south. A sondage was carried out in this room, but no finds were made except for a massive layer of ash, clearly indicating that this was where the ashes from the furnace were stored until being removed from the site.

The last of the bath structure rooms excavated is situated against the southern corner of the previous room. It is comparatively big, measuring 8 x 4.71 m and has two openings facing the great church. The room contained a large number of rough stones but neither sherds of pottery nor other finds were made here.

Frigidarium – piscina
Along the southwest side of the building, in front of the tepidarium and the first part of the caldarium, there is a long cool-water pool, a *piscina* (fig. 35). The two small apses with the windows of the tepidarium and the caldarium face towards this open-air pool, and the two semicircular marble basins inside

Fig. 36. The Baths. The water pool. A room on top of the vault had remains of a mosaic floor (2000).

Fig. 37. The Basilica, Structure D, seen from the north-west with the narthex in front. The apse with the synthronon in the background (2000).

the building are connected to the pool by a small channel running through the wall. The pool is plastered with mortar on the inside, and has two openings by which it could be emptied of water. It may have been about 1.2 – 1.5 m deep.

A peculiar small room with a low, vaulted roof is situated against the short side of the pool towards the southeast (fig. 36). This room must be the *frigidarium* of the bath. On top of this vault there was a room with a mosaic floor, thus indicating that this part of the bath had two storeys.

Clean water was brought to the bath by a channel on a wall along the exterior of the northeast wall of the bath structure. It entered the bath by means of a closed, plastered channel through the northeast wall of the bath building.

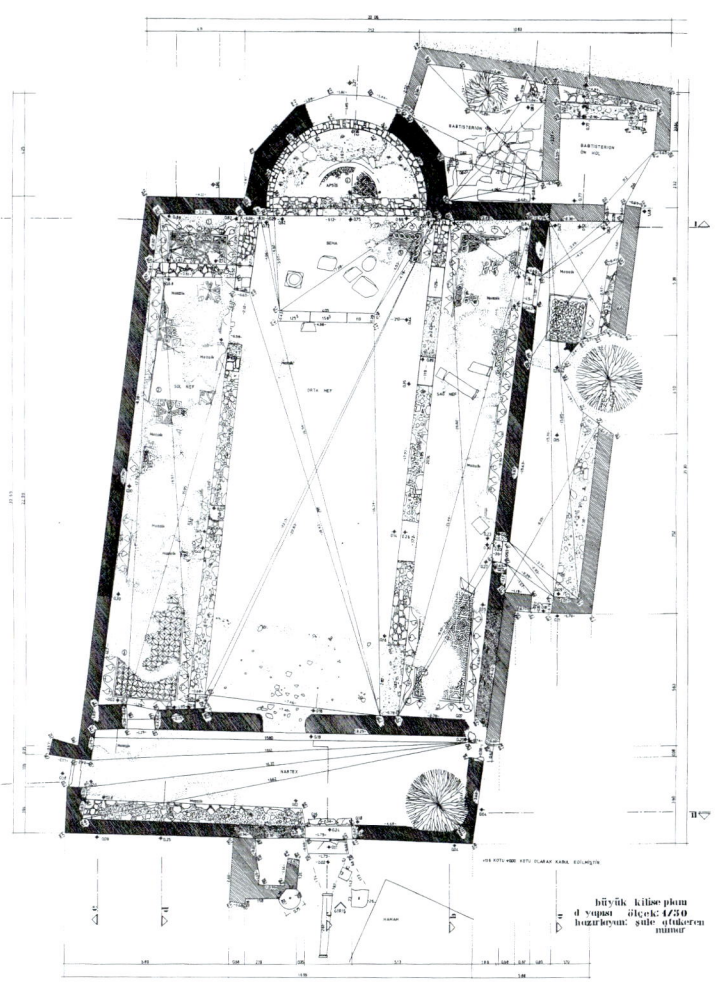

Fig. 38. The Basilica. Plan.

Fig. 39. The Basilica. Entrance to the basilica with large threshold in front and base and fallen column from the porch behind (2005).

The large Basilica (Structure D)

The large church with a central nave and two aisles in the plan of a basilica was uncovered during the excavations (figs. 37, 38). Before the excavation, only some upper parts of the side walls and a part of the apse, with its round interior and polygon-shaped exterior, were visible. Most of the walls are in a very poor state of preservation. The church together with the apse is 34.94 m long and 22.06 m wide. There are two marble column bases in front of the main entrance to the church, one square and the other round (fig. 39). An unfluted, monolithic column lies between the two bases and probably belongs to one or the other of these. The columns probably formed some sort of porch in front of the entrance to the narthex. There was one more entrance in the short northern side of the narthex, by which there was direct access to the "Bishop's House" (Structure B). The narthex has a simple white mosaic composed of large tesserae. The

Fig. 40. The Basilica. Part of the apse and central nave with remains of mosaics and transverse wall (2000).

Fig. 41. The Basilica. The northern aisle seen from the east (2000).

Fig. 42. The Basilica. Mosaic in the northern aisle (2000).

Fig. 43. The Basilica. Part of a mosaic in the central nave (2000).

main entrance from the narthex to the central nave of the basilica is through a centrally placed door. However, another and smaller side door leads directly from the "Bishop's House" into the northern aisle of the church. The plan of the church is not a quadrangle, but more like a parallelogram. The reason for this curious plan is probably that the church had to fit into the available space between the rocky hill and the other buildings on the site. There seem to be several phases in the architecture of the basilica. In particular, the wall running across the apse as well as the wall segregating the easternmost part of the northern aisle must be secondary, as they are partly built on the mosaics (figs. 40, 41).

In contrast to the church, the apse has quite a regular plan with a polygonal exterior and a semicircular interior.[14] There is a large window in the middle of the apse, and a bench runs along the inside of the wall, forming a *synthronon* (fig. 37). The floor of the apse is decorated with a mosaic with geometric motives consisting of intersecting circles (or four-petalled flowers) (fig. 40 and Pl. I, D). The colours are red, black, white and yellow. A black border encircles the central field and outside of this follows a broad band of white tesserae with a few scattered rosettes of simple design.

The floor of the church was originally completely covered with mosaics, but they are not well preserved. In most of the central nave the mosaic floors are completely destroyed, whereas a few more remains are left in both the northern and the southern aisle of the church. In each of the three, the floor is surrounded by a broad border with a decoration of ivy-leaves and tendrils, so that the floor mosaics of the central nave and the two aisles constitute three independent entities.[15]

In the northern aisle the mosaic inside the band of ivy leaves had at least two large mosaic panels with different motives. The eastern panel is no less than about 15 m in length and has a decoration consisting of Maltese crosses and small squares with a motive of intertwined ovals (fig. 41 and Pl. II, A). The motive can also be read as squares and triangles inside an octagonal frame shape. The ivy motive is very similar to the one in the basilica at Iasos.[16] Around the middle of this aisle there is a small panel with a geometric motive of two oval leaves placed across each other. This motive too has a parallel in the basilica at Iasos, which is dated to the 5th – 6th centuries AD.[17]

The western panel in the northern aisle – next to the narthex – is about 4 m in length and quite well-preserved. It has a simple decoration of intersecting circles (fig. 42 and Pl. II, B).

In the nave of the basilica at Torba almost all of the mosaics are destroyed except for a small piece in the south-eastern corner in front of the apse (fig. 43 and Pl. II, C). There are slight remains of the central field of decoration, showing that it was of a geometric character. This field is surrounded by a two-strand twist forming eyelets, and outside of this by a band

Fig. 44. The Basilica. Mosaic in the southern aisle (2000).

Fig. 46. The Basilica. Southern aisle with fallen columns (2000).

Fig. 45. The Basilica. Fragments from a marble balustrade from the bema (2000).

Fig. 47. The Basilica. Polychrome mosaic in the long room along the south-west side of the southern aisle (2000).

of ivy and tendrils similar to those in the aisles, except that the interior of the ivy leaves in the nave is red while in those of the aisles it is white.

The southern aisle has at least two long mosaic panels inside the border of ivy and tendrils, but they differ in length from those in the northern aisle. There are many areas with remains of destroyed mosaics spread over the southern aisle. The eastern part of the aisle

Fig. 48. The Basilica. The pool of the baptisterion (2000).

has a composition of orthogonal pattern of adjacent irregular octagons with four concave sides forming circles[18], while a guilloche and the usual ivy and tendrils surround the central field. In the western part of the south aisle next to the narthex, there is another motive, which may be described as interconnected crosses inscribed in circles or as an hour-glass motive leaving rhombic, concentric squares in between (fig. 44 and Pl. II, D).

The nave is 7.5 m wide and slightly over 20 m long, measured from the narthex wall to the double wall separating the apse from the nave. Four meters west of this last wall, there is a row of three long blocks of marble, which together form a line 4 m in length (fig. 38). The area between the apse and the line of marble blocks can be regarded as the *bema* of the church.

Many fragments from a marble balustrade were uncovered in the area around the three marble blocks of the bema (fig. 45). The balustrade must have consisted of a number of large rectangular slabs, each decorated with an open-work net-pattern within square frames.

Small areas with remains of mosaic are seen in different parts of the central nave, between the row of marble blocks and the narthex wall. A drainage channel crosses the nave next to the south wall.

The north aisle is 20.5 m long and 3.5 m wide. There must have been a row of columns separating the nave from the northern aisle, but unfortunately both the shafts and the capitals of these columns have disappeared into the limekilns, or they were reused for some other purpose at a later time.

The southern aisle is 20.75 m long and 3.5-3.2 m wide. Two pieces of column shafts and two capitals were found, belonging to the row of columns once separating this aisle from the nave (fig. 46). The upper parts of these capitals are rectangular, while the lower parts, which rested on the columns, are square. There are cross motives and volutes on the corners of the short sides of the capitals.

The long room on the south-west side of the church has a plain white mosaic floor, except for a panel with polychrome mosaic surrounded by a border with an ivy and tendril (fig. 47 and Pl. II, E). The motive of the polychrome mosaic is a complicated pattern of intertwined cable ornament in the colours yellow, black and white.

The re-used fragment of an ancient stele was found in the debris of the church walls. It is probably from the Hellenistic period.[19]

The long room along the south-west wall of the church leads up to two rooms at the southern corner of the church: an ante-room and a *baptisterion*. The baptisterion itself was constructed in the corner between the apse and the east wall of the basilica, and it has a cross-shaped pool made of large, thin slabs of marble (fig. 48). The actual pool is square, about 0.62 m on each side and 0.63 m deep, with a water outlet in the middle of the bottom.

Conclusion

The plan of the church shows that it belongs to the early basilica type of Byzantine churches. A parallel to this is the Imrahor Mosque, a three-aisled church which is one of the earliest churches in Istanbul. This church was founded in 463 as the Basilica of Ioannes Prodromos in Samatya. It is one of the most characteristic examples of the early basilica type, having an apse with a polygonal exterior and a semicircular interior and a large central nave (naos), separated from narrow side aisles by rows of columns. This church has great similarity with the church in Torba.[20] The Roman tradition still survives in these large churches of the basilica type.

Fig. 49. Structure D, the Cistern, seen from the north (2000).

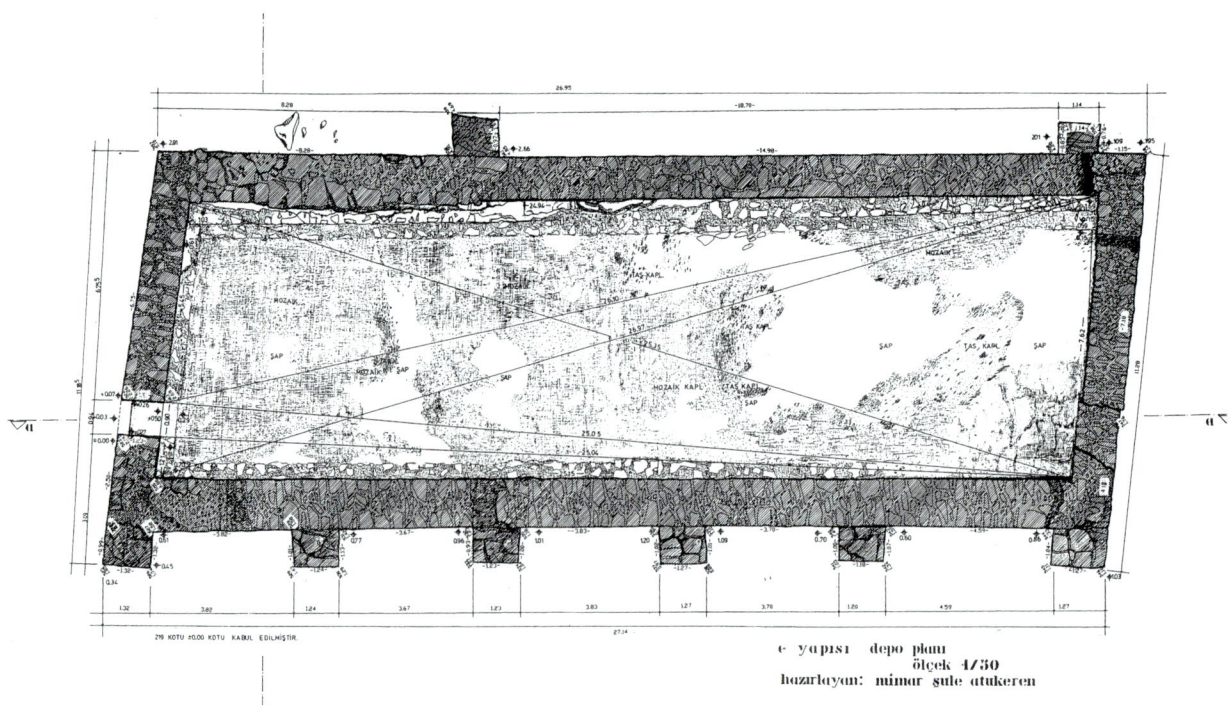

Fig. 50. The Cistern. Plan.

Fig. 51. The Cistern. The northern part of the interior with entrance door (2005).

Cistern (Structure E)

An oblong, trapezoid building, structure E, is situated on the sloping, rocky area south of the bath and the basilica (figs. 49, 50). It is oriented northeast-southwest, and its exterior dimensions are 26.94 (the southeast wall) x 11.28 m (southwest wall including the buttress of about 1 m). The interior measures ca. 25 (southeast side) x 7.62 m (southwest side). The best preserved part of the wall is the central part of the long north-western wall, which reaches a total height on the outside of about 4.62 m.

The walls of structure E are more than 1 m thick, and the building probably either had no roof, or the roof was a wooden construction. The floor was renewed at different periods, and was finally covered with mosaic made with large plain tesserae (figs. 51, 52). The walls too, have had their plaster renewed at different times, and it is possible to see traces of several layers of mortar and plaster on top of each other. As the walls were covered with plaster, which was carefully carried around the corners and down to the floor, it seems clear that the structure was constructed for holding water. A stone bench ran along all four sides of the room, but its purpose has not been understood (figs. 53, 54). One terra-cotta pipe and a water channel were found close to the floor on the northwest wall. The channel most probably was used for taking away the remains of mud that would have settled in the depot.

The long southeast side of the depot is partly built into the slope, so that the ground is much higher on

Fig. 52. The Cistern. Floor of the cistern showing mosaic with several older floors below (2005).

Fig. 53. The Cistern. The interior seen from the north (2000).

the outside of the building on this side. This would have made it possible to direct water from the higher rocky ground to the east into the cistern. The northwest wall was strengthened by 6 buttresses in order to withstand the pressure of the water inside the depot (fig. 55). There are square holes in the walls at a certain level, about 2.5 m above the floor. Their purpose is not known, but perhaps it was to let out surplus water from the cistern.

The only entrance to the structure is an opening in one corner of the short northeast wall (fig. 49). The top consists of an arch in the rubble masonry, but the door has no threshold, and at some period a low wall seems to have been built to block the lowermost part of the opening.

The date as well as the purpose of this door is uncertain. Obviously the cistern could only contain very little water as long as the door was there. Perhaps it belonged to the construction phase to facilitate access and to leave an opening for taking out materials after the construction. If this is correct, it would have been closed afterwards, perhaps only leaving room for a water channel.

But there are, however, a number of puzzles in relation to the interpretation of this structure. In addition to the question of the door-opening there is the question of the benches around the walls of the room, as well as the fact that the entire room was furnished

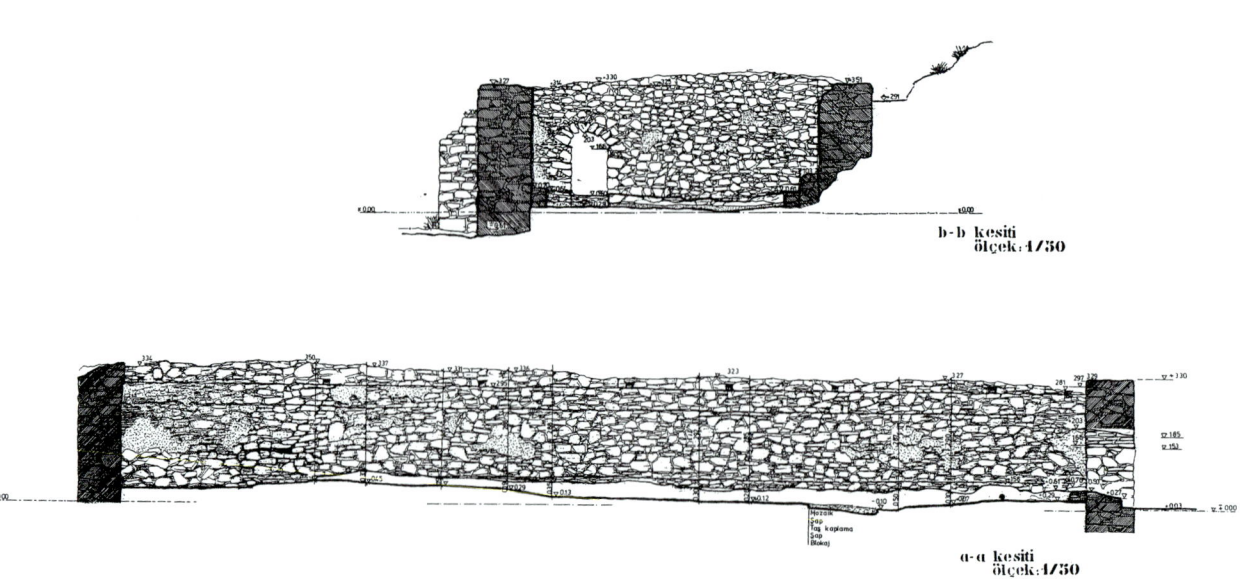

Fig. 54. The Cistern. Section showing the long western wall and short northern wall from the inside.

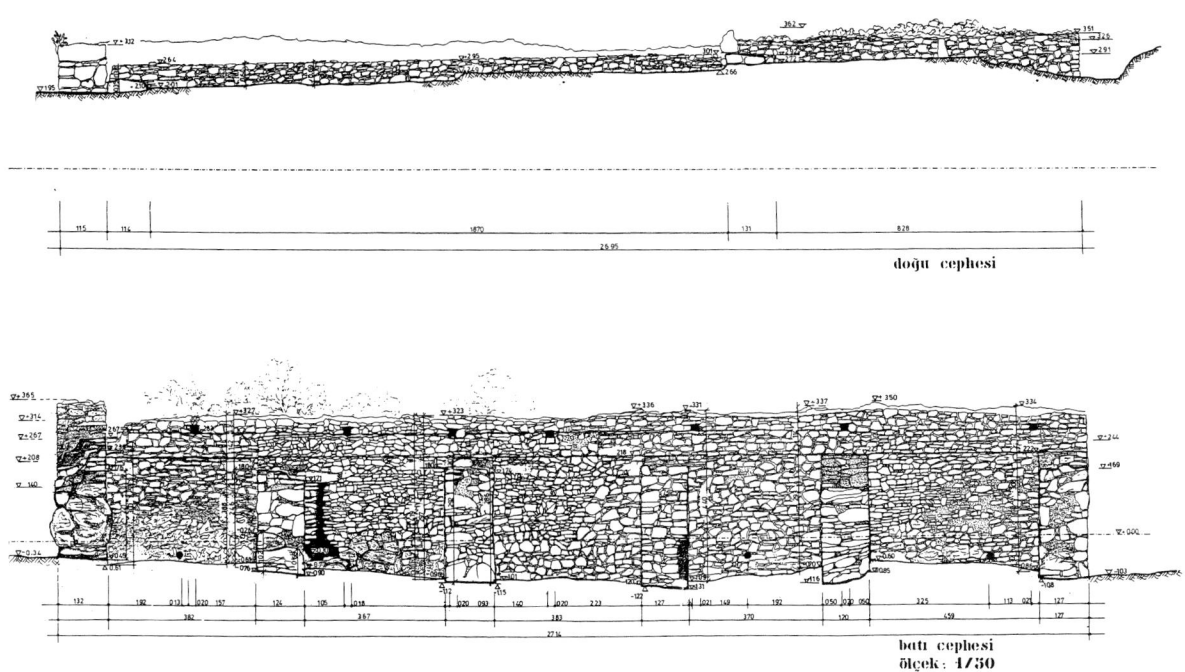

Fig. 55. The Cistern. The long western wall with buttresses seen from the outside.

with a mosaic floor in the latest phase of the building. Although the mosaic is of a very coarse character, it is still quite surprising that the bottom of a simple water cistern should have been furnished with a mosaic.

So perhaps there is another explanation. There can be little doubt that this strong structure was originally erected as a water cistern, but perhaps it was changed to serve some other purpose in its latest phase, and perhaps it received a door-opening on this occasion, as well as a large mosaic floor and a roof consisting of a wooden construction attached to the square holes in the upper part of the walls?

Conclusion

The buildings at Torba were placed very close together; leaving in some cases only small irregular passages open between the walls of the different buildings. Small paths probably led from the entrance of one building to the other, as for instance to the north of the basilica, where the side-door of the narthex faces directly towards the "Bishop's House". The area between the "Bishop's House" and the bath leaves just enough open space for the little columnar propylon of the great basilica to be immediately visible to visitors coming from the harbour. The Mausoleum, which is no doubt the oldest structure on the site, was very significantly situated at the very north of the small group of buildings at Torba. The architecture of the Mausoleum was more rich with ancient spoils and marble than the other structures, and the view of this building continued to be unobstructed by later buildings for anyone approaching Torba from the sea.

It seems that the Mausoleum, the "Bishop's House" and the Bath all belong to the earlier phases, whereas the great basilica was built at a time when only great effort allowed it to be placed in the small area between these structures. On the plan of the Torba complex it is clearly seen that there were entrances to the "Bishop's House", the large basilica, the baptisterion and the bath from the public square and the harbour to the west. But it is also clear that the buildings were also accessible from the courts in between or from neighbouring buildings.

Guests and members of the Christian community from the surrounding area came to Torba by boats

Fig. 56. Ancient road? Sloping terrace south of the cistern – possibly remains of an ancient road leading to the religious site at Torba (2005).

entering the little harbour, or they came from inland, by the road, of which a trace seems to be preserved as a sloping terrace in the rocky hill south of the great cistern (fig. 56).[21] Some would just have attended the services in the church. Others would perhaps have stayed for a time at this religious centre to visit the different places and admire the buildings and their magnificent mosaics.

During the surface cleaning of the area of the church and the bath some coins were found, which had a ship motive and the inscription: "PLUS ULTRA", – coins that were lost here by European travellers, who must have visited the ruins of the once flourishing early Byzantine centre at Torba in the late 17th century AD.

Excavations in the Torba Monastery 37

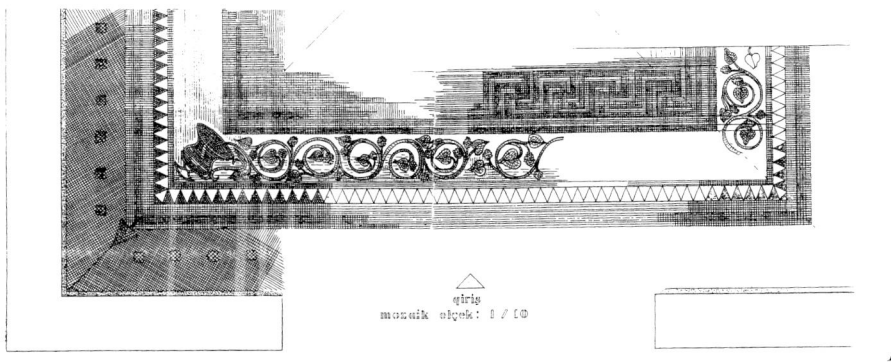

A

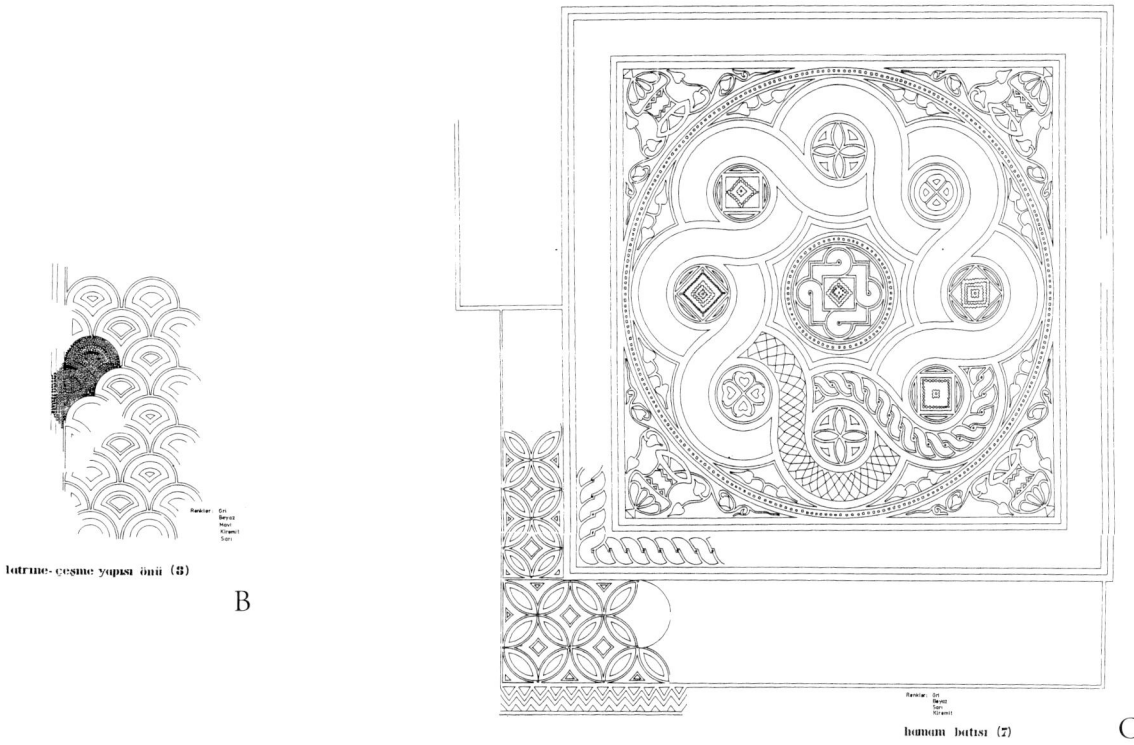

B

C

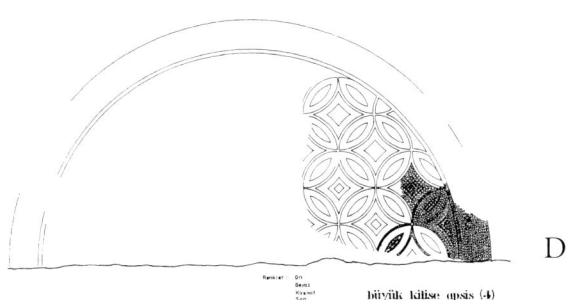

D

Pl. I. Mosaics.

38 *Excavations in the Torba Monastery*

A

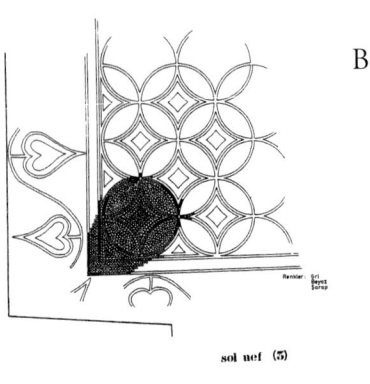

B

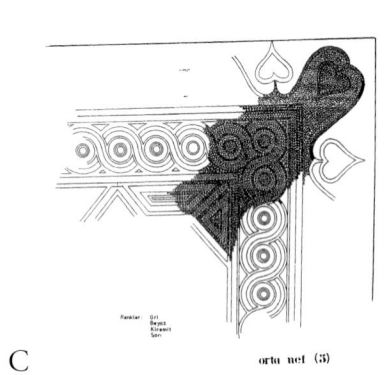

C

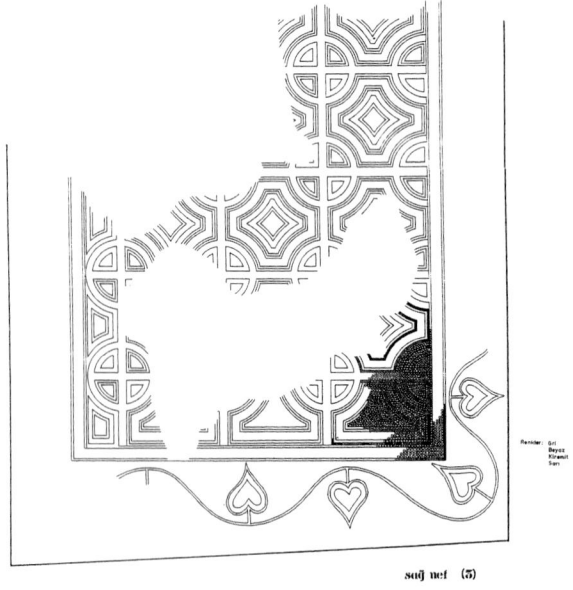

D

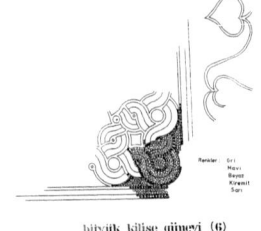

E

Pl. II. Mosaics.

Excavations in the Torba Monastery 39

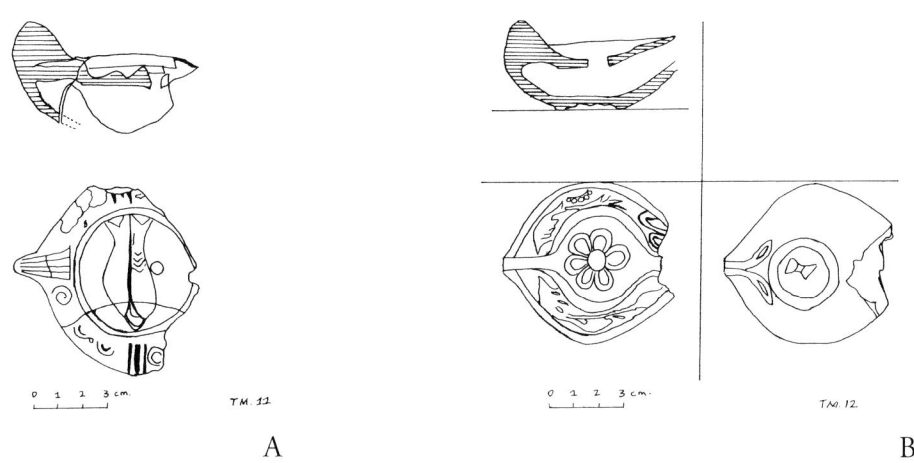

A

B

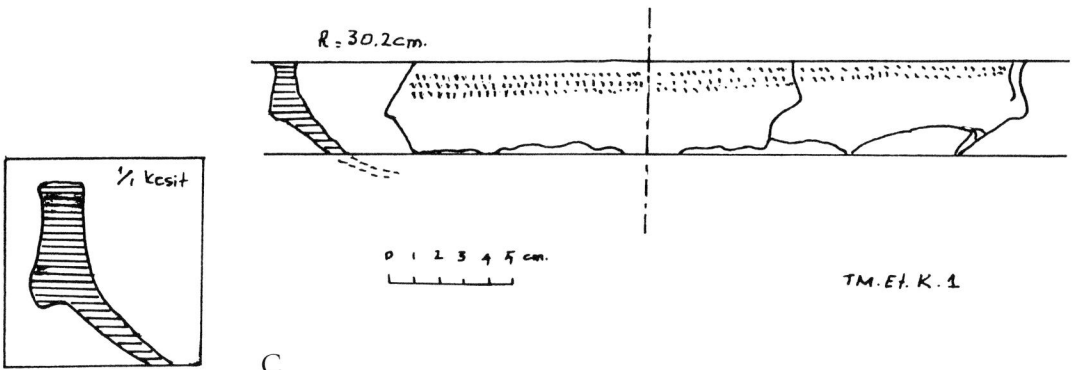

C

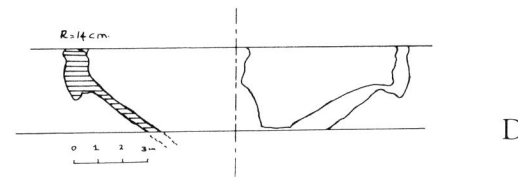

D

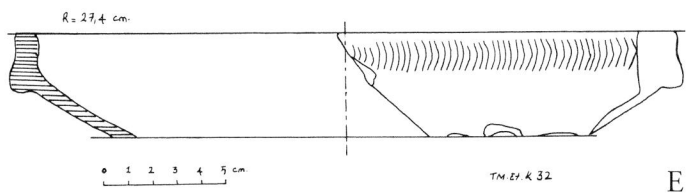

E

Pl. III. Pottery.

40 *Excavations in the Torba Monastery*

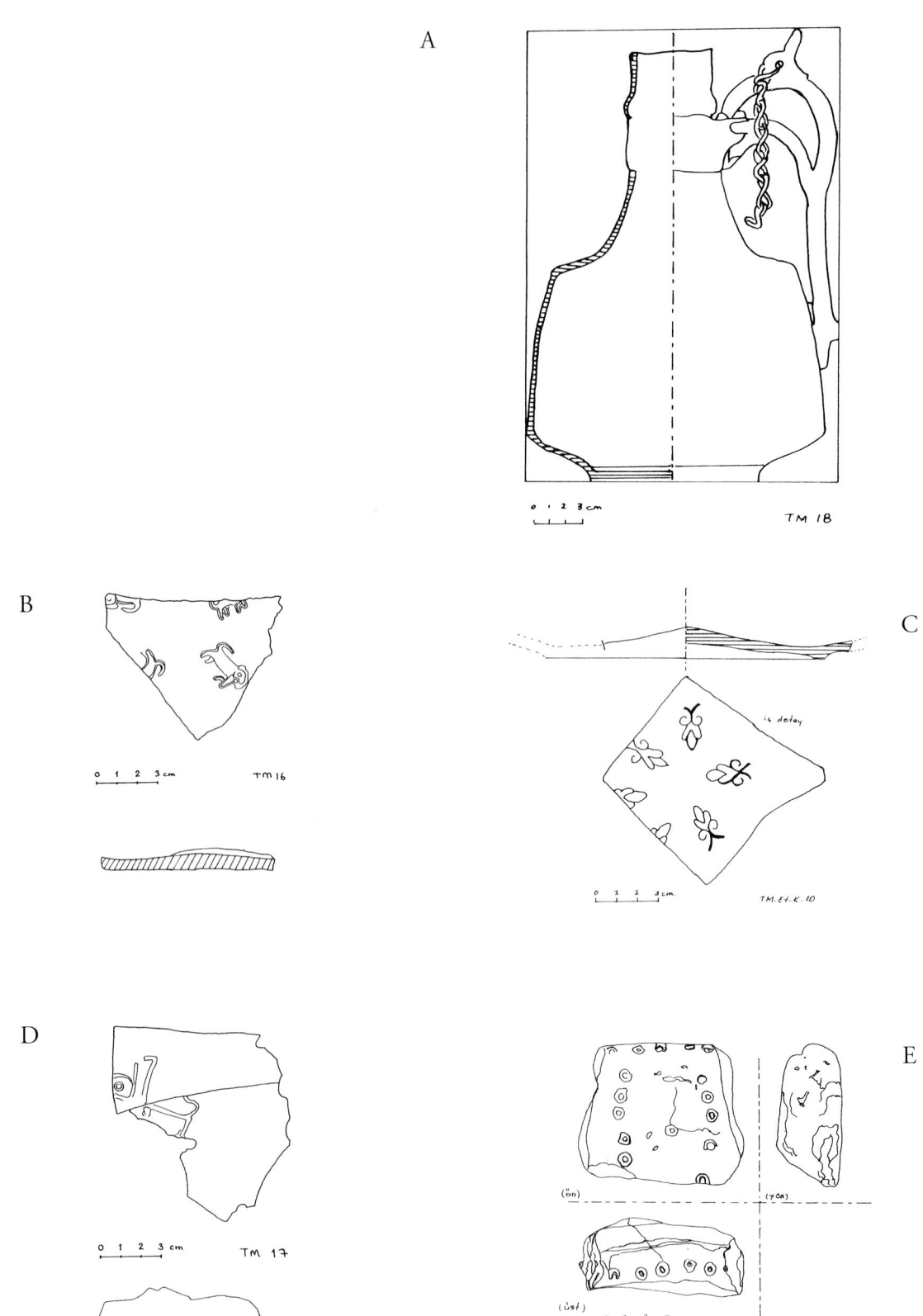

Pl IV. Copper pitcher and pottery.

Bibliography

Bass and van Doorninck 1971: G.F. Bass and F.H. van Doorninck Jr., A fourth century shipwreck at Yassi Ada. *AJA* 75 (1971) 27-37.

Bean 1971: George E. Bean, *Turkey beyond the Maeander*. London 1971.

Berti 1987: F. Berti, I mosaici degli edifici di culto cristiano. In: Studi su Iasos di Caria. Venticinque anni di scavi della Missione archeologica italiana. *Bollettino d'arte, suppl.*, 31-32. Roma 1987, 155-162.

Goodacre 1964: H. Goodacre, *A Handbook of the Coinage of the Byzantine Empire*. London 1964.

Hayes 1972: J.W. Hayes, *Late Roman Pottery*. London 1972.

Hinks 1933: R.P. Hinks, *Catalogue of the Greek, Etruscan and Roman Mosaics and Paintings in the British Museum*. London 1933.

Kuban 1996: D. Kuban, *Istanbul Bir Kent Tarihi Bizantion, Konstantinopolis*. Istanbul 1996.

Newton 1862: C.T. Newton, *A History of Discoveries at Halicarnassus, Cnidus and Branchidae*. London 1862.

Lavan 1999: L. Lavan, The Late Antique Governors: A Gazetteer. In: *"AnTard" 7*, 1999, pp. 135-164.

Pedersen 1997: P. Pedersen, Investigations and Research in Halikarnassos 1995. *XIV Araştirma Sonuçlari Toplantisi, I. cilt*. Ankara 1997, 207-217.

Perlzweig 1961: J. Perlzweig, Lamps of the Roman Period. First to seventh century after Christ. *The Athenian Agora 7*. Princeton 1961.

Poulsen 1994: B. Poulsen, The New Excavations in Halikarnassos, in: J. Isager (ed.), *Hekatomnid Caria and the Ionian Renaissance, Halicarnassian Studies I*, Odense 1994, 115-133.

Poulsen 1995: B. Poulsen, Pagans in Late Roman Halikarnassos I. In: *Proceedings of the Danish Institute at Athens I*, 1995 193-208.

Poulsen 1997: B. Poulsen, The City Personifications in the Late "Roman Villa," in: S. Isager and B. Poulsen (eds.), *Patron and Pavements in Late Antiquity, Halicarnassian Studies II*, Odense 1997, 9-23.

Ruggieri 1997: V. Ruggieri, An Archaeological Survey in the Gulf of Keramos and on the Northern Shore of the Peninsula of Halikarnassos. In: *XV Araştirma Sonuclari Toplantisi I* 1997. Ankara 1998, 201-217.

Ruggieri, Giordano, Zäh 1997: V. Ruggieri, F. Giordano, A. Zäh, La penisola di Alicarnasso in età bizantina I. In: *Orientalia Christiana Periodica, vol. 63* 1997, 119-161.

Sear 1988: D.R. Sear, *Roman Coins*. London 1988.

Notes

1 I wish to thank all my friends in the excavation team, who contributed to the Torba Monastery excavations regularly with their well-informed, self-sacrificing, harmonious and experienced work, and to the contributors on the area and in the administration. When this manuscript was made the article by Ruggieri, Giordano and Zäh was not at my disposal. It has important information about the site at Torba before the excavations as well as some plans and illustrations (V. Ruggieri, F. Giordano and A. Zäh, "La penisola di Alicarnasso in età bizantina. Prima parte" In *Orientalia Christiana Periodica* vol: 63, 119-161).

Sources of illustrations: Aykut Özet 2000: 3, 20, 22, 23, 24, 25, 26, 29, 30, 31, 32, 34, 36, 37, 40, 41, 42, 43, 44, 45, 46, 47, 48, 49, 53. P. Pedersen 1977: 4, 17, 18. P. Pedersen 1995: 1, 19. P. Pedersen 2005: 8, 9, 11, 14, 15, 16, 27, 33, 35, 39, 51, 52, 56.

Drawings by Sule Atukeren and Mustafa Betin: 2, 5, 6, 7, 10, 12, 13, 21, 28, 38, 50, 54, 55.

2 Ruggieri 1997, 205.

3 The same type of spout has been uncovered during the excavations in the site of ancient Halikarnassos, Bodrum, in a joint work between our museum and Odense University.

4 A similar oil lamp discus with twin fish relief is seen in Perlzweig 1961, p. 129, pl. 20, Nr. 945. It is dated to the second half of the 3rd century AD, but similar examples continue into the 4th century AD.

5 The roulette decoration, which is seen on the edges of a plate in Hayes 1972, p. 330 and 332, figs. 67-68, is also found in our examples. The date may be the middle or the second half of the 5th century AD. This kind of pottery was used till the 6th century AD and it is also known as Çandarlı ware.

6 The coin must be dated to the period in which Marcus Aurelius and Commodus reigned together, 177-180 AD. The coin is very indistinct.

7 There is a portrait of the emperor Marcianus on the obverse of the bronze coin, which was found in room B VIII and it can be dated to 450-457 A.D. The coin is very indistinct.

8 Bass and van Doorninck 1971 p. 27-37.

9 Similar to no. 2196 (polychrome orthogonal pattern of adjacent scales) in: C. Balmelle et al., *Le décor géométrique de la mosaique romaine*. Paris 1985.

10 No. 238b and e (bichrome orthogonal pattern of intersecting circles) in C. Balmelle et al., *Le décor géométrique de la mosaique romaine*. Paris 1985.

For parallel in the so-called "Roman Villa" in Halikarnassos: Poulsen 1994, 115-133, fig. 10, and B. Poulsen, Pagans in Late Roman Halikarnassos I. In: *Proceedings of the Danish Institute at Athens I*, 1995 193-208, fig. 10.

11 The mosaic in room F of the "Roman Villa" in Halikarnassos has a similar motive (Poulsen 1997 p. 9-23, fig. 10). It is situated in the part that Newton could not excavate because of a Turkish cemetery there. The mosaic was severely damaged when excavations for graves were made through the mosaic floor, but the main medallion can be seen to be exactly similar to our mosaic in the bath in Torba. An almost exact parallel to the interlaced medallions was found in Room C, cf. Newton 1862, 287-288. A publications of the entire domus is in preparation by B. Poulsen for a forthcoming volume of *Halicarnassian Studies*.

12 A parallel to a sherd with an impressed cross found in the apodyterium can be seen in Hayes 1972, p. 364, fig. 78 no. 67. This kind of pottery with impressed cross and monogram is dated between the end of the 5th century AD and the beginning of the 6th century AD. The sherd with an impressed figure of a lion with a round object on its chin has a parallel in the same publication p. 356 fig. 75 no 38, J and M and is dated to the 5th century AD. Sherds with impressed palmette- and cantharos motives were also found.

13 For a general description of the system see e.g. I. Nielsen, *Thermae et Balnea* I (Aarhus 1990) p. 14 ff.

14 A coin with the diameter of 1.7 cm belonging to the reign of Theodosius I (379-395 AD) was uncovered in the apse of the church. The coin is very indistinct.

15 An exact parallel is at hand in Room C of the so-called "Roman Villa" in Halikarnassos (cf. Newton 1862, 287-288 and Hinks 1933, nos. 52 b and c)

16 This motive is also used in the "Roman Villa" in Halikarnassos in Room F, Room K and Room C, cf. Poulsen 1994 fig. 7 and note 9; Balmelle et al. 1985, no 185 a.

17 Berti 1987 p.162, picture 13.

18 Cf. Balmelle et al. 1985, nos. 168 a and c.

19 The fragment has preserved part of a female figure. Her dress has Archaic features, but these seem to be of an Archaistic character rather than true Archaic. The stele is probably of the Hellenistic period, when an Archaistic style sometimes came in fashion.

20 Doğan Kuban is giving detailed information about the church of Ioannos Prodromus (now called Imrahor Mosque) in his publication "Istanbul Bir Kent Tarihi Bizantion, Konstantinopolis" (Istanbul 1996).

21 The sloping recess in the hill has not been securely identified as a road at present. An ancient road can be seen, however, a few kilometres north of Torba below the modern high-way close to the water front. This road is perhaps the ancient road, which G.E. Bean noticed at a place called "Zeytinli Kahve", which he believed to be originally from the Hekatomnid period (Pedersen 1997 p. 209 and fig. 2).

Bozdağ – an ancient town and marble quarry near Myndos on the Halikarnassos Peninsula

Bahadir Berkaya and Poul Pedersen

In approaching Gümüşlük by the main road from Bodrum, shortly after leaving the villages of Dereköy and Peksimet, you pass over a low saddle on the northeast side of the low, rounded hill named Bozdağ. Bozdağ is about 5 kilometres southeast of the site of the ancient city of Myndos (fig. 1 and 2). It rises from close to the sea at Kadikalesi and thus separates the plain of Turgutreis (Karatoprak) from that of Gümüşlük. From the seaside the barren mountainside appears quite impressive, in spite of the fact that the hill is less than 250 m in height.

While the central part of the Halikarnassos Peninsula is dominated by the high limestone mountains, the southern and western part consists mainly of volcanic stone, forming fascinating and picturesque landscapes inland from Myndos and around Termera further to the southeast.

Bozdağ consists of limestone, and thus differs from the surrounding mountains of brownish andesite typical of this area. Even to the non-specialist it is clearly of a different geological composition than the volcanic material that is normally found here. In 1975 and 1985 the Bozdağ area was subjected to a brief geological survey by a team of German and Turk-

Fig. 1. Bozdağ seen from the northeast. The quarry is on the right side of the very summit of the hill. The terraces on the slope are probably debris originating from quarrying.

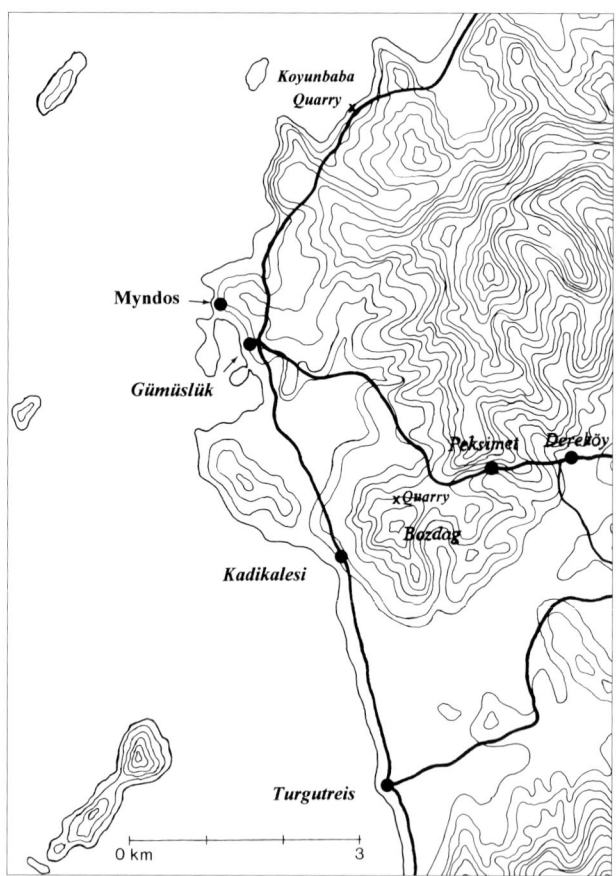

Fig. 2. Map showing location of Bozdağ midway between Gümüşlük and Turgutreis (Karatoprak) commanding the rich and fertile, coastal valleys both north and south of the hill (based on Beil. 11 in W. Radt, Siedlungen und Bauten auf der Halbinsel von Halikarnassos (1970); heights are not precise).

ish specialists. They were particularly interested in the occurrences of metal ore at Bozdağ and in any possible evidence for the exploitations of these resources in different historical periods.[1] They found quarries and plenty of slag resulting from metallurgical work both near the seaside and on the northeast side of Bozdağ, but there is no mention of a marble quarry for building-stones. Is this because what we see as a marble quarry was interpreted by this group as an open quarry for metal ore?[2] According to these specialists the metals extracted here were mainly lead and silver, and this is probably what gave Myndos its modern name "Gümüşlük".

According to the Turkish-German team, quarrying for metal was not abandoned until as late as 1957, but they believe that the name "Gümüşlük" indicates that metal-quarrying also took place here in the Middle Ages, although more recent works have obliterated the traces of earlier activity. Unfortunately, their investigations did not show if silver and lead extraction were of importance to Myndos in ancient times, and the answer this question must be left to more intensive surveys in the future.

Paton and Myres visited Myndos and Bozdağ on their travels to Karia in 1893 and 1894.[3] In their report from 1896 they state that the continuing importance of silverworking here is asserted by both classical and medieval tradition, but they don't give any references to support this. They noticed masses of slag from the silver furnaces on the beach south of the present settlement at Gümüşlük, and they reported that the remains of one furnace were still to be found near the road leading from the beach towards Kadikalesi and Karatoprak. The great silver mine itself could be seen on the range behind the town: "the shaft is very irregular, and of great size, and is filled with water to within thirty feet of the surface. There are still veins of silver-lead in this neighbourhood". We have not seen this silver mine, and it may have been obliterated by more recent quarrying, or perhaps it could be identical with the quarry on Bozdağ, which we believe is a marble quarry.

They do not mention Bozdağ specifically, but they mention a small tower of unwrought stones "On the southernmost and most detached peak above Kadi Kale…" On this spot they found "…fragments of quite primitive handmade pottery, provided with string-holes pierced in the brim, instead of with handles, the paste of which is mere brown mud from the marsh round Karatoprak, and very slightly fired. So far as we know, this is the only record of Karian culture which is earlier than the sub-Mykenaean tombs of Assarlik."[4] This place is probably not the main hill of Bozdağ itself, but rather one of the steep peaks adjoining Bozdağ to the southwest (see fig. 4).

Bozdağ was also visited by Bean and Cook, and was included in their report, published in 1955.[5] They observed a tower ca. 10.5 m square on the summit of the hill, constructed of irregular masonry and with a small Turkish burial enclosure inside its walls. Bean and Cook

Fig. 3. Spur running north from the summit of Bozdağ

noticed pottery sherds from prehistoric down to late-Classical times, as well as some obsidian blades. They found the remains of an irregular ring on the top of the hill, enclosing an area only about 80 metres in width.

Bean and Cook suggested that the settlement on Bozdağ should be identified with the Old Myndos mentioned by Pliny and Stephanus, and which paid one-twelfth of a talent to the Delian league.[6] If Old Myndos was one of the Lelegian towns that were involved in the synoikism of Maussollos, it should be expected to show some of the characteristics of a Lelegian settlement, which they argue that the Hellenistic-Roman town at present-day Gümüşlük does not. The settlement on Bozdağ, however, would be a possible candidate because it has early pottery and walls of simple masonry of unwrought stones.

Bozdağ has not yet been thoroughly investigated, and no excavations have taken place, both of which could provide more precise information as to who lived here and when. However, during the last few years Prof. Mustafa Şahin from Uludağ University in Bursa has initiated new investigations in the Myndos area. Contrary to Bean and Cook's opinion, he has recently suggested that Old Myndos actually was situated on the same site as the Hellenistic-Roman town, and not on the barren mountaintop at Bozdağ.[7]

We have not made any additional studies of the settlement on the top of Bozdağ and thus have no new information to add.[8] But perhaps a few facts deserve to be reiterated. As it may be seen on the map, Bozdağ in fact holds a remarkable position, situated as it is midway between Gümüşlük and Turgutreis (Karatoprak), and commanding the large and fertile coastal plains both to the north and to the south. These two plains must be among the largest and most important agricultural areas on the entire peninsula, capable of sustaining a considerable population. Except for Myndos at the extreme north of the plain, there does not seem to be any other ancient settlement than that at Bozdağ that can be related to this large and fertile area. And the present archaeological site of Myndos may even be a new Hekatomnid foundation, which only

Fig. 4. Peaks south of the summit of Bozdağ.

came into existence when the settlement at Bozdağ was abandoned. At least, this remains a possibility, but it must be admitted that our knowledge concerning the small town on Bozdağ is still insufficient, and for instance the necropolis that might have given some indication as to when the site was occupied has not yet been identified.

Bozdağ actually consists of several spurs and peaks. The main hill has the small, fortified settlement, and from this a rounded, worn ridge runs northwards (fig. 3). Some traces in the barren, naked surface of this ridge may be the remains of an ancient road, which seems to point towards an opening in the enceinte of the settlement at its northwestern extremity. Towards the south and west the summit of Bozdağ is connected by a ridge to two other peaks, of which the southernmost rises quite abruptly above the plain of Karatoprak (fig. 4). This peak seems to have some remains of construction, which may be the tower mentioned by Paton and Myres, and this may also be where they found the remains of prehistoric pottery.[9]

Of the settlement itself, there are clear traces of the enceinte on its north, west and east sides. The houses were mainly or entirely constructed of uncut fieldstones, and have entirely collapsed, so that the debris covers most of the ancient town area. It is difficult to trace any outline of buildings and walls except for the fortification wall (fig. 5). However, the remains are not very extensive, and it is difficult to imagine what kind of town this would have been, and of what period.

Does simple masonry of uncut stones necessarily indicate a Lelegian origin – and what would Lelegian mean here on the western extremity of the Halikarnassos peninsula? Until more investigations have been carried out on this site, one should perhaps keep an open mind to other possibilities. The view from Bozdağ towards the Aegean is amazing, and the proximity of Kalymnos and other Aegean islands is striking.

The marble quarry

The marble quarry was first noticed by staff from Bodrum Museum about ten years ago.[10] It is situated

Fig. 5. Ruined north wall of the fortified settlement at Bozdağ.

Fig. 6. The marble quarry at Bozdağ seen from the east.

48   *Bozdağ – an ancient town and marble quarry near Myndos on the Halikarnassos Peninsula*

Fig. 7. South face of the quarry.

Fig. 8. The western part of the quarry.

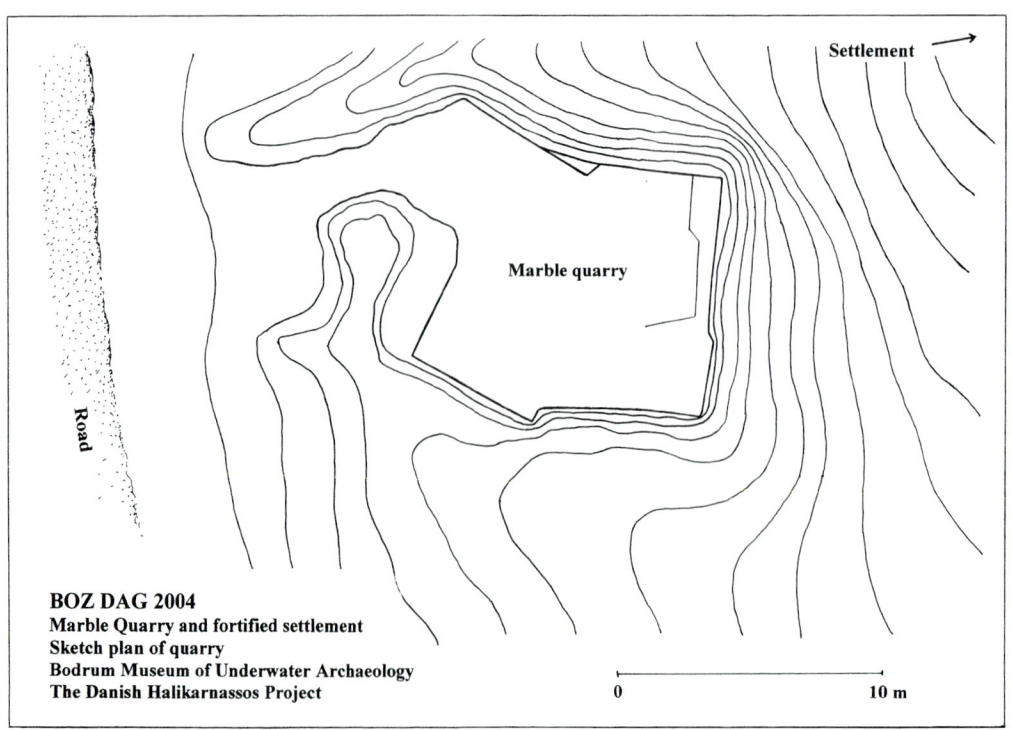

Fig. 9. Sketch plan of the quarry (South is upwards).

on the northeastern side of the summit of Bozdağ and thus is facing inland towards the Bodrum-Gümüşlük road (fig. 1). It can only be discerned with difficulty from the road, but is impossible to overlook for anyone approaching the summit of Bozdağ from this side (fig. 6). It is quite surprising that it does not seem to have been recorded by earlier visitors, and one wonders whether they believed it to be an open mine.

When approaching the summit from the Bodrum-Gümüşlük road, one passes by a number of terraces, probably resulting from the extraction of ore (fig. 1). The actual quarry covers a comparatively small area and is open to the sky (figs. 7, 8 and 9). It is closed on all four sides except for an opening towards the northeast, and the vertical walls reach a considerable height against the higher ground towards the south and west. Shelves and ledges from quarrying remain, and tool marks can be seen everywhere on the walls (fig. 10). It is not possible to tell the depth of the quarry area, as it is partly filled up by deep layers of chippings and fragments.

It is difficult to tell the date of the quarry. There has clearly been quarrying activity immediately to the south of our quarry, and a road, probably of more recent date, leads up to this area, but has now fallen into disuse. It is really surprising that the quarry seems to have escaped the attention of earlier travellers, but the possibility that it is not an ancient building-stone quarry seems, however, to be excluded by the existence of some unfinished square blocks and several columns lying on the slope in front of it (figs. 11, 12, 13, 14). The columns are monoliths of a size and proportions that point to a rather late date.

Fig. 10. Cuttings and ledges in the floor of the quarry.

Fig. 11. Column lying on the mountain slope east of the quarry.

Fig. 12. Broken columns in front of the quarry.

Fig. 13. Roughly dressed block of marble in front of the quarry.

Fig. 14. Block of marble with unfinished channel.

Two samples of the marble were analysed by Prof. Norman Hertz in December 1999. According to Prof. Hertz the samples do not match any classical quarry, and the Bozdağ marble is different from normal calcitic marbles. The one sample was dolomitic (like Thasian marble), fine grained, and had the values: delta-13 C: -0.62 and delta-18 O: -15.15. The other was coarse grained, and may be an iron-rich (ankeritic) marble. It had the values: delta-13 C: -4.88 and delta-18 O: -14.00.

Fig. 15. View towards the north from Bozdağ. The ancient site of Myndos (Gümüşlük) is situated on the coast opposite the rocky island.

Bozdağ is situated about the same distance south of Myndos as the huge andesite quarries at Kouyunbaba are to the north. The greenish andesite from Kouyunbaba was probably used for both Myndos' Hekatomnid city-wall and for the core of the Maussolleion. The quarry at Bozdağ is small, and the isotopic analysis done by Prof. Hertz indicates that this was probably not the source of any of the wide range of marbles that were used at the Maussolleion. The Maussolleion marbles have been analysed by the British Museum and all show very different isotopic qualities.[11]

The marble from Bozdağ is most likely to have been extracted for use in Late Roman buildings or Byzantine churches in Myndos, five or six kilometres to the northwest (figs. 1, 15). The fascinating and yet almost unexplored site of ancient Myndos has ruins from both Roman and Byzantine times.[12] The Byzantine buildings are to a great extent constructed of re-used Roman architecture, to be found in plenty at Myndos. Perhaps we may therefore accept the Roman period as the most probable date for the utilization of the Bozdağ quarry. During this period it was still necessary to quarry new building material, and the proximity of the Bozdağ quarry must have made this an attractive source of marble.

Bibliography

Bean and Cook 1955: G.E. Bean and J.M. Cook, The Halicarnassus Peninsula. *ABSA* 50, 1955, 85-169.

Paton and Myres 1896: W.R. Paton and J.L. Myres, Karian Sites and Inscriptions. *JHS* XVI, 1896, 188-271.

Wagner et al. 1986: G.A. Wagner, E. Pernicka, T.C. Seeliger, I.B. Lorenz, F. Begemann, S. Schmitt-Strecker, C. Eibner, Ö. Öztunali, Geochemische und Isotopische Characteristika früher Rohstofquellen für Kupfer, Blei, Silber und Gold in der Türkei. In: *Jahrbuch des Römisch-Germanischen Zentralmuseums in Mainz*. 33, 1986, 723-752 and Tf. 53-57.

Walker and Matthews 1997: S. Walker and K.J. Matthews, The marbles of the Mausoleum. In: I. Jenkins and G.B. Waywell (eds.), *Sculptors and Sculpture of Caria and the Dodecanese*. London 1997, 49-59.

Notes

1. Wagner et al. 1986, 723-725.
2. The locations of the specific places are given by the Turkish-German team, who also give a scientific description of the geological composition and the metallurgical qualities (Wagner et al. 1986, 724).
3. Paton and Myres 1896, 204.
4. Paton and Myres 1896, 204 and 264.
5. Bean and Cook 1955, 118.
6. Pliny NH V 107 and Steph. Byz. s.v. "Myndos", Bean and Cook 1955, 145 and note 240.
7. Reported by Prof. Mustafa Şahin at the Karien Kolloquium in Berlin 13.-15. October 2005.
8. The observations put forward here are based on abbreviated inspections of the site in 1999 and 2004.
9. Unfortunately we did not have time to go there on any of our brief visits to Bozdağ.
10. The quarry was noticed by Ali Ucarer, who at that time was chief of museum works at Bodrum Museum of Underwater Archaeology. Bodrum Museum has reported the quarry site to the Heritage Protection Board (Koruma Korulu) and the area has now been designated an archaeological protection zone. We were accompanied by Ali Ucarer on our visits to Bozdağ. The sketch-plan is based on measurements made by surveyor Ole Rohde Andersen.
11. For a similar analysis of the Maussolleion marbles and information on the isotopic composition: Walker and Matthews 1997, 49-59.
12. In recent years Bodrum Museum has initiated new investigations at Myndos, including excavations at the site of an early Byzantine church. Another project has been initiated by Prof. Mustafa Şahin from Uludağ University, Bursa.

Tombs of the Halikarnassos Peninsula – The Late Bronze and Early Iron Age

Anne Marie Carstens

The present article contains a diachronic study of tombs on the Halikarnassos Peninsula. It is based on ten weeks of fieldwork in Bodrum and its hinterland.[1]

I have tried to rediscover all the tombs described in early travellers' reports, surveys and excavation publications. Unfortunately, this has not always been possible, either because they disappeared after their original discovery or because impenetrable brushwood made access to the areas impossible. However I then discovered other tombs hitherto unknown.

It is a regrettable fact that the majority of Karian tombs have been looted – either in antiquity or perhaps quite recently – before archaeological investigations were undertaken. Thus we are left with a body of source material often consisting of sepulchral architecture rather than burials. But wherever possible I have included the grave goods in the analyses.

The Halikarnassos Peninsula

The ancient landscape of Karia covers the southwestern part of Asia Minor. Two river valleys, the Maiandros to the north and the Indos to the east, and the coastline defined the region (Fig. 1).

Apart from the west coast, near the mouth of the Maiandros River and the cities of Miletos, Priene and Myos,[2] coastal Greek cities of the type found along the Ionic coast were never predominant in this part of Asia Minor. The coastline with its small bays, peninsulas, and promontories never invited large-scale settlement. In this respect southwestern Karia was more a part of the Dodekanese than of the Anatolian mainland, or even the Aegean as such. Historically Karia often found itself located between neighbours who were, in the political sense, more extensive.

Although the Halikarnassos peninsula is hidden behind the islands of Rhodes and Kos it has always commanded a central position in the east-west traffic of the Mediterranean (Fig. 2).

Small bays and natural harbours characterise the coast, especially west of Bodrum between Bodrum and Çıfıt Kalesi, and on the northern shore from Yalikavak and eastwards. But there are also numerous creeks around Gümüşlük. The landscape is divided up into small fertile pockets by smaller ridges that run out of the higher inland mountains. Northwest of Halikarnassos the mountains stand tall, covered by pinewoods. East of Gümüşlük and in the southern

Fig. 1. Map of Karia (Anne Marie Carstens)

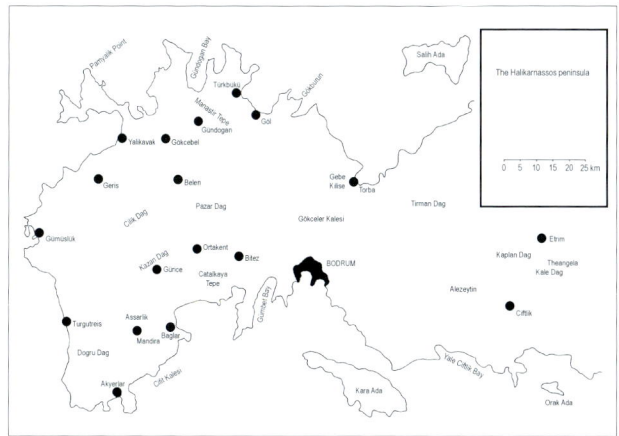

Fig. 2. Map of the Halikarnassos peninsula (Anne Marie Carstens)

The methods of cultivation in the small terraced fields and plantations, as well as the herdsmen's work in the hills seem unchanged through history and may give a glimpse of the ancient exploitation of the land, and thereby also the settlement patterns.

Modern building activities are concentrated in the coastal areas whereas the interior and the area southeast of Bodrum are still relatively unspoiled, and the ancient sites better preserved.

Most of the subsurface of the western part of the peninsula is volcanic andesite of changing hardness, colour, and structure. North and east of Bodrum the subsurface is limestone, often of a reddish/ochre/grey colour and like slate, it is folded in layers that break into slab like flakes.[3] Here huge modern limestone quarries that produce building material scar the hills.

The change between the volcanic andesite and the limestone runs through Bodrum. The native rock at the Myndos Gate in the western part of the city consists of soft white andesite, while in the eastern part of Bodrum near Yokuşbaşi the subsurface consists of

part, north of Akyarlar the mountains are rugged and vegetation is sparse (Fig. 3). It is, however, always possible to find fertile green spots, even in the late summer.

Before tourism set in on a massive scale and made possession of land very profitable the peninsula produced vast amounts of fruit for the inland market.

Fig. 3. The southern part of the Halikarnassos peninsula. View of the highlands from the road between Turgutreis and Gürice (Anne Marie Carstens)

Fig. 4. The Koyunbaba green-stone quarry (Anne Marie Carstens)

reddish limestone. White pozzolana-like andesite is also found in the Ortakent region, whereas the north coast is dominated by a dark grey harder andesite. An impressive quarry of green stone used for the massive inner core of the Maussolleion, the Koyunbaba, is situated on the west coast, north of Gümüşlük (Fig. 4).[4]

The varieties in the geology influenced building techniques and masonry styles. The andesite is fairly easy to work for the stone mason, and it is often used in ashlar masonry, while the limestone breaks into smaller slabs, which is excellent for a very precise rubble dry stone masonry, still used in the building of terrace walls in the countryside.[5]

When the Danish investigations began at the Maussolleion in 1966, Bodrum had only one hotel, the sand beach served as harbour, and the gardens often housed a couple of camels for transport. Although bigger than many of the villages, Bodrum had a decidedly "rural" character. Today, it is still possible to find cattle in Bodrum itself, and part of almost every garden is used for keeping chickens and turkeys. Despite the now almost overwhelming tourism, Bodrum still exhibits many village characteristics and the contrast between modern and traditional life is enormous.

The settlement pattern on the peninsula seems basically unaffected by modern life, mainly because this modernity was only introduced within the last generation and the basic life style is still unchanged. Therefore, a good starting point for an understanding of the ancient infrastructure may be a consideration of the present settlement patterns.

The modern villages are all located at the mouths of wadis or streams that bring water from the higher mountains in the inner parts of the peninsula. The coastal plains are very fertile, in particular the valleys of Ortakent, Bitez, Gümbet, and Turgutreis, and the coastal zone between Kadi Kalesi and Gümüşlük is highly productive. The typical modern village is situated at some distance from the sea, a few km inland, but with an affiliated beach village – examples being Bitez, Ortakent, Göl, and Turgutreis. In some cases the two villages, the inland and the coastal, have merged. During summer the coastal village is dominated by tourism, and therefore at times referred to as the holiday resort, even though it is the anchorage for the locals' smaller fishing boats that both serve the restaurants and the villagers. Some of the towns, however, are situated in direct proximity to a natural harbour, as is the case with Gümüşlük, Torba and Bodrum.

The known ancient settlements, apart from Halikarnassos/Bodrum and Myndos/Gümüşlük, are found on ridges set back from the coastline, towering above good natural harbours or inlets. Fortification walls crowned by a tower or a lookout are often the best-preserved part of the ancient remains (Fig. 5). It is not clear whether these fortified hills formed the basic settlement sites or whether they constituted a series of strategically placed hill forts that served defence purposes. An abundance of pottery on the surface indicates permanent habitation and often series of tombs are found on the slopes or in the immediate vicinity. However, architectural remains of houses are sparse.

Several strategic needs were met by the topographical setting of the 'hill forts'. They divided the region into smaller territories and each hilltop settlement overlooked a reasonable area of fertile land, part of the coastline (and the nearby islands) and was within short distance of neighbouring 'hill forts'. Beacons could, in a very short time, send warning of enemies or pirates approaching the peninsula. However, a collaborative system of that type is indicative of a political organisation, which may not have existed before the late Archaic period.[6]

While evidence of domestic architecture is extremely sparse, many tombs have survived and form an important part of the cultural landscape of the peninsula. Even today the rock-cut tombs with their black quadrangular holes densely grouped on the Göktepe hill north of Bodrum and along the coastal road between Yalikavak and Göl play a striking role in the landscape.

The various concentrations of tombs and their

Fig. 5. View towards the fortified hill at Geriş (Anne Marie Carstens)

topographical setting remain our best ancient source for a consideration of the settlement patterns. In the case of the rock-cut tombs along the northern shore it is characteristic that the concentration corresponds with the natural harbours and small inlets and thereby the modern villages. Normally the preserved tombs are sited a little inland, e.g. on the inner side of the coastal road.

Also many built tombs are well preserved, in particular the many stone tumulus tombs at Gökçeler. Together with the later dynastic tombs, isolated on summits, as in Geriş or at Esentepe, they contain information on territories, major settlements and their importance.[7]

In 1896 W.R. Paton and J.L. Myres published a map of "The Peninsula of Myndos". It included a survey of possible ancient roads.[8] The main roads, the east-west road between Halikarnassos and Gümüşlük, and the coastal road from Gümüşlük to modern Torba follow very closely the orientation of the modern roads. The best-preserved ancient road is the Bodrum-Torba passage, crossing the peninsula north-south at the shortest distance. It connected the Geometric and Archaic settlements at Gökçeler with the coastal regions. Even today it is possible to follow this track and the journey from Bodrum to Torba takes about two hours on foot. The mountainous northern part of the peninsula which includes the Kara Dağ settlement was reached by another north-south road from Göl to Bitez.

Research History

The little picturesque Turkish town of Bodrum has attracted the attention of a wide range of travellers and explorers since the 17th century.[9] Noblemen came by on their way to Rhodes or the Levant. They encountered the ruins of the ancient city that once boasted one of the Seven Wonders of the Ancient world, and they discovered the Barbarians in a romantic setting.[10] Many charming records of the civilized world meeting rural and Muslim Bodrum are preserved. They contain important information, mainly because the reports were often made in a diary style that mixed different impressions of weather, food, supplies, ruins, local inhabitants etc.[11]

Archaeology in Bodrum began with Sir Charles Thomas Newton: In 1846, Viscount Stratford de Redcliffe, the British ambassador in Constantinople, transported thirteen marble slabs incorporated in the Castle of Saint Peter to England.[12] The relief slabs were presented to the British Museum where Newton worked as assistant in the Department of Antiquities. There was little doubt that the sculptures belonged to the Maussolleion and Newton became extremely interested in establishing a "complete elucidation" of both the sculpture as such and indeed the Maussolleion. He argued that "this evidence must be sought for, not in books, but in Budrum itself; that the site whence these marbles were obtained had not as yet been sufficiently explored."[13] In April 1855 Newton visited Bodrum, and in particular he undertook a close examination of the Castle.[14]

During the spring of 1856 he worked for six weeks in Bodrum preparing a large-scale investigation of the monuments. During this stay he also excavated several tombs in the so-called Eastern Cemetery near the Mylasa Gate, and produced a typology, or classification, on the basis of these investigations.[15]

The following autumn Newton put together a scientific team including a small party of Royal Engineers in order to begin excavations at the Maussolleion site. He also went on an explorative expedition "in the neighbourhood of Budrum", and visited Gümüşlük, Kadi Kalesi, Assarlık and Çıfıt Kalesi.[16] Sites on the northern shore, Farilia, Türkbükü and Göl, were also investigated. By the 1st of January 1857, Newton had begun the excavations at the Maussolleion site.[17]

Thirty years after Newton, during the autumn of 1886 or early in 1887 W.R. Paton excavated the chamber tomb necropolis of Assarlık, and in February 1887 he explored the western part of the peninsula in the neighbourhood of the village of Geriş, where he found part of a fortification and a "very remarkable tomb".[18]

Based on their travels in 1893 and 1894 Paton and J.L. Myres published a topographical survey of Karia in 1896. The report also included a meticulous investigation of the Halikarnassos peninsula as well as a typology of "Karian tombs", focussing almost exclusively, however, on tombs from the Halikarnassos peninsula and with Paton's excavations at Assarlık as their point of departure.[19]

The principal drive for the work of Paton and Myres was provided by the literary sources, in particular the works of Strabo and Pliny, but also the Athenian tribute-lists from the fifth century BC.[20] Site names mentioned in these sources were related to the ancient settlements in order to produce a historic overview of the Halikarnassos peninsula.

During the summer of 1921 A. Maiuri and G. Guidi of the Italian Mission on Rhodes conducted a voyage of discovery in Karia. Guidi visited Iasos north of Halikarnassos and included an examination of the rock-cut tombs at Türkbükü and Gümüşlük.[21] An investigation of the so-called "Monumentii Lelego-Carii" at Gökçeler and Aleizeytin was carried out by Maiuri.[22]

In the early 1950s G.E. Bean and J.M. Cook made a survey of the Halikarnassos peninsula, guided by the work of Paton and Myres.[23]

Their impressive work contained a full discussion of all sources available including a large body of epigraphic material: like their predecessors they were preoccupied with the identification of the settlements according to ancient written sources.[24]

In many ways the 1960s broke new ground in the archaeological investigations of Halikarnassos and, not least, its hinterland. In the summer of 1962 Mycenaean pottery from a peninsula site appeared in Bodrum and was shown by local farmers to G. F. Bass.[25] Further investigations revealed that the pottery came from a chamber tomb necropolis at Müsgebi/Ortakent. In two campaigns, 1963 and 1964, Professor Y. Boysal, of Ankara University, excavated the entire necropolis.[26]

W. Radt conducted an impressive one-man survey in the areas north and east of Halikarnassos.[27] In particular the settlements at Aleizeytin, Gökçeler and Kara Dağ were investigated in order to understand the organization of the ancient landscape, mainly in the Archaic period. In contrast to the previous surveyors of southwestern Karia, Radt concentrated on the characteristics of the archaeology left by the indigenous population, analysed through a consideration of the architectural remains.

Since 1966 Danish archaeologists have worked in Bodrum, firstly on the re-excavation of the Maussolleion under the direction of K. Jeppesen. Later investigations and excavations concerning both the late Classical city and later periods have been carried out by the Danish Halikarnassos Project, directed by P. Pedersen in cooperation with Bodrum Museum of Underwater Archaeology.[28]

Early Karia

In the 1880s the British archaeologist T. Bent visited a number of tombs on the Datça peninsula, between Emecik and Resadiye, where many small marble figurines had been found.[29] He described one of them as a seated figure playing a harp, while another was a female figure with a crescent on her head. The figurines are now lost, but C. Renfrew later attributed the harpist to the Keros-Syros culture, ECII-III, the second half of the third millennium BC.[30]

Some seventy years later an Early Bronze Age necropolis was found at Iasos. Between 1961 and 1967 in all 96 cist tombs were excavated in the necropolis situated on the mainland opposite the supposed settlement.[31] The majority (86) of the tombs were rectangular or light trapezoidal. Seven tombs were elliptical and two semicircular, while one was a "tomba a fossa". The rectangular cists were constructed of four slabs overlapping at the corners, while the rounded cists were built of smaller slabs in a dry-stone walling. Another slab formed the cover, and the floor of the tombs was normally earthen. The tombs faced eastwards, from northeast to southeast, and the layout of the cemetery was fairly strict.[32]

Of the 96 tombs 64 revealed only one burial, while seventeen were reused once, eight three times, and four tombs contained four deceased each.[33] The grave goods were sparse; three marble vases, a few spindle whorls and sporadic metal finds, among these a bronze dagger, were included, but the majority of the finds were pottery.[34] Barber dated the Cycladic finds to EC I (app. the first half of the third millennium BC).[35]

In antiquity the settlement at Iasos was separated from the mainland by a narrow channel. Natural harbours framed the island on both sides and the sea was very rich in fish.[36] A marked summit on the southern end of the island formed a natural "acropolis". The naturally defensible coastal position, and the short distance between necropolis and settlement satisfied the needs of a "typical" Early Cycladic site (Fig. 6).[37]

In fact, in many respects, the cemetery at Iasos resembles early Cycladic cemeteries.[38] The construc-

Fig. 6. Iasos (Anne Marie Carstens)

tion of the cists, the reused tombs, the contracted position of the deceased, the marble vases, and much of the pottery belong to the Cycladic culture.[39] But other features differ: the cemetery is rather large, 96 tombs as compared to an average extent of 15 to 20 tombs on the Cycladic islands.[40] The general layout is very strict with a fixed orientation towards the east. Some of the grave goods are Anatolian, in particular the beak-spouted jugs, and both the burnished surfaces and some of the geometric patterns have been found on pottery from inland Anatolian sites, e.g. the necropolis at Yortan and at Troy.[41] The bronze dagger is also considered more Anatolian than Cycladic.[42] The contracted position of the body is very typical in an Anatolian context, where also cist tombs are also occasionally found.[43] The excavator, P.E. Pecorella thus suggestively concluded that Early Bronze Age Karia may be seen as a sort of mediating region – a "zone limitrofe" – between inland Anatolia and the islands – between Orient and Occident.[44]

In 1963 E. Vermeule carried out a survey in the Müsgebi valley.[45] The purpose was to find the settlement belonging to the Late Bronze Age necropolis at Müsgebi, where excavations began the same year. The survey never found this settlement, but on the coastal plain south of the village some Early Bronze Age pottery (second half of the third millennium BC) was collected, including five whole vases. Vermeule placed the pottery in an Anatolian context, while a pyxis (similar to the Iasian "ollae") was defined as Cycladic. Furthermore she believed that a mottled vase might reflect an early prototype of the Minoan Vasiliki ware (EMII)![46]

Minoan remains were also excavated at Iasos in the early 1970s.[47] A building from the Middle Bronze Age ("edificio F") with an almost square plan, ca. 10 x 10 *m*, interior walls, and an entrance on the north side, was found near the Roman basilica.[48] The building has three phases, indicated by three levels of paved floors. The earliest Middle Minoan phase is characterized by both imported and locally produced MMII pottery, among this Kamares ware, a pattern that continues in the following Neopalatial period. The final Mycenaean phase comprises imported Dodekanese as well as local pottery.

Middle Minoan levels were found below the Roman Agora as well and also here a long sequence of second millennium pottery is represented.[49] The lowest level is MBA and consists of local ware (similar to pottery from Aphrodisias) and imported Kamares pottery, MMII. A destruction level follows in MMIII (light-on-dark pottery). The second level, LMI/LMII includes both imported Minoan pottery and local ware.

In the area of the Protogeometric necropolis at the Agora, Mycenean LHIIIA2 or B pottery was found. Only imported or locally produced Aegean pottery was reported from this and the succeeding levels, but that might be due to the manner of publication.[50]

While the evidence of Aegean settlements in Karia in the Early and Middle Bronze Age seems rather scattered, Iasos is different. During the Early Cycladic period Iasos was a significant settlement comprising both Cycladic settlers of the Aegean and an indigenous "Anatolian" people living together. Unfortunately the state of the publications makes it difficult to pursue the mixed nature of the settlement through time. It is not certain what "local pottery" denotes, whether it is locally produced Minoan pottery or what has often been called "Anatolian" ware.[51] What is more, the ratios between Aegean and Anatolian pottery finds are seldom published.

What we are able to conclude is that by the Late Bronze Age the coastal regions of southwestern Karia were also part of the Aegean Bronze Age region and had long been so, maybe not as the results of large-scale, well organized expansion, but rather as being settled by newcomers travelling from the Aegean islands and naturally expanding into the Anatolian coastland. In this respect we may already find that in the Early and Middle Bronze Age, the coastal regions of Karia were part of the Aegean Bronze Age culture. Nevertheless, the local variant of this Aegean culture included or incorporated Anatolian features.

The Late Bronze Age Necropolis at Müsgebi[52]

The Müsgebi valley is probably the most fertile and extensive valley on the peninsula. It is bordered to the north and west by high mountains. It starts off as a narrow gorge enclosing the Uludere Stream which rises in the Gilek Gündoğan. The modern village of Ortakent is sited on the main road from Bodrum to Gümüşlük, where the valley opens. South of Ortakent it widens into a coastal plain. The Late Bronze Age necropolis at Müsgebi is situated in the northwestern outskirts of Ortakent. Today part of it has been destroyed by the digging of a large gravel-pit. The local white, soft, almost clayish andesite is used by the building industry for mortar.[53]

In the summer of 1962 G.F. Bass visited the necropolis together with M.L. Mellink and H. Elbe, then director of the Bodrum Museum.[54] They saw six chamber tombs and found five vases that were brought back to the Bodrum Museum. Earlier that same summer some local farmers had shown Bass two vases from the area. The following year Ankara University began excavations at the necropolis under the direction of Y. Boysal. From 1963 to 1966, 48 subterranean chamber tombs were unearthed and a total of 179 vases from the Müsgebi necropolis were listed in the inventories of the Bodrum Museum. The burials cover a period from LHIIIA1 till LHIIIC, with the emphasis on the LHIIIA2 and LHIIIB periods.[55]

Boysal published the excavations in a series of reports, and a catalogue of the vases appeared shortly after.[56] Later C. Özgünel, who participated in the excavations as a student, added informations on the architectural features of various tombs and published a sketch plan of part of the necropolis (Fig. 7).[57] In his work on Mycenaean pottery in Asia Minor the material from the Müsgebi necropolis has played a central role.[58]

During excavation the necropolis was divided into three areas A, B, and C.[59] The sketch plan published by Özgünel shows that some of the tombs in area B (tomb 6-21) appear to be placed side by side with a fixed orientation towards the north-east. Without a total plan of the entire necropolis it is, however, im-

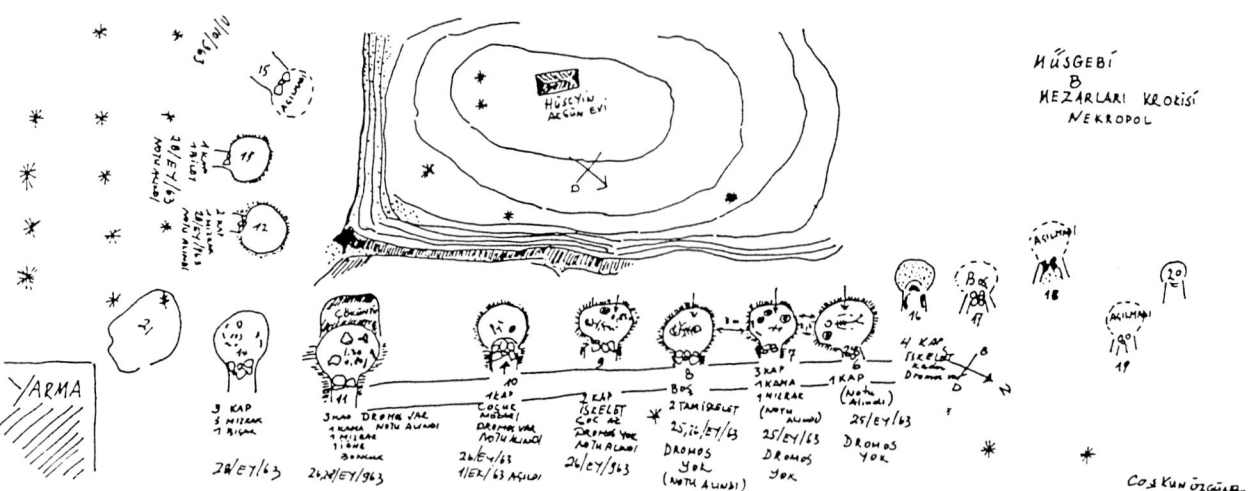

Fig. 7. Müsgebi – the spatial distribution of Tomb 6 to 21 (Özgünel 1987, fig. 1)

possible to draw conclusions on the spatial organization of the tombs.[60]

The tombs are subterranean chamber tombs, cut into the very soft white-greyish andesite (Fig. 8). The best-preserved examples consist of a dromos, in the form of a long trench sloping down towards the entrance; an entrance, closed by a small rubble wall that may be set in mortar,[61] and a burial chamber. The chambers vary in plan from circular to rectangular and the ceiling is made to resemble a dome. In some cases plaster was applied to the lower parts of the walls both in the chamber, and in the dromos.[62] The floor was made of hard packed soil with sandy areas on which the deceased were placed.[63]

Information on architectural details is sparse, but the available measurements and descriptions are listed

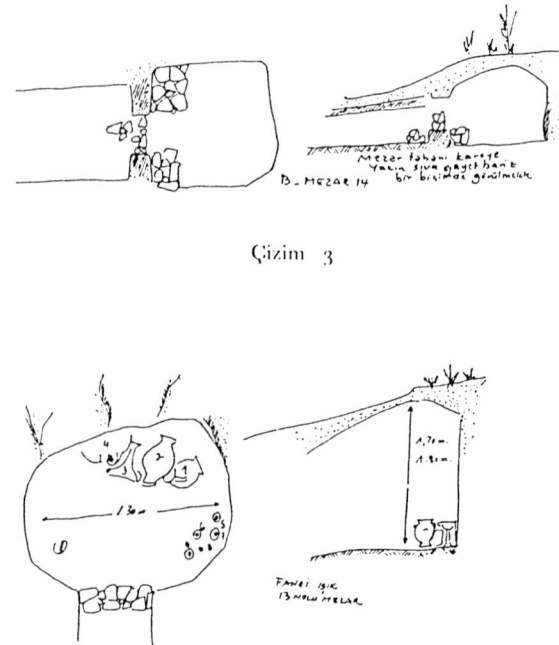

Fig. 8. Müsgebi – Sketch drawings of Müsgebi Tomb 2, 14, and 13 (Özgünel 1987, fig. 2-4)

Tomb no.	Dromos	Length	Width	Height	Entrance	Height	Width	Ø	Depth	Chamber	Height	Width	Depth	Ø
5											1.80			1.75
6	collapsed									elliptical			2.00	1.70
12										collapsed		2.40	1.80	
15	widens	1.80	1.10-1.25					1.00					1.10	
16		2.35	1.10	1.30		0.45	0.60		0.55		max 1.05	1.75	1.30	
22												1.95	1.85	
39		2.05	1.53	3.30						trapezoid	2.50	2.30-2.60	2.47-3.00	
43		3.30	0.90	1.50							1.25	1.30	1.40	
44		4.10	0.80	1.55										
45	plastered	3.55-3.70			plastered		0.65-0.50		0.60		1.60	2.00	1.60	
46											0.85	0.75	0.65	

Fig. 9. Müsgebi – architectonic details and measurements (Anne Marie Carstens)

in the table (Fig. 9). Only tomb 16 was published with a plan and section, probably chosen as the most spectacular and well preserved (Fig. 10).[64] Özgünel later published three sketches, showing the plan and section of tomb 2, 13, and 14 (Fig. 8).[65]

The majority of the Müsgebi burials are inhumations. According to Boysal, three tombs contained cremation burials: tomb 15 contained "bones with a black discoloration or carbonized", and in tomb 39 a skeleton, which had been burnt, was found on the floor of the chamber.[66] In both cases, the tombs also contained inhumation burials. In tomb 3, ashes were placed in a ceramic container.[67] The dating of the pottery in these three tombs did not extend beyond LHIIIB.

The evidence of cremation is not as unambiguous as it was presented in the publication. The relics of a cremation cannot be arranged to form a whole skeleton, unless the cremation took place inside the tomb chamber. This is not likely to have happened. The chambers of the Müsgebi tombs are generally small and the entrances low and narrow. They would not have admitted the oxygen needed for the fire to pass through. Rather, a pyre may have been placed above the body either as part of the funeral or, more likely, as an act of fumigation to clean the tomb. Such a pyre would leave black discoloration on the bones or even carbonise them.[68] Black discoloration may, however,

appear in the process of putrefaction as a result of chemical reactions between the bones, the composition of the soil and the humidity in the tomb.[69]

Only a few metal objects were found in the Müsgebi tombs and unfortunately they were never published. However, Boysal mentioned that the excavation in 1967 had yielded 20 metal objects: "Unter den Beigaben aus Metall sind Messer, Dolche und Lanzenspitzen

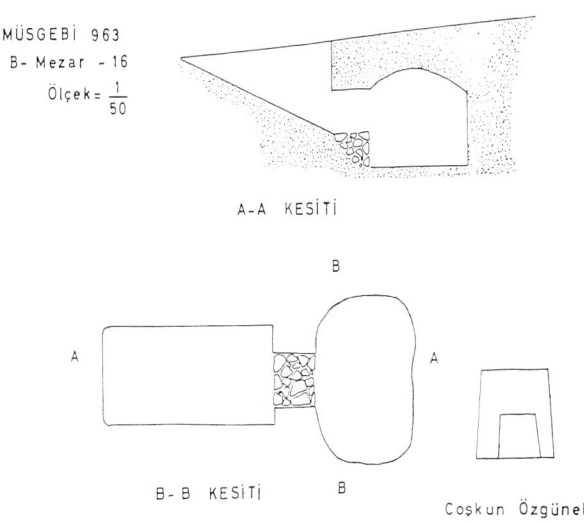

Fig. 10. Plan and section of Müsgebi Tomb 16 (Boysal 1967a, fig. 5)

Tomb no.	2	3	4	6	7	9	10	11	12	13	14	15	16	18	20	21	22	23	24	26	27	28	29	30	31	32	33	3
Undated										1				2	1													
LHIIIA1		1																										
LHIIIA2	19	1	1	1				2	1	1		5	1	1	1	3	11	1	5	1	2					19		
LHIIIA2-B		2			2	1	1		1		1		2	1			2		2	1	2	1	1				4	
LHIIIB		2							4	1	1			1↓				1	3								4	
LHIIIC1									4																			
Total	19	5	2	1	2	1	1	2	2	9	3	6	3	5	2	3	11	3	5	1	5	4	2	1	1	19	8	
Piriform jar	2							2		2		1					5		1							1	1	
Stirrup jar	6	2							1			1				1		1	1		1	3	1			6		
Amphoriskos										2																		
Alabastron																	1											
Pyxis			1	1						1	1						1	1	2							1	1	1
Flask	2								1					1	1													
Askos																										1		
Brazier																	1	1								2		
Basket vase	1																											
Bowl		1							1	1																		
Jug		1	1			1	1		1	1	2		2	1			1		1	1	1					1	3	
Kylix	4	1							1	2			2	3	1	2												
Cup or mug	4		1		1					1	1			4		1					1					7	3	
Total	19	5	2	1	2	1	1	2	2	9	3	6	3	5	2	3	11	3	5	1	5	4	2	1	1	19	8	

Fig. 11. Müsgebi – pottery finds in context (Anne Marie Carstens)

in qualitätvollen Exemplaren vertreten."[70] Later C. Mee reported that the exhibition at the Bodrum Museum included seven spears, three knives, one razor, and one dagger.[71]

C. Mee examined the pottery from the necropolis at Müsgebi in an article from 1978.[72] In 1996 Özgünel published a contextual catalogue of the Müsgebi pottery in his monograph on Mycenaean pottery in Anatolia.[73] The catalogue only deals with 176 pieces of pottery, whereas the total amount of pottery published by Boysal was 179 pieces. I have listed the pottery finds in their context in the table (Fig. 11).[74]

Pottery was found in 39 of the 48 tombs.[75] The most common shape is the traditional funeral vase, the stirrup jar (35 pieces), presumably preferred for its content of aromatic oil,[76] followed by cups (32 pieces),[77] jugs (28 pieces), kylikes (24 pieces), and piriform jars (24 pieces).[78] The majority, 103 pieces, can be dated to the LHIIIA2 period. The period of greatest use covers the LHIIIA2 and LHIIIB period with 166 vessels. Only six pieces can be dated later, in the LHIIIC period, and one earlier, in LHIIIA1.

The distribution of shapes in the tombs forms a somewhat uncharacteristic picture. One or more jugs were found in 21 tombs, whereas stirrup jars were found in 18 tombs and cups and mugs in 15 tombs. The piriform jugs appear in 14 tombs and kylikes were

36	37	38	39	40	41	42	45	46	47	no context	TOTAL
						1					6
											1
3			4		2		6		2	6	103
1	1	1		1				2		6	36
					1					2↓; 3	27
						1				1	6
4	1	1	5	1	2	2	6	2		18	179
1					1		1	1		3	24
1		1	1				2	1	2	2	35
							1				3
											1
		1						1		2	16
											5
											1
											4
											1
										1	5
1			1	1		1	2	1		2	28
			2				1			3	24
1					1		1	1		3	32
4	1	1	5	1	2	2	6	2	2	18	179

found in 12 tombs. If the group of drinking vessels are regarded as one (then comprising cups, mugs and kylikes) they appear in 24 tombs.

Almost half the vessels were made locally, with a predominance of jugs, cups and pyxides (Fig. 12). According to Mee, the jugs "look local" and share with Koan jugs the pinched, almost trefoil lip usually considered to show the influence of Hittite, beak-spouted jugs.[79] Most of the cups are undecorated and rather unpretentious. The pyxis is uncommon in the Dodekanese area, but its popularity in Müsgebi suggests that it may have been local. The fabric of the local vessels does not contain mica, which is very characteristic of the local Mycenaean pottery production at Miletos, but also frequently found in wares presumably produced in the region around Milas.[80] Even though the high concentration of mica is a generally accepted characteristic of Asia Minor fabrics, its absence should in no way preclude a local production.[81]

At the conference *Problems in Greek Prehistory*, Manchester 1986, K.B. Gödecken presented results of petrologic analyses of pottery from both Miletos and Müsgebi. She was able to find two different workshops producing LHIIIA2 and LHIIIB1 pottery in Miletos and even proved that a number of Müsgebi vessels were produced in these Milesian workshops.[82] However, her investigations have never been published and it remains uncertain to what degree the interpretations may hold good. The vessels ascribed to the Miletos workshops belong predominantly to the group that Özgünel and Mee considered to be of local production. Thus, while it does not reflect the number of Dodekanese imports, it may result in a rather reduced number of vessels made locally.[83]

Most of the imported pottery is Dodekanese, especially Rhodian. These imports are found among the piriform jars (seven pieces), stirrup jars (four pieces), some of the flasks (?), at least one jug, and the basket vase. The majority of the undecorated kylikes (12 pieces) are Rhodian, as are all the braziers and amphoriskoi. The majority of the stirrup jars (15 pieces) may be Argolid imports, while only two piriform jars are unquestionably imports from the Argolid.

The pottery found in the Mycenaean tombs in Müsgebi represents both local production and imported ware. In this respect the material may be representative of other Mycenaean centres on the Anatolian west coast, especially Miletos. The greater proportion of the imported ware is Dodekanese, and Karia seem to have been closely connected to the Dodekanese. The region – what we may call the south-east Aegean (then comprising the Karian coast and the adjacent islands) formed a natural entity, topographically as well as geographically. Travel by sea was safe only in terms of the shorter crossings. In this respect we may consider trade with two kinds of import: the regional Dodekanese (and Milesian?) and the few interregional imports, mainly Argolid.

Shape	Local	Rhodian	Koan	Dodekanese	Argolid	Mycenaean	Minoan	Import	?	Total
Piriform jar FS35	1	7								8
Piriform jar FS45	3				4					7
Piriform jar - others		1		8 (?)						9
Stirrup jar	4	4			4+6(?)	5	1	1	10	35
Amphoriskos			3							3
Alabastron	1									1
Pyxis	16(?)									16
Flask	4(?)			4(?)				1		5
Askos									1	1
Brazier		4								4
Basket vase	1									1
Bowl	2	1				1		1		5
Jug	28									28
Kylix	1	12			4				7	24
Cup or mug	27							5		32
Total	84 or 88	29	3	8 or 12	18	6	1	8	18	179

Fig. 12. Müsgebi – pottery production centres (Anne Marie Carstens)

If we consider Gödecken's results to be valid, the situation at the Müsgebi settlement can be summarized as follows: A Mycenaean necropolis was in use in the late LHIIIA1 period, grew rapidly through the LHIIIA2 and LHIIIB period, and by the end of the Bronze Age it went out of use, either because the settlers moved or because they chose another burial area. During this period strong relations with both Rhodos to the south and Miletos to the north characterised the community – pottery at least was imported from both places.

Where did these Mycenaeans come from? Unlike the situation at both Iasos and Miletos the Müsgebi settlement seems to have no antecedents in the earlier part of the Bronze Age.[84] Did the settlers on the Halikarnassos peninsula emigrate early in the LHIII period from either the Dodekanese / Rhodes or Miletos? It may seem to be stretching the archaeological evidence too far to claim that this could be proven by the finds from the necropolis. However, as the majority of the imported vessels in Müsgebi were produced in the region – either the Dodekanese or Miletos – reachable within a shorter distance than, for instance, mainland Greece, the presence of both these kinds of pots in Müsgebi may reflect direct relations between Milesians, Rhodians, and the Müsgebi people.

This close contact with the southeast Aegean and the Bronze Age settlement at Miletos illustrated by the Müsgebi necropolis may have constituted the starting point and the solid basis for cultural change and exchange within these regions. Through time these activities fluctuated but always remained an important part of the southwestern Karian culture.

Anatolia, the Aegean, and a Bronze Age *koiné*

Hittite texts tell of intensive exchanges on political and military levels between the Ahhijawa and the Hittite kingdoms in the Late Bronze Age.[85] The kingdom Ahhijawa has been interpreted as the Mycenaeans, maybe with the nucleus of this kingdom at Mycenae, while Millewanda, an Ahhijawan city located between the Hittites and its "motherland" may be the Aegean settlement at Miletos.[86] These conclusions are, however, results of an interpretation based on rather circumstantial evidence, and other views have, since the first presentation of the theory in 1924, been debated among Hittitologists and Aegean archaeologists.

The nature of the Aegean settlements in western Anatolia and their relation to the Hittites have been aspects of this discussion, but the archaeological evidence is fairly meagre, though, however, increasing in recent years. The new excavations of prehistoric Miletos have as their objective the determining of the nature of the Minoan and later Mycenaean influences in Miletos, and are also concerned with providing a better answer to the hypothesis of Miletos as Millewanda.[87] While a satisfying answer to the latter question may put an end to the Millewanda discussion, it seems more interesting, in a wider perspective, to explore the nature of the settlement at Miletos and its relation to both Anatolia and the Aegean.

In the archaeological tradition Miletos has been regarded as both the Mycenaean outpost and the leading Mycenaean city on the Anatolian west coast.[88] The discussion of the relations between the Aegean city and its Anatolian neighbours has focused mainly on the late Mycenaean fortification wall, its masonry and layout. Previous excavations in Miletos only paid attention to the finds of Aegean pottery, while Anatolian undecorated wares were only published at random and with no indication of the quantitative relations between Aegean and other pottery.[89]

Traditionally the excavations of prehistoric Miletos have been divided into three building periods, and the new excavations, initiated in 1994, also follow this practise. The first building period is characterised by imported MMIIIB and LMIA pottery, and much locally-made domestic pottery, in particular conical cups. In this period only two percent of the pottery is Anatolian. More spectacular finds have also been made: a serpentine vase with a hole in the bottom and an alabaster jug, both interpreted as cultic vessels. Fragments of fresco-decoration depicting a lily, but in rather bad condition, may also derive from a sacral context, maybe a shrine.[90]

Some architectonic remains belong to the second period, among these an oikos house, where pottery kilns have also been found.[91] They represent three different types, the first mainly found on the Greek mainland, the second found only in Miletos, while the third is a Minoan type, and apart from this example it is only known from Crete. Thus, a local production of Mycenaean pottery in Miletos is clearly evidenced by the kilns and their contents.

A destruction level datable to LHIIIA2-LHIIIB, divides the third from the second building period. In one of the Hittite texts, the Annals of King Mursili II (*CTH* 61) a rebellion against the Hittites is described: In the upheavals, which followed Mursili's accession to the throne, Millewanda took sides with the King of Ahhijawa and abandoned its Hittite allegiance. In response Mursili sent his two generals, Gulla and Malaziti, who attacked and destroyed Millewanda. This event has been dated to 1318 or 1314 BC.[92] It is of course tempting to interpret the destruction levels as the remains of Gulla's and Malaziti's attack. However, in order to present convincing evidence, it is necessary to find a significant amount of undisturbed and datable pottery from the period in question. Hitherto the material confirming the correspondence consisted of 27 pieces of fragmented pottery and the transition between LHIIIA2 and LHIIIB was dated to the beginning of the 14th century BC.[93] This chronological frame has recently been down-dated by dendrochronological examinations of a wooden beam, which formed part of the cargo in the Uluburun Shipwreck. The tree was felled in 1305 BC, and the pottery on board the ship belonged to the transition between LHIIIA2 and LHIIIB.[94] The Niemeiers state, however, that the pottery material from the destruction level is still rather limited so while the chronology is now more consistent with the historical date of a Hittite sack of Millewanda, the material evidence is still meagre.[95] Only five percent of the pottery in the second building period is Anatolian. The third period, covering LHIIIB and LHIIIC, is, as yet, only sparsely represented and only a few architectonic remains can be dated to the final phase of the Mycenaean period.[96]

While only a very little material is Anatolian pottery – in the first period two percent, in the second five percent – and the production, as illustrated by the finds inside and near the kilns, is clearly concentrated on Aegean wares, we cannot hastily conclude that Miletos was a pure Aegean settlement. Indeed a vast number of coincidences may have disturbed the results excavated. The excavated area may simply have formed the Aegean quarters of a town, while other ethnic groups occupied other districts.[97] Nevertheless, this presents a picture of a Mycenaean city with contacts to the Hittites. While architectural remains and local pottery production were clearly Mycenaean, patchy pottery finds, related to the Beycesultan ware, are the only evidence of Anatolian influences.[98]

In the discussion of cultural exchange between east and west certain architectonic features have been put forward as evidence of exchange of either craftsmen or engineering skills. The "Cyclopean" masonry has been interpreted as a Hittite invention that was brought to mainland Greece from Anatolia. However, a recent study of Mycenaean architecture has proven that the so-called Cyclopean masonry *de facto* is a worked rubble masonry style, while the Hittite masonry is pure polygonal masonry without the smaller stones used as fill between the bigger ones in the Cyclopean masonry.[99]

In the case of the subterranean "galleries" in both Tiryns and at the south gate of Boğazköy the roofing principle is, however, identical. In both cases a corbelled barrel vault roofed the galleries and even the function of these was most likely identical: the galleries formed a protected entrance or way out of the fortification.[100] The reason for choosing the corbelled vault may, however, be that it served as the practical answer to a simple construction problem. In that way it is hardly evidence of direct contact between Hittite and Aegean engineers.

The Late Bronze Age fortification wall at Miletos, dated to the LHIIIB period, has been the subject of similar discussions. The wall has been interpreted as a Hittite-inspired fortification or as a hybrid form combining both Mycenaean and Hittite fortification techniques.[101]

At Troy we encounter a Hittite fortification and a layout of the city, with a *Burgberg* and an *Unterstadt*, a plan not yet found on the Greek mainland.[102] While the Mycenaean pottery found in Troy used to be explained as Argolid imports and the "Greekness" of the town questioned,[103] recent studies prove otherwise. On the basis of visual examination of more than 500 shards P. Mountjoy has identified a number of distinct features that differentiate the Trojan pottery from the possible Argolid imports. Abundant gold mica and the softness of the clay characterise this local production. The same clay was also used in the following Geometric and Archaic pottery. Mountjoy has emphasized that the situation is paralleled in Miletos, where, originally, the Mycenaean pottery was also regarded as Argolid imports.[104]

The excavated part of Bronze Age Miletos reflects an Aegean settlement with only sporadic use of pottery which was not Aegean. Indeed the evidence of local ceramic production emphasized that the Aegean settlers were self-sufficient. Apparently indigenous and Aegean people did not live together in an integrated society, but rather in adjacent enclaves. Perhaps certain buildings, such as the fortifications, were influenced by Hittite architecture, but the people who lived in the now-excavated part of the town, were Aegean. At least that is what archaeology tells us.

Troy on the other hand may represent a town with a more mixed population, where locals and Aegean settlers lived together in a town laid out according to Hittite principles.

Both texts and archaeology thus speak of common life between Aegean peoples and Anatolians in what has been called a Late Bronze Age *koiné*.

Cremation

While much of the discussion on the relations between Anatolia and the Aegean has concentrated on specific sites, like Miletos, Troy and Iasos, certain themes have also been described with the model of adoption of cultural elements as starting point. Among these themes the introduction of cremation in the Late Bronze Age Aegean has been debated, especially in connection with the necropolis at Müsgebi.

I have already argued that it is highly unlikely that the three cremation burials at Müsgebi actually existed. If so, the notion of interpreting Müsgebi as a link in an adoption of cremation from east to west collapses. But the idea has been the object of much debate and this debate constitutes a good example of the way archaeology has traditionally argued over cultural exchange.

In the publication of the Perati Necropolis, S. Iakovidis presented a study of the distribution of cremation activity in the Mycenaean world in which he concluded that the practice of cremation did not appear on the mainland until the LHIIIC period.[105] In the Perati Cemetery, dated to LHIIIC, 18 persons had been cremated.[106] These persons were indistinguishable from those inhumed.[107] Iakovidis argued that the introduction of this new practice came from the Hittites via Müsgebi and pointed to evidence contemporary with Müsgebi (LHIIIA2-LHIIIB) of cremation burials on Kos and Rhodes. However, in M. Benzi's re-publication of the Ialysos material the cremation burials have been down-dated to the LHIIIC period.[108]

Still, the theory of an adoption of Hittite burial rites – understood as cremation burials – remains intriguing, particularly so if down-dated since the line of development proposed by Iakovidis, from Müsgebi via the Dodekanese to Crete, follows the area of influence known from a much later period, when Rhodes in the Hellenistic age was the leading power in the southeastern Aegean, controlling a large part of Karia.[109]

The argument involves the assumption that cremation was widely practised, almost exclusively among the peoples of Anatolia.[110] This has been generally accepted to such an extent that evidence of cremation burials has been taken as being indicative of a Hittite presence.[111] However, J. Seeher has pointed to the fact that the practice of cremation burials among the Hittites was always concurrent with inhumation burials.[112] Normally the cremation remains were placed in a separate cluster of tombs within a cemetery that also contained inhumations.[113] But in some cases, such as the Middle Bronze necropolis at Demircihüyük-Sarıket[114] at Eskişehir, the Late Bronze cemeteries at Panaztepe at Izmir and Beşiktepe in Troas,[115] the cremation remains were deposited in the same tombs as the inhumation burials.

The burial practice, either cremation or inhumation, was used as a means of distinguishing members of the society – either illustrating ethnic differentiation, for example caused by intermarriage between ethnic groups – or indicating a special rank or status, for example priests or chieftains.[116]

Seeher questions the generally accepted theory of an east west line of development in the use of cremation in the Bronze Age: "Die Verbreitung der Sitte hat früher und wohl auch schneller stattgefunden und dürfte eher mit der Übernahme durch verschiedene lokale Volksgruppen zu erklären sein, wobei noch nicht einmal klar ist, ob die Brandbestattung wirklich aus dem Osten gekommen ist, denn auch auf dem Balkan und in Griechenland war die Totenverbrennung seit dem Neolithikum bekannt. Sogar die autochthone Entstehung, allerdings kaum ohne einen Impuls von aussen, ist noch immer als Möglichkeit in Betracht zu ziehen."[117]

While the cremation rite may have occurred or been "invented" independently in different periods and regions, the random diffusion in the Late Bronze Age may of course be the result of movements of people, which were not necessarily part of large migrations. Rather it may reflect the high level of contact between the Late Bronze Age people, and a desire to differentiate groups of people by another burial practice.

More evidence of cultural encounters and contact has been found in recent years at Panaztepe, north of Izmir. Here A. and E. Erkanal are excavating a settlement with continued habitation from the third millennium into Archaic times.[118] LHIII cemeteries have been excavated both west and north of the tepe; they show a significant combination of Aegean and Anatolian features and a frequent reuse of tombs. The cemeteries include both small pithos burials in stone settings and cist graves as well as tholoi. This is quite definitely an exciting place, providing apparent evidence of both continuity and interaction. The excavators have reported finds of Mycenaean pottery, as well as the grey Minyan ware.[119] The Panaztepe finds may give us more information about a multicultural site, where a mixed population lived together in a peaceful assimilation of Mycenaean settlers with an indigenous population, as early as the Late Bronze Age period.

Libation

Libation was an important element in Hittite ritual behaviour.[120] It was performed several times in the course of the Hittite royal funeral rituals. These are known from text fragments, probably written down in the 14th century BC but originating before the middle of the second millennium BC. The Hittite texts describe different types of sacrifices associated with the funeral, including libations, followed by deliberate breaking of ceramic vessels used in the ritual. Animal sacrifice is also described, especially the burnt offerings of the heads of horses and cattle, but also that of minor "chthonic" animals such as birds.[121] A survey of the archaeological evidence of burials from inland Anatolia indicates that libation sacrifices took place in the context of funerals in general.

The excavations of the Hittite cemetery at Yanarlar, near Afyon, revealed 36 pithos burials, all inhumations.[122] Smaller objects, such as spindle whorls, knucklebones and bronze pins were put inside the pithos. However, the pottery finds, which consist almost exclusively of pouring vessels,[123] were placed near the rim of the pithos. This may indicate that libations were offered at the funeral and afterwards the libation vessels were placed next to the burial pithos and buried in the same pit.[124]

The pithos burials from the cemetery at Gordion[125] are similar to the Yanarlar evidence in that pottery (jugs and bowls)[126] was placed outside the pithos, thus also indicating a libation performed at the funeral before filling in the pit. Some of the grave goods were deliberately broken.

Of the 131 cremation burials placed in beak-spouted jars in the cemetery at Ilıca,[127] only 14 contained pottery other than the urn jug. Here, a drinking vessel, either a cup or a small bowl, was present in nine burials, while beak-spouted jugs were found in five burials. As in the two previous examples, the pottery was placed near the urn.

A cemetery at Kazankaya, north of Hattusa / Boğazköy, which had been severely plundered before the excavation, seems to confirm this picture.[128] The grave goods consisted of bowls, teapots and beaked pitchers, but more specific conclusions could not be drawn. The four cemeteries at Yanarlar, Gordion, Ilıca, and Kazankaya can all be dated to around the middle of the second millennium BC.

More unusual are the burials at Osmankayası, probably the necropolis of Hattusa, where the burial ground was formed by an overhanging rock creating a cave.[129] Both cremation and inhumation were practised and most of the pottery belonging to the burials was deliberately broken. Animal sacrifices – horses, mules, cattle, and sheep – were also performed at the funeral and buried in the cave.[130] The cemetery was in use during the Old Hittite Kingdom, from the 17th to the 14th century BC.

In the Hittite burials, the grave goods are generally few in number; often only one vase is included. But the overall picture shows that the ceramic containers chosen for this purpose all belonged to the group of pouring and drinking vessels. They are often placed outside the burial as such, but in the same pit. The animal sacrifices at Osmankayası are so far a remarkable exception, which contrasts with the generally very modest burial gifts. But, on the other hand, the rituals performed at the burials at Osmankayası conform fairly closely to the literary descriptions of the funerary rituals.

A set of drinking vessels, consisting of a jug and a cup or a kylix, is frequently included in the burial gifts at Müsgebi. Indeed, if the pottery is arranged according to function, the drinking vessels, both cups and kylikes, exceed in number all other shapes by 56 pieces.[131] In 17 of the 39 tombs containing pottery, a drinking or a pouring vessel, or both, were deposited. Moreover, in the very poorest tombs with only a few vessels, jugs or cups were preferred to other shapes.[132] Whether the presence of a drinking service in the tombs is a mere coincidence or has a significance in a ritual sense, either as a banquet, a funeral meal or a liquid sacrifice performed at the funeral, needs closer examination.

The repertoire of grave goods must represent a conscious selection. In spite of the large number of publications on cult and burial rites in the Greek prehistoric period,[133] an analysis of burial gifts and their significance has yet to be carried out in the archaeological discipline.[134] In 1986, R. Laffineur put forward a theory concerning the animal rhyta in the

Mycenaean shaft graves.[135] He argued that the rhyta were deposited in the graves as a substitute for animal sacrifice.[136] Thus, the sacrifice was not (only) performed at the grave but (also) given to the dead inside the tomb.

The theory that the animal rhyta were meant as an abbreviated sacrifice or a symbolic representation may be applied to other types of grave goods, for instance, the ceramic containers. However, the difficulties regarding whether these vessels, and their contents, were meant as a meal for the dead, as a meal at the funeral or as an abbreviated sacrifice remain crucial.[137] These three meanings could, on the other hand, be included in the presence of only one (set of) vessel(s) – illustrating both the meal for the dead, the meal at the funeral *and* the sacrifice. An interpretation of the grave goods as the symbolic representation of a sacrifice must be regarded as a hypothesis. However, if we assume that the hypothesis holds good, the set of drinking vessels in the Müsgebi tombs may be understood as a representation of or a substitute for a liquid sacrifice performed at the funeral.[138]

The liquid sacrifice is one of the most common rites in Bronze Age religious practice, and furthermore it was extremely widespread both chronologically and geographically.[139] The ritual act could be performed in various ways, such as pouring liquid into a container, on an altar or on the ground.[140] The archaeological evidence for liquid sacrifices in Mycenaean cult shows that this cultic behaviour constituted a basic ritual performed on various levels, in the everyday family cult, at more public or communal celebrations, and at the funeral before sealing the tomb.[141] The liquid sacrifice in a Mycenaean context should be seen as an act which could be performed as liquid poured out, as liquid drunk, or as liquid placed in a cup on a table as a show dish. In that way, both a jug or a cup would indicate a liquid sacrifice, either as poured out, drunk or presented forward,[142] thus including both libations and drink-offerings.

Libations performed in connection with funerary and tomb cult are known in a quite developed form in the Middle Helladic tumulus tombs in the Argolid. Here, cover slabs with holes for pouring libations into the tumuli have been found. In addition, drinking and pouring vessels were preferred as grave goods.[143] At the Mycenaean tombs at Prosymna, evidence for libations performed at the sealing of the chamber tombs is indicated by kylikes found in the dromos.[144]

I suggest that a connection between a liquid sacrifice at the funeral, as represented by the grave goods, and an established tomb cult, performed by pouring libations into the tumuli, existed. The presence of libation vessels among the grave goods may even indicate a commitment to continuing the cult at the grave. Thereby, the sacrifice at the closing of the tomb includes a promise to establish a tomb cult at the grave.[145]

A Ritual *koiné*

Rather than indicating specific influences following specific routes, the apparent synchronism and similarities in the burial rites reflect the religious *koiné* in the eastern Mediterranean area in the second half of the second millennium BC.[146] This *koiné* probably covered the Aegean area, Anatolia, northern Syria and the Canaanite city-states, which all shared a palatial society and may best be characterised as a familiarity rather than a real unity, since the interrelations between the protagonists in question are to a large degree unknown.[147] Investigations in the eastern Mediterranean have so far focused on the relations between the Bronze Age Levant and the Minoan-Mycenaean areas, while the evidence from Anatolia and the Hurrian kingdom of Kizzuwatna, between Syria and Anatolia, has been somewhat ignored.[148]

Given the spread of relations between the Aegeans and the Hittites, as testified by both textual and archaeological evidence, one may be tempted to suggest that Hittite libation rites at the funeral were adopted in the Mycenaean tombs in Müsgebi. However, it seems more reasonable to argue, on the basis of, admittedly, sparse evidence, for a ritual coherence within the framework of a large cultural *koiné*. A search for a rigid system of evolution between one group and another would not take into account the nature of the close contact on many levels between the peoples of the eastern Mediterranean in the second half of the second millennium BC.[149]

A liquid sacrifice performed at the funeral seems to have formed part of the burial ritual in the Hittite world and may be represented by the pouring and drinking vessels among the grave goods at Müsgebi. These vessels should then be understood as an abbreviated sacrifice, a theory that has also been suggested for the iconography of Minoan larnakes.[150]

Whether the assumed similarity in the burial rites should be regarded as evidence of contact or as an emphasis on the *koiné,* understood as similarities originating from similar life conditions, remains an open question. It seems evident, however, that a common concept of ritual behaviour at the funeral existed between the Hittites and the people of the Aegean. In connection with the wide range of similarities in many different aspects of the archaeological material, this common concept may be interpreted as evidence of fairly intense contact between the peoples of Anatolia and the peoples of the Aegean area, suggesting that not always did these people see each other as opponents, merely as different.

I find it attractive to regard the Hellenization of western Anatolia as already embedded in the Bronze Age Aegean settlements. Routes of contact – physical as well as metaphysical – between the Aegean area and Anatolia were established then and they were never forgotten.

The Submycenaen Necropolis at Çömlekçi

Çömlekçi is a small village halfway between Bodrum and Milas, two km east of the modern road. The necropolis is situated in the southern outskirts of the village, and local villagers discovered it in 1967. During two campaigns, in 1968 and 1969, Y. Boysal excavated the necropolis, and the pottery from Çömlekçi was included in the collection of the Bodrum Museum and published together with the pottery from Müsgebi in 1969.[151]

The exact number of tombs excavated is not known and neither a plan of the excavation site nor any indication of the internal distribution of the tombs was published. Two types of cist tombs were found here, rectangular and circular, built in rubble masonry of smaller stones (0.1-0.3 m). The state of preservation was poor, mainly because of ploughing in the area and the information on the tombs likewise summary and unclear (Fig. 13).[152]

The size of the cists varies considerably and one may speculate whether the smallest cist, Tomb 11, once contained a cremation burial. The much larger Tomb 9 was apparently used for inhumation burials.

The floor was covered with stone slabs in most of the rectangular tombs (C, 1(?), 3, 4 and 9). Apparently some tombs had two floor levels, separated by a pavement of slabs placed on the floor.[153] In Tomb 2 slabs were set horizontally in the ground so as to divide the tomb into two compartments. Slabs set on edge formed the walls of Tomb 11. At least in some cases, the roofs of the rectangular tombs were roofed with stone slabs. The cover stones were found in situ in Tomb 11.

The circular tombs had a diameter up to 3 m, and the walls were preserved to a height between 0.3 and 0.6 m. Tomb 10, apparently the best preserved, had inclined walls, perhaps intended to form a domed roof. In every case the roof had collapsed.

Tomb	Chamber shape	W	L	H	Lower Ø	Upper Ø
1	Rectangular	0.92-0.98	1.02-1.11	0.80		
9	Rectangular	1.20-1.37	2.44-2.64	1.23		
11	Rectangular	0.45-0.46	0.34-0.36	0.34-0.40		
10	Circular			1.95?	1.20-1.27	0.95-1.12

Fig. 13. Çömlekçi – architectonic details and measurements (Anne Marie Carstens)

No entrance or dromos was found, but these features may very well have been destroyed by local cultivation.

Apparently both inhumation and cremation were in use in the necropolis. Tomb 9 contained two skulls and "other human bones"[154] while Tomb 2 revealed "small bone fragments, possibly burnt".[155]

A preliminary report of the 1968 campaign mentioned the find of a fibula,[156] and in the publication Boysal stated that Tomb 6 contained a fibula and a footed vase.[157] However, in the catalogue of the pottery no vases from the Çömlekçi excavation were marked with Tomb 6 as context.[158] According to the catalogue only Tomb B, 4 and 10 yielded pottery, in all five vessels, while the remaining 14 vessels were published without context. They may belong to the group of pottery which was handed over to the Bodrum Museum before the excavation.[159] The most common shape is the jug (four pieces) but amphoriskoi, cups and bowls are also frequent (three, two and three pieces respectively). However, with such limited material, mostly without a specific context, it becomes rather meaningless to draw any conclusions based on the representation of pottery. All the pottery belongs to the Sub-Mycenaean period and was characterised as local ware by both Boysal and Özgünel.[160] Özgünel has remarked that the material reveals a preference for ovoid shapes in the Sub-Mycenaean pottery. This may perhaps add to the theory suggesting a local production, as more depressed shapes are also found in later pottery probably produced in the Milas region.[161] As is the case with the presumed local production of the Müsgebi Necropolis, the clay contains no mica.

The Protogeometric Necropolis at Assarlik

Situated on a steep mountaintop in the southern part of the peninsula, the ancient site of Assarlik offers a perfect view of the coast towards both east and west, while to the south, this prospect is in the shadow of the hills between Akyarlar and Assarlik. Nowadays one reaches the site from the coastal road east of the village of Mandira. A wadi runs in a narrow valley between the village and the site. It continues in the direction of Çıfıt Kalesi, on the coast southeast of Assarlik. The most prominent remains of the ancient settlement are the still very well preserved gate and the rather long stretch of the fortification wall that once surrounded the hill.[162]

C.T. Newton visited Assarlik with Lieut. Smith in the autumn of 1857.[163] They came from the west coast and at Turgutreis[164] they turned northeast towards the village west of Assarlik, Akçaalan.[165] Here they proceeded southeast towards the hill of Assarlik and discovered three chamber tombs, the first located on the side of a hill (Newton 1), the next two some 200 m away, presumably in the direction of the hill of Assarlik, built on the same slope (Newton 2 and 3). Newton and Smith climbed the hill and described the ruins on the plateau. Descending from the summit they found "…several tombs of a very ancient form." Two of these were described as located on the slope of the Assarlik hill itself (Newton 4 and 5), while a third may have been sited some distance away (Newton 6).[166]

In 1886 the necropolis at Assarlik was examined and partly excavated by W.R. Paton.[167] He assumed that the tombs described by Newton were situated in "a valley running north", but apparently Paton only referred to the tombs that Newton described as he descended the hill (Newton 4-6).[168] Paton excavated two tumulus-tombs (Paton A-B) and several "circular and rectangular enclosures" (Paton C-O). These tombs were situated "on a ridge facing the acropolis to the S.E., and beyond this on both sides of a torrent bed, the direction of which is south-easterly, and which joins the sea near Chifoot-Kale-si".[169] This topographical description indicates that Paton's tombs were located southeast of the hill of Assarlik and on both sides on the ravine, which continues to Çıfıt Kalesi. When Bean and Cook visited the site in the early 1950's they found that "there are tombs on the edges of the site, in the valley to the west, and on the watershed east of the main gate of Assarlik towards the hamlet of Madıra… there are built tomb complexes still visible on the ridge leading down to Aspat."[170]

Tomb	Dromos	W/L/H	Entrance	W/D/H	Chamber	W/L/H	Roof	Krepis wall
1	Facing east; isodomous courses of oblong blocks, more massive masonry than the rest	1.37/2.28/1.22	Two frame-blocks, regularly dressed	nm/nm/1.22	Oblong blocks	2.59/3.20/nm	Egyptian arch Dromos: large slabs	Preserved up to 1.06; thickness: 0.90
2			Facing southeast		Good masonry	2.90/3.20/1.22	The walls leant inwards to each other	Partly preserved
3	Facing northeast	0.98-0.88/ 3.40/1.45	Doorway marked by slight groove; two square holes on each side		Isodomous courses of squared stones	2.64/3.45/nm	Egyptian vault; all four walls inclined	Preserved up to 2-3 courses
4					Beautiful ex. of isodomous masonry	3.05/nm/1.83	Angular roof	
5					Isodomous masonry	3.66/3.84/2.44	Beehive	
6					Very large stones	3.20/4.45/nm	Not preserved	

H = preserved or measurable height; nm= no measurements provided

Fig. 14. Assarlık – architectonic details and measurements of the tombs investigated by C.T. Newton (Anne Marie Carstens)

Newton's Tombs

Apparently the tombs found and described by Newton were empty when he examined them. The descriptions concentrate on the architecture. It was especially the roofing system which attracted his attention. Unfortunately he described the various constructions in a somewhat ambiguous way, which makes further interpretation uncertain. I have listed the features and measurements of each tomb in a table (Fig. 14), quoting Newton's terminology.

Newton 1 was published with a sketch plan and consisted of a rectangular chamber placed in "a circular enclosure". A passage built in isodomic masonry led into the chamber, which was roofed with a corbelled barrel vault. The circular enclosure outside the tomb may be a krepis wall, surrounding a tumulus raised above the chamber. The passage or dromos was very carefully built and roofed with large slabs (Fig. 15).

Newton 2 was also built in isodomic masonry, but only the chamber was preserved. As in the first tomb the walls leaned inwards, maybe to form a corbelled barrel vault. However, the description may indicate that the inclination was found on all four sides, which

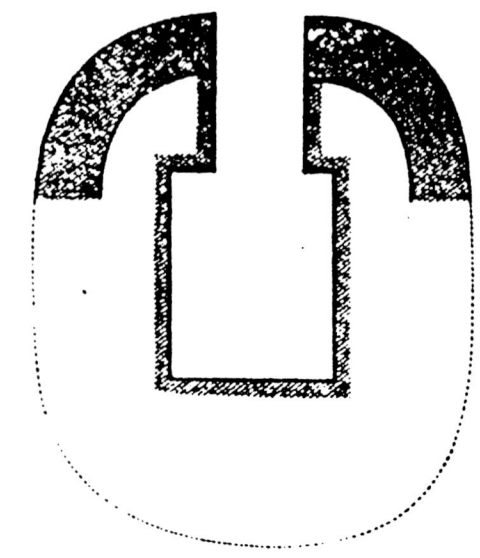

Fig. 15. Assarlık – Newton's tomb 1 (Newton 1862-1863, plate LXXXIII)

would then imply that the roof was constructed as a pyramid vault. Part of a krepis wall was found on the "back" of the tomb.

The best preserved of Newton's tombs, Newton 3, was also built in isodomic masonry of "squared stones". It consisted of a chamber, a doorway and a dromos. The doorway had two square holes cut below the lintel on each side of the doorframe so as to make provision for a bar. The walls in the chamber were preserved up to one course above the lintel and Newton described them all as incurving "showing that the chamber had been covered by an Egyptian vault". Here the description clearly indicates curving on all four walls, meaning that the roof was constructed as a pyramid vault. The krepis wall surrounding the tomb was preserved to a height of two to three courses.

The three following tombs seem to have borne different roofs. Newton 4, built in "beautiful" isodomic masonry, was covered by an angular roof described as "two stones converged at the top so as to form an acute angle". This seems to indicate a pitched roof. Newton 5, also in isodomic masonry, was covered by a corbelled "dome", which began at the third course where the walls curved inwards and the corners disappeared into a circle. Newton described the dome as a beehive. The last tomb, Newton 6, was constructed of very large blocks, but only a single course was preserved. Two of the blocks were provided with a notch, which Newton thought might have served as a "binder" for the next course. The chamber was rectangular with an entrance in one of the short sidewalls.

Apparently a corbelled barrel vault covered Tomb 1, while Tomb 4 had a pitched roof. But the remaining Tombs 2, 3, and 5 (6 was only preserved as far as the first wall course) were roofed with pyramid vaults, which in the case of Newton 5, closely resembled a beehive dome.

Newton used the term "isodomous masonry" in the description of Tomb 1, 3 and 4. Without illustrations of these walls, it remains unclear to what degree the individual blocks were drafted. In Tomb 3 and 4 the masonry is described as, respectively, "isodomous courses of squared stones" and "a beautiful example of isodomous masonry". We must assume that these blocks were carefully dressed, whereas the masonry of Tombs 1, 2 and 5 may have been less precise. Newton never suggested a date for the tombs.

Paton's Tombs

The tombs excavated by Paton in 1886 yielded both pottery and metal finds, but they also provided more detailed information on the architecture and not least the construction of the roofs. Details and measurements provided by Paton are listed in the table (Fig. 16).

Paton's Tomb A and B were built next to each other, southeast of the hill of Assarlık. Tomb A was published with a plan and section, and described in detail. The tomb consisted of a dromos, roofed with slabs and an entrance/doorframe constructed of four large rectangu-

Tomb	Dromos	W/L/H	Entrance	W/D/H	Chamber	W/L/H	Roof	Krepis wall
A	Facing northwest	nm/13.96/nm	Frame, threshold and lintel of ashlars	0.92-0.76/nm/0.99	Polygonal masonry, dressed stones	2.08/2.33/2.95	All walls curve inward, the side walls most	Preserved up to two courses, rubble masonry
B	Facing southwest		Loosely built		Polygonal masonry, dressed stones		As A	?
C	Facing southwest			0.91/nm/1.07		2.95/3.55/1.98 at top: 1.82/2.74/nm	Collapsed	Placed in circular enclosure
D	Facing northwest			0.69/nm/nm		2.13/2.64/1.83	?	

nm = no measurements provided

Fig. 16. Assarlık – architectonic details and measurements of the tombs excavated by W.R. Paton (Anne Marie Carstens)

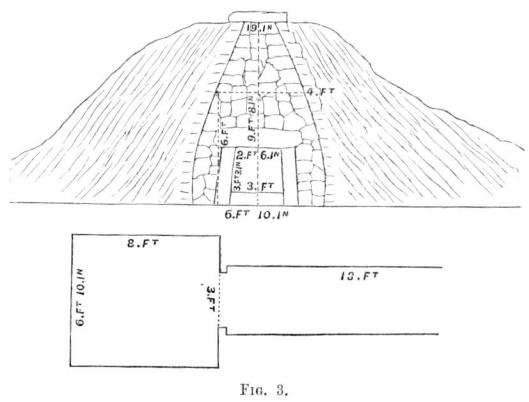

Fig. 17. Assarlık – sketch of Paton's tomb A (Paton 1887, fig. 3)

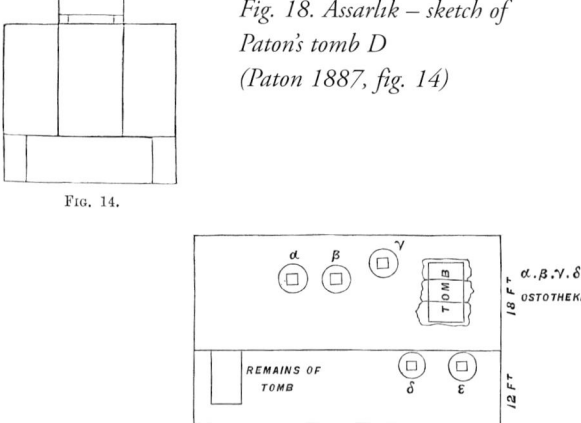

Fig. 18. Assarlık – sketch of Paton's tomb D (Paton 1887, fig. 14)

Fig. 19. Assarlık – sketch of Paton's tomb N (Paton 1887, fig. 16)

lar blocks. The chamber had incurving sidewalls, but the short walls also curved, although "less sensibly".[171] Two large blocks covered the top of the roof (Fig. 17) A krepis wall preserved to a height of two courses and built of "irregularly shaped stones",[172] surrounded the tomb and kept a rubble tumulus in position. Both Tomb A and B were built in a polygonal masonry of dressed stones. Tomb B was somewhat smaller (but no measurements were provided) and the doorway was "loosely built".

Paton found at least seven circular and four rectangular "enclosures" southwest of tomb A and B. He noted that each of the rather poorly-preserved circles contained a chamber covered by two or three large blocks. Paton interpreted the circular enclosures as the remains of krepis walls for tumuli raised above the chambers. These tombs may very well have been constructed as Tomb A, covered by "a kind of arch, on the top of which rest the covers."[173] The rectangular enclosures were found empty apart from one which contained a cist tomb lined with terracotta slabs covered by a circular stone.[174]

Tomb C, D, and E apparently belonged to this group of circular enclosures. Tomb C consisted of a dromos, an entrance and a chamber. The roof had fallen in and left the chamber much disturbed. Inside Tomb D, a tomb "of similar construction within circle", three cists were placed along the walls in a ∏-shape (Fig. 18). The cists were equal in size, 1.83 x 0.56 m, and apparently the top of their sides reached 0.43 m above the floor level. They were lined with terracotta slabs. Tomb E was also a tumulus tomb. It was only partially cleaned and Paton did not describe it further.

Down the hill to the south in the direction of Çıfıt Kalesi Paton observed a series of rectangular enclosures. Three of these (Tomb M, N, and O) were examined and some of their architectural details were described. Tomb M was a very long enclosure with two small cists (0.46 x 0.30 m) lined with stones, at the east end. They both had their circular cover placed in situ. Tomb N consisted of two long enclosures, built together and containing five small cists and two other larger cists (ca 1.8 x 1 m) (Fig. 19). In one of the small cists the ashes were placed in a large vase.[175] Tomb O included two small cists, and at least five other cists, one of these a pithos burial.[176]

Paton also examined two tombs placed on the same slope as the tumulus Tombs C, D, and E (southwest of A and B) but "higher up".[177] It is unclear whether these two tombs belonged to the tumulus group, but it seems most likely. Paton remarked that "the tops of both had been carried away", and also that the tombs contained fragments of terracotta sarcophagi.

Paton and Myres included a survey of Karian tombs in their report on travels made in 1893 and 1894.[178] Here the Assarlık material was more clearly presented. The rectangular enclosures were described as tomb terraces: "it should be observed that, from whatever cause, the level of the ground was frequently higher within the enclosure than outside; and that where the ground was naturally uneven, an attempt had been

Fig. 20. Assarlık chamber tomb (courtesy of Jan Zahle)

made to level the enclosure, with a low supporting wall on the down-hill side."[179]

The roofing system of the tumulus tombs was described as: "(a) simple device of bracketing out the last few courses of the wall and laying the roof slabs across the narrower opening which is thus left."[180] Thus, all four walls were inclined and they must have formed a pyramid vault, in some cases with courses that turned from angular to rounded ones (Newton 5). This kind of vault was also used in the stone tumulus tombs at Gökçeler north of Halikarnassos, a technical correspondence that Paton and Myres also observed.[181]

Paton and Myres considered Newton Tomb 1 and 3 a more sophisticated version of the same tomb type (Fig. 20). This was especially true of the presence of a doorway, constructed of large blocks, forming a threshold and lintel, and the flat covering stones of the dromos in Newton 1, but also the "superior finish" of the masonry, led Paton and Myres to suggest a date in the 7th or 6th century BC, which is somewhat later than the tombs excavated by Paton himself.[182]

The Burials

Information on burial rites and finds are presented in the table (Fig. 21). Fragments of a large urn filled with bones and ashes were found in Tomb A, placed on a flat stone opposite the entrance.[183] The same position of the urn appeared in Tomb B, and in Tomb C "portions of two cinerary amphorae" stood on a similar flat stone in each corner opposite the entrance.[184] A third urn was placed in the corner to the right of the entrance.[185] The three cists in Tomb D did not yield any human bones or ashes; at least none were mentioned.[186] One of the small cist burials in Tomb N contained ashes in a large vase.[187] The tombs southwest of A and B contained fragments of terracotta

Tomb	Cremation	Urn	Inhumation	Sarcophagi / cists
A	x	1 urn (fragments)		
B	x	1 urn (fragments)		
C	x	2 urns (fragments)	In sarcophagi?	TC w. lead dowels (fragments) Urns placed in sarcophagi
D			In cists?	3 cists along the walls
M	x			2 small cists
N	x	1 pithos in small cist	In larger cists?	5 small cists, 2 larger
SW of A+B			In sarcophagi?	TC (fragments)

Fig. 21. Assarlık – assumed relation between burial rites and finds (Anne Marie Carstens)

sarcophagi.[188] In his summary of the results Paton stated: "The bodies have in all cases been burnt."[189]

Yet, later, in the 1896-report, Paton and Myres concluded otherwise.[190] All the small cist graves were used for cremation burials, while the larger cists also placed on the terraces with all probability contained inhumed burials. The size alone suggests inhumation, and a similar argument may hold true in the case of the tumulus Tomb D. The three cists in this tomb approximately correspond in size to the larger cists in the terraces. However, Paton and Myres refrained from any discussion on the burial rites in the tumulus tombs.

It seems that both cremation and inhumation were practised in the Assarlık tombs. Whether this reflected a development through time, from early cremation to later inhumation, is impossible to state; the material is limited and the datings imprecise.

The Finds

The pottery and other finds yielded during the excavation in 1886 were brought to the British Museum.[191] The metal finds included iron weapons, among these

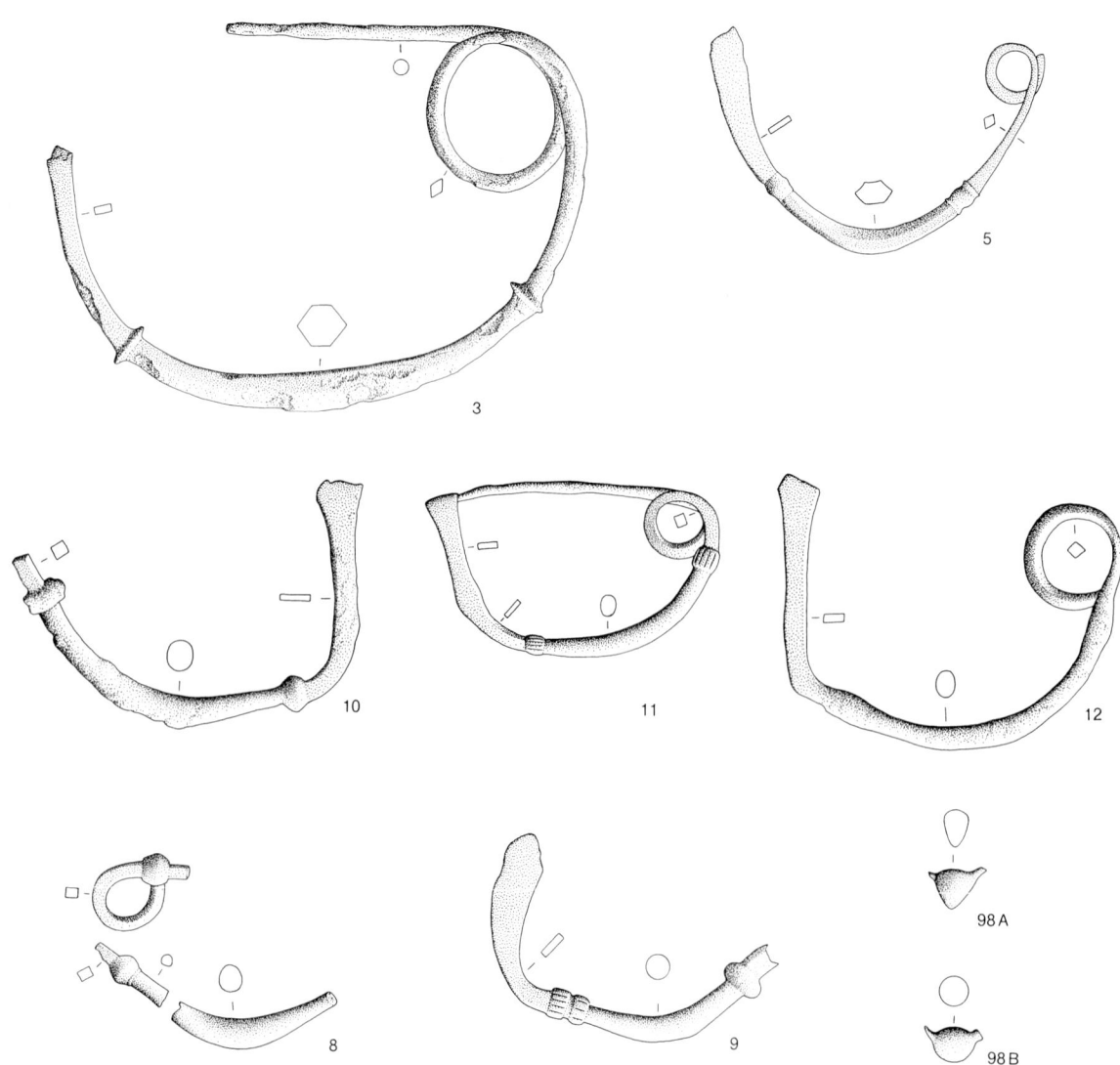

Fig. 22. Assarlık – bronze fibulae (Caner 1983, Tafel 1, 2, and 6)

Tomb	Pottery	Iron	Bronze	Gold
A	A1103 spouted bowl A1104 amphora A large urn	Weapons, incl. 1 spearhead and 1 knife		
B	A large urn	Weapons	Thin bronze plate	1214-1215 hair spirals
C	A1105 skyphos A1106 jug A1107 amphora A1109-2 lid A1109-3 lip A1110 TC sarcophagus	Weapons, incl. 1 spear and 2 knives	Fibulae, Caner type IId (Caner 8; 8a, and 9)	1212 disk 1213 plaque 1216 tapered hoop ring
D	A1108-1 large vessels Sherds: thin kylix, black glazed	Weapon, incl. 1 knife		
E	A1109-1 incised ware			
F			117 pair of tweezers Fibulae Caner type Va (Caner 98a-b)	
G			Fibula Caner type IIb (Caner 5)	
M			Fibula Caner type IId (Caner 11)	
N	A pithos; a large vase; a bowl with concentric circles		Fibula Caner IId (Caner 12)	
O	A1101 stirrup jar A1102 askos Sherds of a large closed vessel		Fibula Caner type IIa (Caner 3)	
Tombs SW of A+B	A1111-1116 TC sarcophagi		115 two spiral armlets 116 two armlets	
÷ context			Fibula Caner type IId (Caner 10)	

Fig. 23. Assarlık – contextual overview of finds (Anne Marie Carstens)

knives, and spearheads. However, these finds do not appear in the catalogues of the British Museum, and Paton did not provide any specific description of the weapons, other than that two of the knives were curved and one was small.[192]

The bronze finds were mostly fibulae, but also included a pair of tweezers and a curved plate (Fig. 22). Walters never mentioned the latter in the catalogue, where only the pair of tweezers and six fragmentary fibulae were described.[193] E. Caner presented a corpus of the Anatolian fibulae in 1983.[194] On the basis of a substantial catalogue he analysed the Assarlık bronze finds, and in connection with this work Caner studied the inventories of the British Museum thoroughly, and presented the fibula-material from Assarlık as indicated in the table (Fig. 23).[195]

The types IIa (Tomb O) and IIb (Tomb G) are also known from Crete from the Subminoan and Early Protogeometric periods.[196] Type IId (Tomb C, M, and N and one without specific context) from the Geometric period is especially known from Cyprus, where it was probably first produced. Caner emphasized, however, that the fibulae from Assarlık were probably produced in Karia as they represent a variant known neither on the Aegean islands nor on Cyprus.[197] The two balls found in Tomb F belong to the fibulae of the Va type and date from the Late Geometric period.[198] The pair of tweezers in Tomb F was compared with Cypriot material.[199]

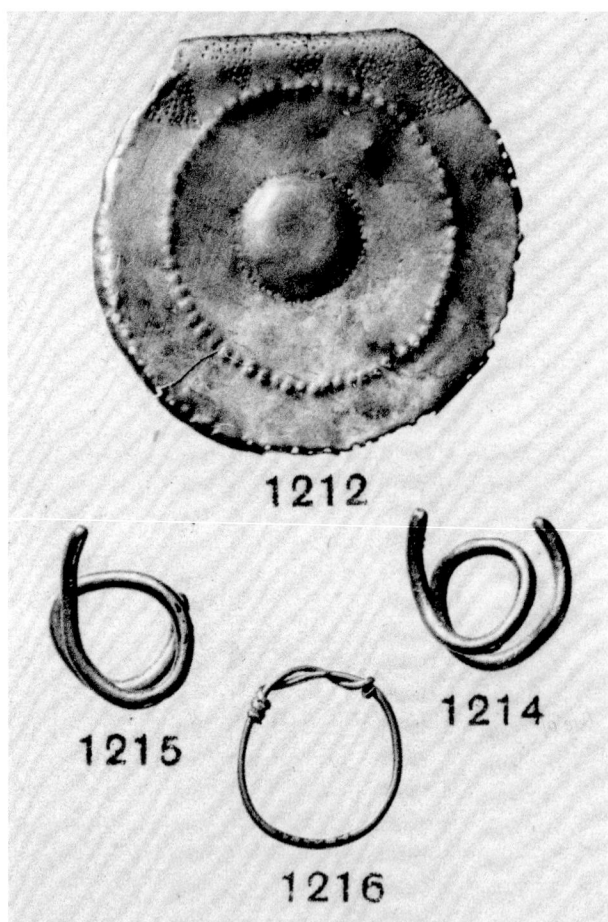

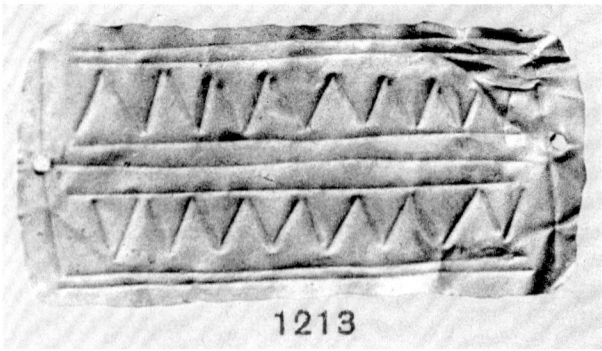

Fig. 24. Assarlık – gold jewellery. Tomb C: 1212, 1214, 1216. Tomb B: 1214, 1215 (Marshall 1911, plate XIII)

Jewellery was found in three or four tombs (information on the tombs southwest of A and B was collective), in the form of bracelets, pendants and rings (Fig. 24). The golden disk (1212) found in Tomb C may represent a Rhodian type of pendant of Syrian inspiration,[200] while the ring (1216) from the same tomb is less distinctive. The bronze bracelets (tombs SW of A & B) were not depicted in the British Museum catalogue, and from the description they seem rather insignificant. The same seems to be the case with the hair spirals, (1214-1215), from Tomb B, which belong to a large group of rather undistinguished spiral jewellery made of plain gold wire. R. Higgins has dated them to the 10th century BC.[201] The gold band with a simple zigzag decoration (1213) is likewise difficult to identify, but the sparse ornamentation may confirm a date in the Geometric period as suggested by the pottery finds.[202]

The pottery found in the Assarlık tombs has attracted considerable attention. V.R.d'A. Desborough included a detailed study of the vessels and presented them as the bulk of the evidence from western Asia Minor in his monograph on Protogeometric pottery (Fig. 25).[203] The fact that the vessels were brought to the British Museum after the excavation and published both in the following year (1887) and in the catalogue of prehistoric Aegean pottery from 1925,[204] made the finds accessible and much easier to study than material from the excavations at Miletos (Fig. 26).[205]

Desborough emphasized that the frequent use of circular decoration was seldom present in the local Dodekanese style.[206] Based on the rather limited material (consisting of two imported pieces) he suggested that the pottery finds reflected a migration, that the settlers form Assarlık emigrated from Attica by the time of the transition to the Protogeometric period. They brought with them both the practice of cremation and their own pottery style.[207]

In 1971 Snodgrass, however, concluded that probably all the Assarlık pottery was made locally, though the earliest finds might be imports.[208] In his discussion on "The Advent of Protogeometric" he reiterated the conclusion already drawn by Desborough: "…among these new schools is that of the Greek settlements on the western coast of Asia Minor: the finds at Miletus, Assarlık and elsewhere suggest an early dispersal of pottery, and probably of actual migrants carrying it, beginning in the first half of the eleventh century. This is perhaps our material testimony for the beginning of the Ionian migration".[209]

Coldstream placed the pottery of Tomb C in the Dodekanese group of the East Greek Middle Geo-

Pottery	Provenience	Decoration	Date	Context
A 1101 stirrup jar	Attic	Semicircles, handmade	Transition to PG	Tomb O
A 1102 askos	Attic	Linear	Transition to PG	Tomb O
A 1108 -1 skyphos	Local	Concentric circles	PG	Tomb D
A 1106 jug		Cross-hatched triangles	Geometric	Tomb C
A 1107 amphora		Bars divided by an X	Geometric*	
A 1105 bowl		Undecorated?		Tomb C
A 1103 amphora		Concentric semicircles	PG?	Tomb A
A 1104 spouted bowl		Undecorated		Tomb A
A 1108, 2 skyphos	Local?	Concentric circles	PG	
A 1108, 3 skyphos	Local?	Concentric circles	PG	
A 1108, 4 skyphos	Local?	Band	PG	
A 1108, 5 amphora?	Local?	Set of circles	PG	
A 1108, 6 krater	Local?	Sets of circles	PG	

* ...and not the earliest, Desborough 1952, 220.

Fig. 25. Assarlık – Desborough's consideration of the provenience and date of the pottery finds (Anne Marie Carstens)

metric pottery.²¹⁰ This group was characterised by a composite style, which combined Attic, Cypriot, and indigenous elements.²¹¹

Özgünel later subscribed to the theory of a close Attic influence in the Middle Geometric period, and he even suggested that the amphora 1107 was an Attic import.²¹² The close affiliations with Attic Geometric pottery in western Anatolia present a quite marked distance from the Dodekanese Geometric style, which may be surprising, not least in this southwestern corner of Karia.

The Protogeometric Tomb at Dirmil/Gökçebel

Gökçebel is the modern name of a village in the northwestern part of the peninsula. South of the village on a hilltop is a "hill fort", first described by Paton and

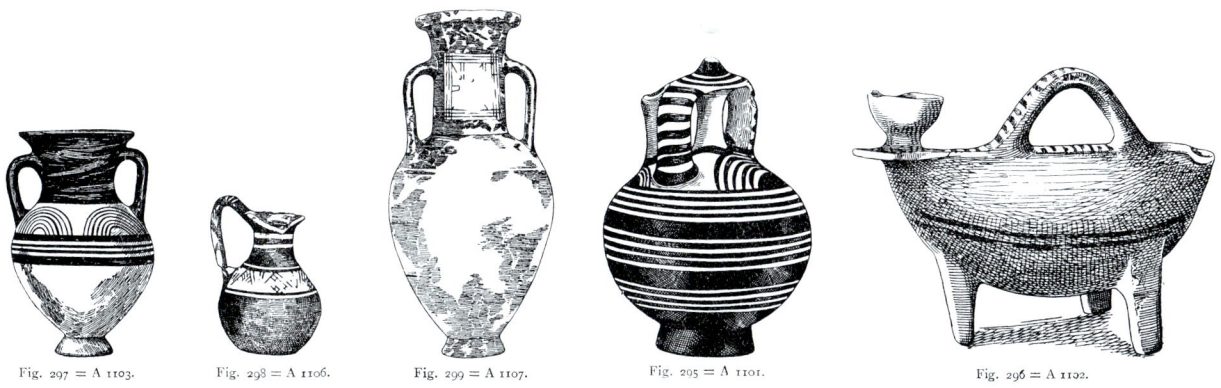

Fig. 26. Assarlık – pottery finds. Tomb A: A1103. Tomb C: A1106, A1107. Tomb O: A1101, A1102 (Forsdyke 1925, fig. 295-299)

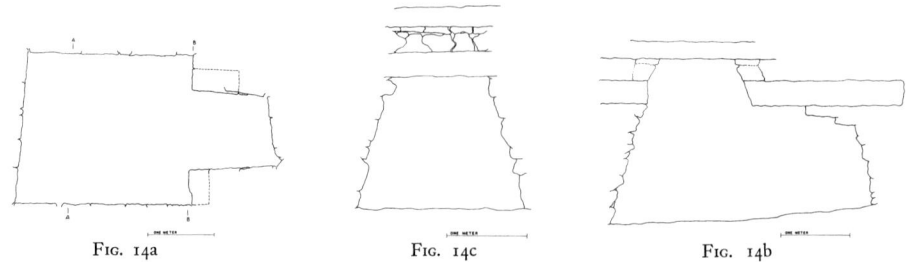

Fig. 27. Gökçebel/Dirmil – plan and section of the Dirmil chamber according to Bass (Bass 1963, fig. 14)

Myres in 1896, and later visited by Bean and Cook.[213] Paton and Myres also found rock-cut tombs "below the village".[214]

G.E. Bass first discovered the Protogeometric tomb in 1962, when he visited the site together with H. Elbe of the Bodrum Museum. Before that a local captain that worked for the American underwater excavations at Yassi Ada had shown him some pottery from the tomb. A local farmer had found the tomb on the southern slope of the hill.[215] In 1963 Bass published the finds and a sketch plan of the tomb (Fig. 27).[216] The same year E. Akurgal excavated the tomb[217] (Fig. 28).

The tomb consisted of a chamber and a dromos, facing south. A "bedding" was presumably cut in the rock, before the tomb was built.[218] When it was discovered, it was completely hidden in the slope, and Bass's team entered the chamber through a hole in the roof. The tomb was built in polygonal masonry of un-worked stones, with the best masonry in the lower courses of the dromos. The dromos was rather short (1.2 m long; 1 m wide; 1.15 m high at the outer end) and roofed with a corbelled vault, which began at approximately 0.5 m height. Three large slabs roofed the vault. A wall built in roughly rectangular stones closed the outer end of the dromos. In Akurgal's description this wall is not mentioned, but a stone wall between the dromos and the tomb room was said to be 0.6 m

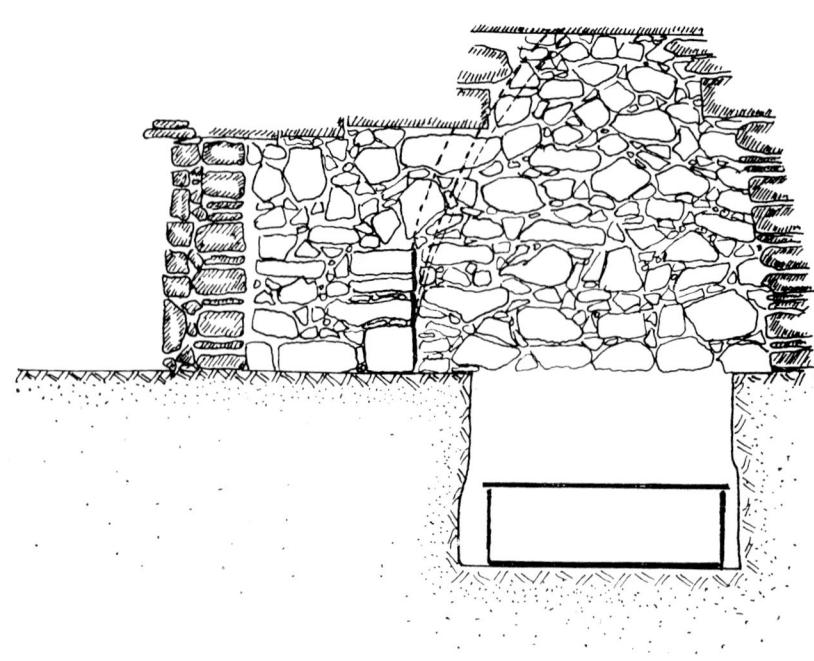

Fig. 28. Gökçebel/Dirmil – section of the Dirmil chamber according to Akurgal's excavation (Boysal 1967a, fig. 24a)

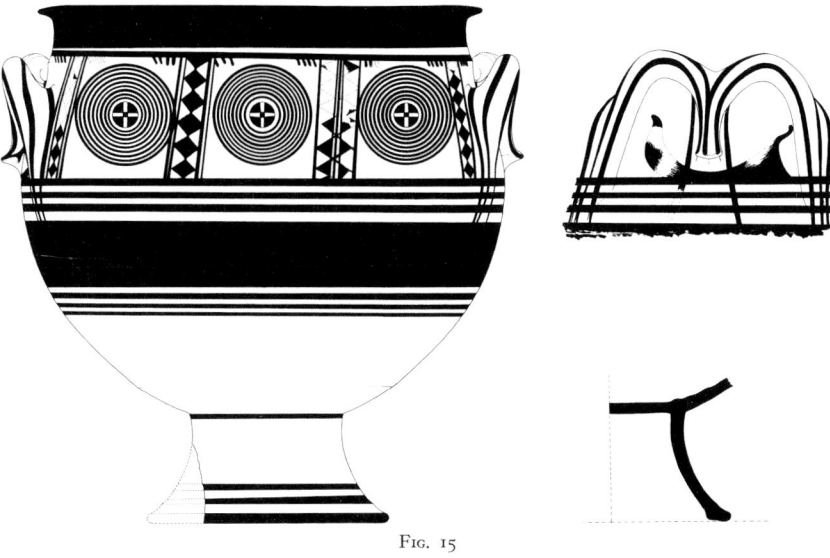

Fig. 29. Gökçebel/Dirmil – the krater from the chamber tomb (Bass 1963, fig. 15)

deep.[219]

The chamber was roughly rectangular (south 2.15 m; north 2.14 m; east 2.45 m; west 2.55 m) in plan, but already at the second course the walls began to incline and the corners disappeared into a circle. Approximately at the same height as the roof of the dromos, but opposite the entrance, a large slab was set into the wall, otherwise constructed of rubblework. Bass found the use of the slab peculiar and thought it might have been inserted to strengthen the roof. At app. 2.31 m height the width of the chamber was only 1 m and a large slab roofed the remainder of the gap.

Bass had not examined the floor of the chamber, but Akurgal cleaned it and found a rectangular pit cut into the rock floor.[220] The pit was 1.85 m long and 1.4 m wide at the bottom, narrowing to 0.92 m (south) and 0.82 m (north), and 1.4 m deep. A terracotta sarcophagus (0.62 m x 1.7 m, inside depth 0.55 m) was discovered inside the pit. Apparently a skyphos was found in this pit, while the rest of the finds must have been placed in the tomb chamber itself. It is not clear how the pit was covered, but Bass noted that the floor of the chamber appeared to be earthen.

An examination of the anthropological material concluded that the person buried in the sarcophagus was a tall male c. 65 years old.[221] He was placed in a dorsal position and near his feet a separate pit contained the contracted burial of a woman c. 30-35 years old.[222] There was no indication of cremation.

Bass published the first pottery finds from the tomb in 1963. Later Akurgal reported that the burial gifts included a bronze fibula.[223] Boysal included the pottery from the Dirmil tomb in the catalogue of the Bodrum Museum published in 1969.[224] The finds comprised 2 skyphoi, 1 krater, 2 amphorae, and 2 oinochoes (Fig. 29).

Coldstream placed the Dirmil pottery in his East Greek Late Protogeometric group, which is characterised by three ancillary ornaments: a) groups of pendant tongues or simple strokes; b) one or more vertical rows of dots; and c) one or more wavy scribbles, either vertical or horizontal; if horizontal they link as sets of concentric circles.[225] He found all these ornaments illustrated in the pottery from the tomb, although he stressed their similarity to "Attic prototypes".[226]

In Özgünel's monograph on Karian Geometric Pottery from 1979 the pottery from the Dirmil tomb was reconsidered according to both shape and decoration in an analysis of Attic, Dodekanese and Ionic Geometric pottery. Although Özgünel agreed on the Attic influence he was able to point to specific elements of shape and decorations, which made him conclude that the pottery was most likely local Karian ware. Indeed he characterised the Karian Protogeometric style by its combination of different schools: "In the Carian region, we see the interwoven influences of different places."[227]

The krater had already been compared by Bass to the kraters from Marmariani in Thessaly.[228] Özgünel emphasized that the connection with Marmariani as indicated by only this one krater should be used with care.[229] Yet, sherds from a skyphos with similar decoration were found during the Danish excavations at Vigli on Rhodes in the early 20th century.[230]

Çömlekçi, Assarlik, and Dirmil – basic conclusions

Both cist tombs of various sizes but also at least two circular tombs apparently roofed with a kind of vault were found in the Çömlekçi Necropolis. The evidence is meagre and only when considering it in relation to the built tombs at Assarlık might one suggest that the circular tombs at Çömlekçi were typologically connected with these.

The tomb chambers at Assarlık are all rectangular and considerably larger than the small tumulus tomb from Çömlekçi. Also the chamber of the Dirmil tomb was rectangular. In most cases these built tombs were roofed with a kind of vault, either a pyramid vault with inclining walls on all four sides or a two-faced corbelled vault. A slab closed the top of the roof. In some cases, for example in the Dirmil tomb and in Newton 5, the corners of the ground plan disappeared into rounded courses. The only circular chamber is Çömlekçi Tomb 10.

The tumulus tombs built at Assarlık have been considered in relation to the prehistoric tholos tombs, which survived into the Protogeometric period in both Thessaly and on Crete.[231] These might, of course, have influenced the sepulchral architecture in Assarlık. But the line of development is broken if not in time then in space, and what is more, the tombs at Assarlık all have rectangular chambers. I suggest that they were a local "invention" rather than deliberately imitative of other "foreign" tomb types.[232]

The cist tombs of Çömlekçi vary in size, from very small pits to the "full length" type which would easily contain a body stretched out to its full length. This variation is also seen at Assarlık and it may be suggested that the smaller cists were used for cremation burials, while the larger were used for inhumations. The cist tombs in Assarlık were placed in tomb terraces, the Çömlekçi cist tombs may have been single sepulchres; for all we know they were not incorporated in an architectural context.

Both at Assarlık, and in the Çömlekçi Necropolis, cremation and inhumation seem to have been practised. In the burial cist of the Dirmil tomb only inhumation burials were found. In general, it is believed that by the early Iron Age the burial practise in the Aegean area changed from inhumation, common in the Bronze Age Aegean, to cremation.[233] Therefore, the evidence in favour of cremation burials at Assarlık was regarded as an indication of an Attic settlement that brought along two Attic vases and the practise of cremation. Indeed, it was even suggested that the Dirmil tomb contained cremation burial, "below a tumulus" because it would fit a picture which had this migration theory as its starting point.[234]

The metal finds from the Assarlık tombs, especially the fibulae, were probably produced in Karia, but with Cretan and Cypriot characteristics. The most significant piece of jewellery, the disc pendant, is related to Rhodian material. However, the pottery found in the tombs remains the most obvious group for a wider study of the external affairs of the peninsula in the Submycenaean and Protogeometric periods.

While the pottery from Çömlekçi is generally agreed to have been produced locally, the Assarlık and Dirmil ceramic material has been the subject of more studies and more debate. But, with the possible exception of the stirrup jar and the askos from Tomb O in Assarlık, this material may also have been produced locally. The micacious incrustations that are typical in the local wares of Milas and Miletos were never noted in the clay descriptions of both the Assarlık and the Dirmil pottery. The descriptions may not be as accurate as modern scholarship would wish, but in general the amount of mica is striking in these fabrics. Such a marked feature would hardly be left unnoticed.

The pottery from the Middle Geometric Tomb C at Assarlık was influenced by the Attic Geometric styles both regarding shape and decoration, and Özgünel suggested that the amphora (1107) might be an Attic import.

The Protogeometric Necropolis at Iasos

The Protogeometric necropolis at Iasos covered an area later incorporated in the Greek agora and it was excavated in 1969-1970. About 50 tombs were found, both cist tombs with inhumation burials (in some cists more than one burial) and pithos tombs with cremations.[235] Some of the cist tombs contained large quantities of grave goods. The grave goods were normally placed inside the cist, but occasionally they were found outside the tomb in the pit at the short end.[236] The publication of the necropolis is summary, and does not permit a contextual analysis, but the grave goods from six tombs were depicted in the preliminary report.[237] The pottery consists of locally-produced Protogeometric vessels of micaceous clay and rather monotonous decoration patterns.[238] The shapes depicted in the publication are mostly jugs, drinking vessels (mugs, skyphoi, and kylikes) and amphoriskoi.

A total of 18 fibulae were found in the necropolis, but only ten of them were brought to the Izmir Museum. According to Caner they seem to constitute the earliest examples of each type (type IIIa, IIIb, Ivc, and VIa) otherwise only known from the Geometric and Archaic periods. In the publication the metal finds were dated to the latter part of the 10th century BC.[239] One type IVc fibula had a close parallel from Lindos dated to the end of the Geometric period, the two type VIa fibulae had parallels mainly in 8th and 7th century BC contexts.[240] The grave goods also included some spiral bracelets and earrings of bronze.[241]

The situation at Iasos in many respects mirrors the sparse evidence from the Halikarnassos peninsula. The cist tombs and pithos burials were also found at Assarlık and the cists also at Çömlekçi, as was the evidence of both inhumation and cremation. While the pottery repertoire differs somewhat, for example by the lack of amphorae at Iasos, the pottery stylistically seems close to the peninsula material, especially the local wares.

Continuity?

The most crucial problem encountered in the Submycenaean to Protogeometric period, is the matter of continuity from the Bronze Age to the Iron Age. Here we come up against the tradition of various migrations in the Early Iron Age. The traditional view of the migration theories implies an invasion of a Greek-speaking people from the north (Thessaly), the Dorians, forcing the Ionians living in Achaea to leave their land. The Ionians came to Athens and from here they later settled in Ionia.[242] These movements of peoples may (or may not) be reflected in the distribution of the Greek dialects by the Classical period. The historical tradition classified the colonization of the Anatolian west coast in three tempi, the Aeolians as starters on the northern part of the coast, and then followed by the Ionians, occupying the middle, and in the southwestern corner the Dorians settled in the Dodekanese and Karia.[243]

Whether these migrations actually took place remains a question of belief, but they were treated as a political fact by the fifth century.[244] This, indeed, may tell us more of the societies where the tradition was established than of the historical fact they may (or may not) represent. Characteristic for the literary sources describing these migrations is their remoteness from the events they describe and the political situation in which they write. They indeed have a vested interest in stressing the origins of certain population groups for their contemporary audience. First and foremost the Persian occupation of the Ionian cities demanded stiff resistance, and thus the historical claims to the land were emphasized.[245] The history of tradition may find its roots in many ways and the objective truth is without meaning in this context.[246] Clearly the migration myths served to underline the "Greekness" or rather the close relations between the Attic people and the people living on the Anatolian west coast.

In the archaeological discussion of the Early Iron Age migrations, it is especially the finds at Assarlık which have been used as evidence, confirming the theory. This implied that the cremation burials as well as the Protogeometric pottery were brought to the site by newcomers, settlers from Athens. The Dirmil tomb, discovered later was also used in this argument, and a hypothesis of a cremation burial here was also put forward in 1963 before the actual burials were excavated in the following season.[247] As already shown the material evidence is extremely sparse, and hardly to be interpreted as clear evidence of a new Attic settlement, nor a ramification of an earlier Bronze Age one, although the Submycenaean cemetery at Çömlekçi and the earliest Tomb O at Assarlık may hint at a transitional phase.

The Protogeometric necropolis at Iasos revealed a larger number of both burials and ceramics. The pottery found here was all locally produced. The study of the Karian Protogeometric and Geometric pottery by Özgünel emphasized that back in the Early Iron Age the settlements in Karia were already self-sufficient as regards pottery (and thereby the goods that came with the vessels). By way of a rather heavy eclecticism they created their own style of pottery and probably produced it at several centres. It is difficult to see just one stylistic feature as the most prominent, rather the Karian pottery was "Karian" from the beginning. This confirms a hypothesis of continuity and development of the Late Bronze Age situation. It is possible that, for a generation or more, life was modest and unpretentious, settlement patterns may have altered from lowland to hilltops, and by the beginning of the Geometric period we see the beginning of a local style not only in pottery, but also in the sepulchral architecture.

Instead of arguing for a connection between the late tholos tombs on the Messara or in Thessaly I suggest an interpretation implying local innovation. The tumulus tombs are constructed on fairly simple principles, and the roofing technique, either the pyramid vault or the two faced vault presents a simple principle depending on weight and gravity, which makes it possible to cover larger rooms than could be done with a flat roof. The earthen or stone tumulus above the built structure kept it all in place, and made outer facing of the built structure unnecessary. All in all, this was a good straightforward solution, which would need no outer influence to develop. As with the local pottery style these tombs may be interpreted as a result of an acquired innovative power after a tranquil period in the transition from the heyday of the Bronze Age.

Interestingly, the rather closed nature of the regional imports and contacts between the Halikarnassos peninsula and the Dodekanese seems to have persisted as most visible in the pottery style, although the pottery of the Dirmil chamber tomb is closer to the Attic styles. The pronounced distance between the Protogeometric tombs at Iasos, which only included cist tombs and pithos burials, while the built tumulus tombs invaded the Halikarnassos peninsula, may be a significant expression of another type of settlement and cultural interaction here. This may have to do with the geographical and topographical situation. The Halikarnassos peninsula is closely related to the Dodekanese, and while Iasos is indeed located on the coast, the bay can only be reached from the south by passing around the Halikarnassos peninsula. From a south-eastern Aegean standpoint Iasos was a remote place, which would more logically be approached directly from the west or north.

Snodgrass characterised the shift from the Bronze Age to the Iron Age detectable in archaeology by two innovations, a) the mass acceptance of single burial and b) the adoption of cremation.[248] While this still seems to hold true in some areas, for example at Iasos, and at the north cemetery at Knossos[249] – maybe in a slightly moderated form – I find it difficult to argue that these innovations also characterised the transitional phase on the Halikarnassos peninsula. The single tombs at Assarlık appear all to have been enclosed in built terraces or temenoi, together with other tombs. Cremations have hardly ever been found in Çömlekçi, and while the publication may only reveal a proportion of the finds, inhumation and cremation seem to have gone hand in hand at Assarlık, and the Dirmil chamber tomb only contained inhumations. The single tombs, on the other hand, only found acceptance much later if at all, and chamber tombs continued to be built, used and reused throughout antiquity.

The *Lelegian* Archaic Stone Tumuli

In Radt's monograph from 1970 a consideration of the cemeteries at Gökçeler and on the Kaplan Dağ was included.[250] Both sites are located in the mountainous inland of the peninsula, Gökçeler to the north of Halikarnassos and Kaplan Dağ east of the city, southwest of the village of Etrim. Gökçeler had previously been described by first Paton and Myres, and later Bean and Cook, while in both reports the name Kaplan Dağ was used for a hilltop farther to the north, the Tirman Dağ, and the remains at Kaplan Dağ were not included.[251] Radt included a study of the topographical distribution of the tombs at the necropolis at Gökçeler, as well as a new identification of the so-called compound-buildings in the area. These buildings had previously been interpreted as tombs, an identification Radt rejected.[252]

The Italian Mission situated on Rhodes in the early 1920's conducted sporadic excavations at Gökçeler. They examined and emptied some of the tombs and found here: "…ceramica di tipo geometrico, fibule di bronzo a globulo sferico sul'arco, armi in ferro".[253] To my knowledge these finds were never fully published. Maiuri concluded on the basis of the finds that a date in the 9th or 8th century BC might be reasonable. The variety of finds corresponds neatly to the finds from Assarlık, especially Tomb C.

In the almost thirty years since the publication of Radt's work, more investigations of Archaic Karia have been undertaken, which adds to the conclusions presented then. The following pages are by nature strongly dependent on the previous research, but appear in a new light provided not least by the investigations of the Milesian peninsula and inland Lykia.

The Tombs at Gökçeler and Kaplan Dağ

An ancient road leads from the eastern slope of the hill of Göktepe north of Halikarnassos to the north coast at Torba. The ruins of the Gökçeler Kalesi tower above the middle of the mountainous hinterland. Here a detached hilltop surrounded by a fortification wall

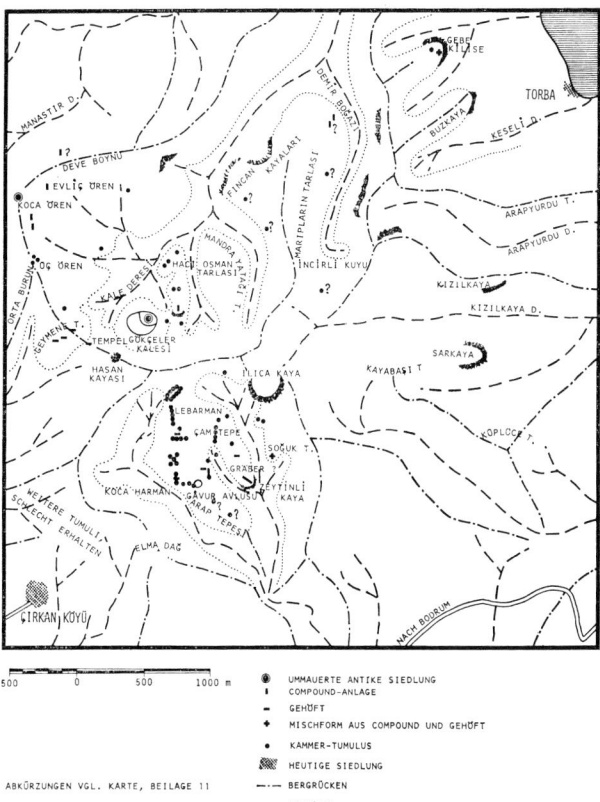

Fig. 30. Gökçeler – map of the settlements and cemeteries (Radt 1970, Abb. 18)

with towers and bastions enclosed a habitation area.[254] An outer perimeter wall was found south of the fortification. Bean and Cook saw tiles and Hellenistic and Roman sherds on the surface and they found Early Archaic pottery to the southeast near the tumuli. A detailed map of the region shows the distribution of the tumulus tombs (Fig. 30). The majority of the tombs were located southeast of the settlement, but tombs were also found north of the site and the best preserved example, the Gebe Kilise Tomb, crowns a peak that rises above Torba.

The average size of the tumuli varies from 6 to 8 m in diameter, with roughly quadrangular chambers of at least 2 m length. The biggest tomb has a diameter of 14 m, while the chamber walls measure approximately 5 m, and the dromos is 3.8 m long.[255] The chambers are often displaced from the centre of the tumulus.

The roofs of the chambers are constructed as pyramid vaults. In some cases the courses in the corners were set diagonal to the original corners turning the

Fig. 31. Gökçeler – pyramid vault of a stone tumulus tomb (Anne Marie Carstens)

shape from rectangular to octagonal, alluding circular courses.

I examined one of the Gökçeler tombs in June 1996.[256] It was roughly quadrangular with very precise corners and a pyramid vault roof (Fig. 31). Coarse sherds, probably from terracotta sarcophagi and pottery with geometric design lay scattered on the floor, in between rubble that had fallen into the chamber from the opening in the vault (Fig. 32). The fabric of the pottery was dull grey-beige with no mica. The Geometric pottery may belong to the Middle or Late Geometric period, in the latter half of the 8th century BC.[257]

The best preserved and most prominent of the Gökçeler tombs, Gebe Kilise was built on a levelled terrace and consists of a krepis, 12.90-13.80 m in diameter and 1.75 to 2.25 m high (Fig. 33).[258] This is crowned by a cornice with two thin courses of "slabs",

Fig. 32. Gökçeler – geometric pottery from the tumulus tomb (Anne Marie Carstens)

Fig. 33. The Gebe Kilise tomb at Torba (Anne Marie Carstens)

which project 0.20- 0.25 m from the krepis wall. From here the roof begins, on the outside in the form of a rounded roof with circular courses of masonry. The first seven courses were well preserved when Radt investigated the tomb, but the higher parts of the tomb appeared to be covered (also originally?) with a mass of more "loose" rubble.

The inside consists of a roughly quadrangular chamber and a dromos (Fig. 34). The chamber measures c. 3 m on the sides, and the floor is neatly paved with slabs. The walls are of isodomic masonry and incline slightly. After their construction they were smoothed with a point chisel. At a height of 1.25 m the pyramid vault begins. It consists of 29 courses and it is closed by a slab. The total height from the floor to the slabs was 5.10 m (Fig. 35).

In the opening from chamber to dromos is a rabbet, perhaps a "bedding" for a closing wall. Its conical shape would prevent intruders simply pushing the wall inwards. An almost stepped corbelled vault of seven courses covers the dromos.[259] The dromos is 3.60 m long, 0.90-1.00 (below) to 0.55- 0.75 m (above) wide, and 1.55-1.65 m high. The outer opening of

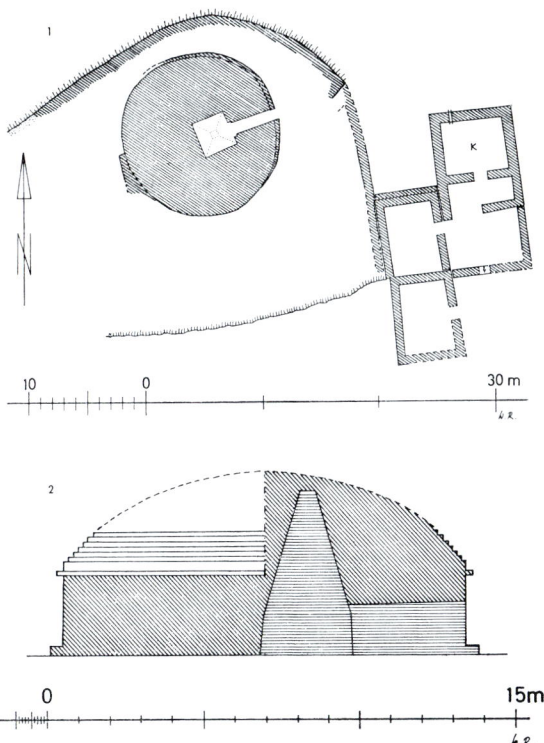

Fig. 34. Plan and section of the Gebe Kilise (Radt 1970, Abb. 19)

Fig. 35. The pyramid vault of the Gebe Kilise (Anne Marie Carstens)

the dromos was apparently left open. Radt suggested that this might indicate that worshippers could enter the dromos and perform rituals there.[260]

The settlement at Kaplan Dağ is situated southwest of Etrim, opposite Theangela. It occupies two hilltops, both surrounded by fortification walls. The southern hill was occupied by habitation and perhaps a temple, while the larger hilltop to the north may have served as both refuge and necropolis.[261] Here Radt found four tumulus tombs in the north-eastern part, while a bigger tumulus was located in isolation near the western edge on the highest point of the plateau. This tumulus had a diameter of c. 15 m and the chamber was preserved 4 m high. As in the Gökçeler tombs a pyramid vault with 'rounded' corners, formed the roof.[262]

Buildings, farmsteads or pens, were found in connection with some of the tombs of the southeast necropolis at Gökçeler.[263] It is impossible to say whether these buildings were contemporary with the tumuli, but no matter which building structure was constructed first, the proximity to either tomb or house must have been evident. They were in that way related.

Such a farmstead was also near the Gebe Kilise tomb, and here the structures were more thoroughly examined (Fig. 34).[264] A small building consisting of rectangular rooms was built in connection with the terrace constructed for the tomb. The room to the north (marked K) was covered with a corbelled vault. A short distance to the east stood a compound building. Radt considered the two buildings to be contemporary, but somewhat later than the tomb.[265]

The Milesian Peninsula

In the early 1980s Walter Voigtländer began a survey on the Milesian peninsula, concentrated on the area around the bay of Akbük and the hills to the north, the Karavelitepe and the Saplatansirt.[266] A number of rural buildings, either farmsteads or dwellings for the herdsmen, were recorded, among these oval houses and compound-like structures, somewhat similar to the ones found by Radt in the Halikarnassian region.[267] A number of monumental tombs were likewise investigated.[268]

These tombs all have a trapezoidal shape and are built in rubblework with fairly good corner bonds. Generally the preservation is poor and it is difficult to imagine the precise structures from observation with the naked eye. Many of the tombs have rectangular elements built onto them at some later point, as if the core of the building had been enlarged. These roughly rectangular buildings form the outer structure within which a number of corridors and smaller chambers or niches were built, covered by corbelled vaults either on two sides, as a barrel vault, or from all four sides, as pyramid vaults. Channels were discovered which may have served as drains for the buildings, which would probably have collapsed if the penetrating rainwater had been allowed to remain within the structure.[269]

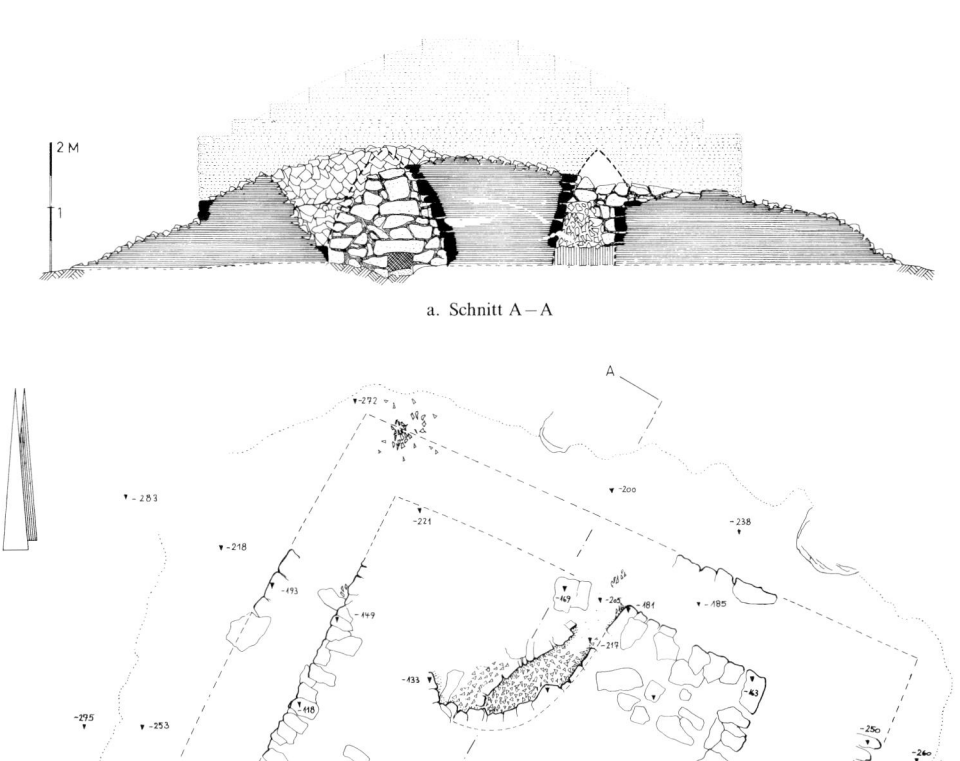

Fig. 36. Plan and reconstructed section of Heroon 12 in the hills north of Akbük (Voigtländer 1988, Abb. 25)

Voigtländer reconstructed the tombs as covered by an outside pyramid structure.[270] However, this feature does not seem to be documented, and only in the case of the "Heroon 12" what may be three steps are visible on one side of the building (Fig. 36).[271] They rather resemble a pile of stones, as in the shape of a rubble tumulus although the plan suggests a square.

Voigtländer generally dated these tombs to the Archaic period.[272] Despite the correspondence with the Halikarnassian tumulus tombs, the employment of corbelling techniques for the roofing and the rubble-work, they completely lack the fairly spacious chambers and regular dromoi we find in the Halikarnassian region.

Lykian Stone Tumulus Tombs

In 1973 and 1974 J. Zahle investigated six tumulus tombs at Phellos, north of Kaş in central Lykia.[273] He divided the tombs into two different types, A and B. The type A tumulus consisted of a krepis built of small and large stones, and a dromos gave access to the

Fig. 37. Reconstruction of Phellos tumulus type B (Zahle 1975, fig. 12)

rectangular chamber, which was covered by a corbelled pyramid vault. The type B tumulus had a one-course krepis of larger stones with a rounded facade (Fig. 37). One or two huge stone blocks, only smoothed on the side visible in the chamber, roofed the chamber. A tumulus crowned both the type A and type B tombs. In some cases it consisted of an inner core of stone fill with an earthen sealing above, while others may have been covered entirely by a stone tumulus.[274] The krepis wall of the type B tumuli may have supported a further architectonic element, maybe a cornice as in the Gebe Kilise tomb; some of the stone blocks were dressed with a c. 0.20-0.35 m wide rebate.[275] The type A tumuli correspond typologically to the Gökçeler / Kaplan Dağ tombs and Zahle suggested a date in the Archaic period, 9th/8th to 6th century BC, while the type B may be slightly later, forming a typological development of the type A tumuli (Fig. 38).

For quite a long period of time these tumulus tombs were thought to be rare in the Lykian region, but survey activities in the region of the ancient town Kyaneia have now altered the situation. The Kyaneia fieldwork has established that, indeed, the tumulus tombs of the Phellos type form a substantial proportion of the Lykian tombs, often found in connection with settlements datable to the 6th and 5th century BC, although they may have remained in use even longer.[276]

The stone tumulus tomb, Agios Milianos, north of

Fig. 38. Pyramid vault of Phellos tumulus (Zahle 1975, fig. 6)

Lindos on Rhodes seems to be related to the type B tumuli at Phellos, regarding the krepis.[277] And Maiuri investigated a similar chamber tomb on Simi and suggested a date in the 5th century BC for both the Agios Milianos tomb, and the tomb on Simi.

It seems reasonable to suggest a typological development from the Gökçeler / Kaplan Dağ tumuli and the type A in Phellos to the type B, sharing at least the cornice of the Gebe Kilise tomb, and again to the Simi and Lindos examples, reaching down into the Classical period.

Other Archaic Tombs

During the excavation of the chamber tomb at Dirmil in 1963, other investigations were made in the neighbourhood of the tomb. In 1976 Özgünel published pottery finds (eight vessels) deriving from the exploration, but he did not indicate the contexts.[278] Later, in his monograph on Karian Geometric pottery, these contexts were, however, included in the catalogue.[279] Without any plan of the excavation it is rather unclear where the finds were made, other than "at Dirmil, near the chamber tomb".

A Middle Geometric neck-handled amphora was found in a tomb labelled "Child Tomb 2". According to Özgünel the amphora was influenced by Attic pottery, both in shape and decoration.[280] Another amphora and an oinochoe were found in Tomb 3, the amphora also from the Middle Geometric period, while the oinochoe was dated to the Late Geometric period.[281] Like the first amphora this was Attic in style, but doubtless a local product. The oinochoe combined Attic and Dodekanese elements, but the very plump shape is also found in the later Karian pottery.[282]

The contexts of the five remaining vessels were only indicated as particular areas of the excavation. A Late Geometric oinochoe of conical shape, a Rhodian bird bowl, an Attic or Cycladic skyphos and a locally-produced kantharos with plastic snakes on the handles were all found in Area II, Plan I. All these finds were dated to the Late Geometric period.[283]

Sherds from a krater or dinos were found "between the A and B walls, Area I, Plan I". This appears to be a Karian workshop, with the very characteristic use of the metope decoration in the central panel.[284]

With the poor state of contextual evidence, one is forced only to draw the conclusion that apparently more tombs were located in the vicinity of the chamber tomb, and the ones excavated were somewhat later, probably from the second half of the 8th century BC.

Only in the case of a few of the Geometric finds from the vicinity of Milas are the contexts certain. In 1953, a cist tomb was found during the construction of the main road from Milas to Ören.[285] Inside the tomb two skyphoi, four kotylai, two amphoriskoi, two olpai, one plate, five cups, and two lekythoi, a total of 18 vessels, were found. Özgünel dated the ceramics to the Late Geometric period (second half of 8th century BC), the kotyles to the Subgeometric (first half of the 7th century BC), and it was his opinion that the pottery had been produced locally.[286]

Near Beçin a number of cist tombs were excavated around 1965.[287] Two of these tombs were described in some detail. Tomb 2 was a cist covered by a lid consisting of one or more slabs. The cist was 1.82 m long, 1.02 m wide, and 0.74 m deep, and built in rubble work. It contained 15 skeletons placed with different orientations. In all nine vessels were found near the corners of the cist, two cups, three skyphoi, two amphoriskoi, one spouted jug, and one lekythos, all belonging to the Late Geometric period and probably produced locally. Tomb 3 was likewise built in rubble masonry, 1.70 m long, 1.05 m wide, and 0.76 m deep. It contained nine skeletons found in disarray. One of the dead was a child. Here only three vessels were found, one skyphos, one amphoriskos, and one oinochoe, also Late Geometric and probably produced locally.

Especially in the case of Tomb 2, where 15 skeletons were found, one may speculate whether the tomb was not in fact used for second burials, whether the excarnated skeletons were deposited some time after the burial. Even if the tomb had been in use for a long period, the grave goods (all belonging to the Late Geometric period, dated by Özgünel to the second half of the 8th century BC) may only have derived from the later burials. However, without a more detailed publication this remains pure speculation, the only sure fact being that all the burials in the two cist tombs were inhumations, and the grave goods relatively sparse, with less than one locally produced vessel per body buried.[288]

Southeast of the village of Etrim, the ancient settlement Theangela has revealed rather early finds, though unfortunately, these were yielded by unauthorized excavations.[289] In 1980 F. Işık published a monograph on the terracottas, probably deriving from a well or bothros excavated on the eastern slope of the acropolis, and later in 1990 more finds were found to derive from looted tombs at Theangela. A number of these finds were eventually handed over to the Bodrum Museum, while others were discovered on the local art market in Bodrum. The earliest of the finds were fragments of two Late Geometric skyphoi, which can be easily fitted into the system of local pottery production as described by Özgünel.[290] But, what is more, Işık suggested a local, and rather early production of terracottas at Theangela, beginning in the late 8th century BC. This may have continued until the Hellenistic period.[291]

The material from Milas and Theangela merely emphasizes the fact that in the Geometric period, local pottery and terracotta production were probably successfully established. The tombs from Milas demonstrate that here the cist tomb tradition, established at Iasos in the Early Protogeometric period, was still in use.

Özgünel characterized the local Karian pottery as an eclectic style, influenced by Rhodian, Ionic, Attic, Argolid, and Euboean pottery.[292] This mixture forms the basis of a distinct Karian style, and may be interpreted as evidence of an extensive, wide-ranging contact with the Greek world, a contact, which was reflected and subsequently translated into something Karian.

Built tombs similar to the ones from Gökçeler and Kaplan Dağ have not been found at Iasos or at Beçin/Milas. One may speculate whether the more monumental built tombs were in use by some communities marking different dynasties or ethnic groups, while others represented a difference by using only cists. However, at Assarlık both tomb types seem to have been used simultaneously in the Protogeometric period, although here the early cists were placed in terrace complexes. On the Halikarnassos peninsula only the built tumuli continued into the Archaic period. Again, however, this apparent conclusion may be a false one, only demonstrating that cist tombs were not found on the peninsula. Unlike the built tumuli they would leave no traces in the landscape and would only be recognized at random, by construction work for instance. As the settlements in the Archaic period seem to have been concentrated in the mountainous hinterlands, protected from the rapid growth in the resort buildings concentrated on the coastal areas, they are not likely to have been discovered.[293] Of course, here also other explanations, like that of clandestine excavations, may be put forward, moreover, since this has proven to have been the case with the Theangela tombs.

Stone Tumulus Tombs – a diffuse phenomenon

The "indigenous" Assarlık tumuli developed into the tumulus tombs of the Gökçeler type. Built in dry stone masonry and crowned by a stone tumulus these tombs characterise the Archaic sepulchral architecture on the Halikarnassos peninsula. For many years they constituted a quite remarkable unit of monuments and they were, by reference to Strabo, linked to the so-called Lelegian people, regarded as the original indigenous inhabitants of Karia.[294]

Later archaeological fieldwork has shown that this type of tomb spread to a wider area, as did the style of herdsmen's compound buildings, also at first regarded as especially characteristic of the Halikarnassos peninsula in the Archaic period.[295] A small number of tumulus tombs were found in the early 1970s at Phellos in Lykia, but for almost 20 years these tombs were regarded as unique in Lykian sepulchral architecture. Later fieldwork in inland Lykia has shown that this type of tomb was widely used here in the Archaic period, maybe as early as from the 9th century BC and perhaps still in the Late Archaic period.

Also on the Milesian peninsula rubble chamber tombs built in dry stone masonry are related to the Gökçeler type. Although the tombs here have square or trapezoidal plans, the construction principles seem connected with the round tumuli, in spite of the less strict interior organization of the chambers. In contrast to the Lykian tombs, here the similarities may thus be of a more structural and technical nature. The similarities were based upon technical solutions, dictated by the nature of the building material, the small rubble, more than anything else. Both constructions are dry stone masonry buildings with a massive core of masonry intersected by chambers, in the Milesian tombs with more, smaller, and more irregular chambers, while in the Gökçeler tombs there are regular rectangular chambers with well-defined corners. But in both cases these chambers were covered with vaulted roofs, using the corbelling technique. As argued above this building technique is straightforward and may develop independently at various places. But also the rural buildings, in particular the so-called "Oval Häuser" are found both on the Halikarnassos and the Milesian peninsulas.[296] Not only a common conception of such buildings, built to fulfil similar demands, but also closer relations between the peoples living in the two regions may be suggested not least since the distance is short, at least by boat. In other words, it falls within a frame of regional interaction.

The Lykian tumuli of the Phellos type seem closely related to the Gökçeler tumuli, but the distance between Lykia and southwestern Karia is much greater, separated as they are by high mountains. Still, a Phellos tomb would not have seemed "foreign" if it was located between the tombs at Gökçeler.

Why this similarity? Without a more precise dating of the tombs, the answer is not readily apparent. We have little historical knowledge of the earlier Archaic organization, especially that of the hinterlands. A possible hypothesis, one which is also particularly founded on our increased knowledge of settlement patterns, is that both the Karian and the Lykian landscape were organized in minor dynasties, each with a limited territory, determined by the lie of the land. It was not until the time of the Persian conquest in 540 BC that these dynasties developed into more unified and politically coherent structures: the external stress exerted by the Persian supremacy and the need for an organization to match this threat may have produced a greater unity than was ever the case before.[297] These similarities in settlements between the two areas may be arbitrary: this is how any Archaic hinterland would have been organized. I suggest, however, that the two parts of southwestern Anatolia formed more closely related cultural groups, perhaps achieved by aristocrats who enjoyed mutual contact, even before the Persian presence.

While this early Lykian connection is rather tenuous, the later period brings more examples of a cultural link with Lykia, but also perhaps a Cypriot connection. Both these links may be related to a framework of élitist contact that the Persian rule encouraged, an élitist contact within and between the Persian satrapies. I suggest that these contacts were established earlier between local peers both in central Lykia and on the Halikarnassos peninsula. A cultural network resulted in closely related sepulchral architecture; a network established in the Archaic period, an era more receptive to ideas than is often believed.[298] I find that, for the time being, the best explanation is that the cultural webs did indeed "entangle" distant regions and that what to the naked eye appear rather closed entities of minor fortified settlements in the highlands were not isolated. One may indeed argue that the fortifications constitute more evidence for a suggestion of a high level of interaction with others settlements, other people, and other regions. As a matter of course, this interaction need not always have been peaceful.

The Development of a Sense of Being Karian?

Southwestern Karia was always linked to the Aegean, particularly to the Dodekanese. The Early Bronze Age necropolis at Iasos belonged to a Cycladic / Anatolian settlement, and from the Middle Minoan period a Minoan group of people lived in Iasos and produced their own pottery. However, the excavations of the

1970s at Iasos are only summarily published and our knowledge of the contacts and relations with Anatolian or indigenous people at Iasos is limited. The Aegean settlement at Iasos survived into the Mycenaean period, and possibly also into the succeeding Submycenaean and Protogeometric period. It is also clear that as far back as the Early Bronze Age coastal Karia was part of the Aegean Bronze Age culture.

Early finds are extremely sparse on the Halikarnassos peninsula, until the large necropolis at Müsgebi was used in the LHIIIA period. Müsgebi was a Mycenaean settlement, possibly with a local production of pottery and with close relations to the Dodekanese, especially Rhodes and maybe Miletos as well. The few Argolid imported vessels merely emphasizes the general relation to the Mycenaean centres. Contacts with inland Anatolia and the Hittites are not particularly accentuated in the Müsgebi material, but it is obvious that the Late Bronze Age saw multiple cultural relations in the Eastern Mediterranean, forming a *koiné* culture, where, not least, religious practises were widespread and shared.

It seems that the transition to the Early Iron Age brought with it the birth of a distinct local style, both in the sepulchral architecture – the stone tumulus tombs at Assarlık and later Gökçeler – and in the local pottery production. Maybe the people on the peninsula lived a quiet and modest life for some generations, with fairly little contact with the outside world. Out of this modest life in relative isolation grew new ideas. It is clear that relations to the Dodekanese area were still vital, but Ionic and Attic inspiration can also be discerned in the pottery styles.

The Early Iron Age gave the Karians a sense of being Karian. With this self-identification as a solid basis the Karians, with their eclectic sense, re-entered the outside world.

Notes

1. The article had its genesis in my Ph.D. dissertation *Death Matters. Funerary Architecture on the Halikarnassos Peninsula* from 1999 (Carstens 1999). Fieldwork was carried out in the period from 1996 to 1998 as part of the Danish Halikarnassos Project, directed by Dr. Poul Pedersen, and with the kind permission of the Turkish General Directorate of Monuments and Museums. I received kind and generous help from the Bodrum Museum, its director Dr. Oğuz Alpözen, and not least Mr. Ali Uçarer. I wish to express my heartfelt thanks to Poul Pedersen, who supported my work in the best way.

    The Danish Research Council of the Humanities financed the work. The manuscript was completed in June 2002 and since then there have only been minor additions.
2. Herodotus 1.142 includes these three cities in the territory of Karia, and classes them as a unity because they shared the same language. The *Copenhagen Polis Centre*, however, excludes the cities, Flensted-Jensen 2004; Blümel 1998.
3. Bean & Cook 1955, 85, indicates controversies between the geological descriptions of respectively Paton & Myres 1897, 44 and Philippson 1915, 51. However, both state that the bedrock probably consists of gneiss with a volcanic subsurface above. Indeed the gneiss may also form the bedrock below the limestone in the eastern part of the peninsula.
4. Bean & Cook 1955, 169; Carstens 2002a.
5. This change in the native rock is clearly traceable, when following the ancient city wall of Halikarnassos, where it influenced the masonry styles. Pedersen 1994, 221-222.
6. Such a level of organisation may be suggested by literary sources referring to the federal organisation of the Karians in the early 5th c. BC. Hornblower 1982, 55-56.
7. Carstens 2002a; 1999, 84-89, 169.
8. Paton & Myres 1896, pl. XI.
9. Newton 1862-63, 72-85.
10. Dalton 1751-52; Hamilton 1842; Ross 1852.
11. Ross 1852, 30-33.
12. Newton 1862-63, 80-84.
13. Newton 1862-63, 81.
14. Newton 1862-63, 82-84.
15. Newton 1862-1863, Chapter XII, 333-341. The classification of the Bodrum tombs comprised ten types of Late Classical to Late Roman tombs: 1) subterranean (?) chamber tombs; 2) vaulted chamber tombs, built of rubble and concrete; 3) slab-lined cist tombs; 4) plain monolithic sarcophagi; 5) terracotta cists; 6) cist tombs lined and closed with roof-tiles; 7) pithoi, all found empty; 8) cinerary urns, containing bones; 9) slab-lined or built cist with saddle-roofed lid; 10) rubble cists closed by slabs.
16. Newton 1862-63, 573-601.

17 On the history of Newton's excavations inside Bodrum, particularly at the Maussolleion site, Jeppesen 2000, 2002. The Danish excavation of a Late Roman Villa can be related to Newton's excavations in the field of Hadji Captan in 1856. Newton 1862-1863, 280-310; Poulsen 1994.
18 Paton 1887.
19 Paton & Myres 1896, 242-264.
20 Paton & Myres 1896, 205; Carstens & Flensted-Jensen 2004.
21 Maiuri 1921-22; Guidi 1921-22.
22 Maiuri 1921-22, 425-459.
23 Bean & Cook 1955.
24 See Carstens & Flensted-Jensen 2004.
25 Bass 1963.
26 Boysal 1964, 1965, 1967a, 1967b.
27 Radt 1970.
28 For a history of research concerning the Maussolleion, Jeppesen 2000, 2002. An overview of the fieldwork of the Danish Halikarnassos Project from 1989 onwards, is found in Pedersen 1992, 1993; Guldager Bilde 1995; Briese, Carstens and Pedersen 2002.
29 Bent 1888, 82.
30 Renfrew 1969, 13-14.
31 Early Cycladic pottery has been found on the bedrock at the theatre. Pecorella 1984, 100.
32 Pecorella 1984, 91-92.
33 Pecorella 1984, 93.
34 11 metal objects were found, among these a bronze dagger, cat. no. 7. Pecorella 1984, 75-76. The marble vases were a small bowl, and two beakers. Pecorella 1984, 66-67. Two fragments of a terracotta figurine were found as well as three spindle whorls or weights in stone and four stone beads. Pecorella 1984, 76-78. The pottery was divided into five groups: small bowl: 7 pieces; small mugs and jugs: 6 pieces; other jugs: 12; amphorae: 3; ollae (containers): 32. Pecorella 1984, 94, table p. 80, and plan Figura E.
35 Barber 1987, 76. Pecorella discusses a more precise chronology, including the Ayio Gala publication, Hood 1981-1982.
36 Strabo 14.658. Although Strabo refers to the Augustan period it is most likely that this was also the case in the first half of the third millennium BC, as it is today.
37 Doumas 1977, 29. Barber 1987, 43-44.
38 Doumas 1977.
39 Doumas 1977, 67-68. Pecorella 1984, 96-97, 102. Renfrew (1972, 166, fig. 10.4 and 10.5) attributed the marble vases to the Grotta Pelos Culture.
40 Doumas 1977, 31.

41 Renfrew 1972, 133 and Pecorella 1984, 104. The Iasian "Anatolian" pottery and pottery from the Early Bronze Age levels at Beycesultan share certain similarities. Lloyd & Mellaart 1962-1972, vol. I. Beak-spouted jugs: Pecorella 1984, cat. no: 21 corresponds to Lloyd & Mellaart 1962-1972, EB2: P. 25:8 (p. 148). Geometric patterns on burnished ware: Pecorella 1984, cat. no. 60 corresponds to Lloyd & Mellaart 1962-1972, EBI: P. 14:1 (p. 118). Juglet: Pecorella 1984, cat. no. 11 corresponds to Lloyd & Mellaart 1962-1972, EBI: P. 16:13 (p. 122). Near Yatağan between Milas and Muğla an Early Bronze Age cemetery yielded pottery, similar to finds from the Iasian. The pottery was collected in the Bodrum Museum and no further publication was undertaken. Mellink 1966, 149. Pecorella 1984, 104.
42 Again a parallel can be found in Early Bronze Age Beycesultan, Lloyd & Mellaart 1962-1972, 284-285.
43 Wheeler 1974.
44 Pecorella 1984, 104.
45 Vermeule 1964. Müsgebi is now better known as Ortakent, but the site is archaeologically known and referred to as Müsgebi (Episkopi on the map by Paton & Myres).
46 Vermeule 1964, 249.
47 Laviosa 1978, 1097-1098; Mee 1978, 129. See also: http://archeo4.arch.unipi.it/Benzi/ricerca_iasos.html
48 Laviosa 1978, 1098, compared the Middle Minoan building to houses from Mallia and Messara.
49 Mee 1978, 129.
50 Traditionally, the Bronze Age excavations on the west coast only published the Aegean pottery in detail. See e.g. Niemeier & Niemeier 1997, 193.
51 The research program *Bronze Age Carian Iasos* will hopefully alter this situation.
52 Part of the following pages concerning the Müsgebi burials has previously been published in the proceedings of the Internordic colloquium *Ceramics in Context*, Stockholm June 1997. Carstens 2001.
53 In June 1996, I visited the site together with Mr. Ali Uçarer from the Bodrum Museum. We engaged a local guide and visited some of the bigger chamber tombs. Part of the area is still cultivated with olive trees, but the gravel pit has clearly cut through a major part of the necropolis area. It was not possible to obtain any idea of the spatial organization.
54 Bass 1963.
55 Boysal 1969. Mee 1978 reconsidered the Müsgebi-pottery. I have used his work as my starting point and added information regarding date and production centres

56 Mountjoy 1986 and Leonard 1994. Preliminary reports of the Turkish excavation: Boysal 1964, 1965, 1967b. The most complete publication of the excavation is Boysal 1967a. The well-illustrated catalogue: Boysal 1969.
57 Özgünel 1987, table 1; fig. 1-4.
58 Özgünel 1979, 1996. There exist controversies between the information provided by the excavator Boysal and Özgünel. Published shortly after or during the course of excavations, I consider the information provided by Boysal to be the more reliable.
59 Group A: tomb 1-5, 28, 30-41. Group B: tomb 6-16, 18, 20, 21, 43-47. Group C: 22-27, 29, 38, 48. Boysal 1967a, 33-34.
60 Boysal's group B does not include tomb 17 and 19. These tombs are located here on Özgünel's plan, but tomb 17 is marked boş (empty) and tomb 19 açılma[d]ı (disturbed).
61 Boysal 1967a, 35. The mortar consisted of a simple mixture of water and andesite dust. It has a certain pozzolana like quality and hardens like concrete.
62 Boysal 1967a, 36. The plaster is similar to the "mortar".
63 Boysal 1967a, 36.
64 Boysal 1967a, 34, plate V.
65 Özgünel 1987, fig. 2-4.
66 Boysal 1967a, 39.
67 Boysal 1967b, 79: "..in Grab Nr. 3 eine Urne mit der Asche." Boysal did not provide any information about the urn. Çiner (1964) published skeletal remains from the 24 graves excavated in the 1963 season. Only in the case of three burials could the sex be determined: grave no. 6 (male), grave no. 8 (female and male).
68 Temperatures around 400°c blacken the bones. Herrmann 1990, 259.
69 Gejvall 1960.
70 Boysal 1967b, 79.
71 Mee 1978, 137.
72 Ceramic evidence from a large number of prehistoric sites on the Mediterranean coast of Anatolia was investigated here in order to devise a tool for further research in the trade and settlement pattern between the Aegean world and the Eastern Mediterranean. Mee 1978, 137-142.
73 Özgünel 1996, 153-166. The overall approach here is chronological and in the case of the Müsgebi pottery minor variations according to shapes, motives and dates occur.
74 Boysal 1969. Özgünel 1996. The dating follows Mee's suggestions corresponding to Mountjoy 1986 and Leonard 1994. See appendix.
75 Boysal 1969.
76 Bell 1979-1980. Tournavitou 1992.
77 The group "cup" includes both cups and mugs.
78 18 pieces are published without context.
79 Mee 1978, 139. Mee stated in his study of the pottery that some of the locally produced small beak-spouted jugs may have been inspired by Anatolian pottery, but clearly in a Late Bronze Age Mycenaean context. Although such "Anatolian" inspired shapes can be found in much Bronze Age pottery in the Aegean area (maybe especially because we never quite bothered to define "Anatolian" more precisely) it may be interesting to examine whether there may be more Anatolian features in play in the Müsgebi burials, and also if these features are found in the region as such. The new focus on the Bronze Age in western Anatolia, represented, for instance, by the new excavations in Miletos, and the *Bronze Age Carian Iasos* team will hopefully alter this situation.
80 Mycenaean pottery production at Miletos, Niemeier & Niemeier 1997. R.M. Cook recently identified the so-called Karian Fikkellura pottery, presumably produced at a Milas workshop. Cook 1980, 1993, 1999.
81 Mountjoy 1997, 259, has pointed to the fact that mica particles may be hard to see in the sections because they have a tendency to lie parallel to the outer surface in the levigated clay. However, Sanne Lind Hansen who is responsible for part of the publication of the late Roman pottery from the Roman domus excavated in the early 1990s in Halikarnassos, informs me that the local wares normally contain so much mica that after contact with the potsherd, the hands of the investigator are literally sparkling.
82 Gödecken 1988.
83 In the proceedings of the conference Gödecken refers to 28 vessels, which seem to have been a group selected in order to investigate a wide repertoire of ceramic shapes.
84 This may, of course, be associated with the find situation and the state of investigation, namely that the settlement itself has not been located.
85 T.R. Bryce has presented a consideration of the state of evidence in a series of articles in the latter part of the 1980s. Even though the Hittite texts form the bulk of this evidence Bryce has incorporated also archaeological material, mainly by referring to Mee 1978. Bryce 1989a and 1989b give a thorough commentary and discussion on the texts including references to the Hittite text corpus *CTH* and a commonly accepted date and translation.
86 E. Forrer first presented this theory in 1924, Forrer 1924.

Later contributions to this discussion can be found in Güterbock et al. 1983. Mellaart 1968, Macqueen 1986, and Foxhall & Davies 1984 present other interpretative models. Niemeier & Niemeier 1997, 200-205, give a short history of research and lists the many locations posited for the Kingdom of of Ahhijawa.

87 Niemeier & Niemeier 1997.
88 This view is shared by both researchers working with the Anatolian material (Naumann 1971, 488-489 and Bittel 1976, 18, 135) and Aegean archaeologists (e.g. Dickinson 1994, 230).
89 Niemeier & Niemeier 1997, 193.
90 Niemeier & Niemeier 1997, 229-240.
91 Niemeier & Niemeier 1997, 219-229.
92 Bryce 1989a, 6.
93 Niemeier & Niemeier 1997, 195, 196.
94 Niemeier & Niemeier 1997, 247-248. The date 1316 BC was revised during the work of 1997 BC to 1305, see: www.arts.cornell.edu/dendro/96adplet.html and www.arts.cornell.edu/dendro/97news/97adplet.html
95 Niemeier & Niemeier 1997, 225.
96 Niemeier & Niemeier 1997, 218.
97 The nature of the settlement is also discussed in the Niemeiers's report, placed in the framework of Branigan's three types of Minoan colonies. Branigan 1981. Niemeier & Niemeier 1997, 194, 242-243.
98 Four swords or daggers found in the Mycenaean tombs on Değirmentepe at Miletos are probably Hittite. Niemeier & Niemeier 1997, 203, compare with Geiger 1993.
99 Küpper 1996, 119.
100 Küpper 1996, 119.
101 Niemeier & Niemeier 1997, 196-197, present an overview of the previous theories.
102 Siebler 1994, 86-87.
103 Hooker 1976, 25: "This lack of real harmony between the material culture of Troy VI and that of Middle Helladic Greece ought to dissuade us from concluding, without serious reflexion, that the two areas were settled by different branches of the same intrusive people… They had in fact nothing significant in common, except that they both used a grey pottery of the same type [the grey Minyan Ware].
104 Mountjoy 1997, 266-267.
105 Iakovidis 1970, 43-57.
106 219 tombs were excavated; approximately 60 had been plundered. Iakovidis estimated that some 500 – 600 people were buried here. Paidoussis & Sbarounis (1975) published the bones from the cremation burials at Perati.
107 Iakovidis 1970, 423.
108 Benzi 1992, 227-231. Mee 1982, 9, note 12, also suggested a down-dating of these burials.
109 Bean & Fraser 1954; Gabrielsen 1997; Berthold 1984. The Hellenistic "international" character, leading to a large degree of uniformity throughout the Mediterranean, may, to a large extent, be comparable with the Late Bronze Age *koiné*.
110 For Hittite burial customs, see Emre 1978, 123-132 and Kull 1988, 91-96. For cremation in the Late Bronze Age Aegean, see Bouzek 1985, 208, fig. 101.
111 Seeher 1993, 219. See Mee 1982, 87.
112 Seeher 1993, 224-226.
113 For example Ilıca, Orthmann 1967. Osmankayası, Bittel et al. 1958. Gordion, Mellink 1956.
114 Seeher 1993, 219; 1991; 1992.
115 Erkanal 1987; Korfmann & Kossatz 1988.
116 Seeher 1993, 225; Schlenter 1960. Metcalf & Huntington 1993 of mortuary rituals, also underlining the multiple differentiations in this field.
117 Seeher 1993, 226. For the connections between the Aegean area and the Balkans, see Bouzek 1985.
118 So far the excavations that began in 1988 have been published as a series of preliminary reports in Turkish, but the final publication of the cemeteries should be forthcoming. Erkanal 1996 offers a bibliography until 1994.
119 Erkanal 1996, 333; www.geocities.com/Athens/Forum/8635/bibliog.html
120 Carstens 1998.
121 Hout 1994. Carstens 1997, 122-144.
122 Emre 1978.
123 Twenty-four burials contained pottery: 41 jugs or pitchers in 24 burials; 1 teapot (burial no.4); 2 bowls (burial no.4); 1 two-handled vase (burial no.25).
124 Emre 1978, 137. Kull 1988, 90-96.
125 Mellink 1956. The cemetery consists of three types of burial: pithos burials, cist graves and inhumations. No cremations of the Hittite period were encountered.
126 Eighteen bowls in 15 burials; 8 jugs or pitchers in 6 burials; 3 cups in 3 burials; 2 jars in 2 burials; 1 teapot in 1 burial.
127 Orthmann 1967. Only evidence of one inhumation burial, tomb 56. Orthmann 1967, 36.
128 Özgüç 1978.
129 Bittel et al. 1958.
130 Bittel et al. 1958, 60-80.
131 The five most frequent shapes are: stirrup jars (35 pieces); cups (32 pieces); jugs (28 pieces); kylikes (24 pieces); piriform jars (24 pieces).

132 Tombs 4, 9, 10, 12, 18, 20, 30, 40, 42 and 46.
133 Among them, Hägg & Nordquist 1990; Hägg, Marinatos & Nordquist 1988; Antonaccio 1995.
134 Recently, D.L. Wieland has undertaken an analysis of the grave gifts. Here, the site was the Manicalunga necropolis at Selinunt (6th – 5th c. BC). Wieland 1997.
135 Laffineur 1986.
136 For rhyta as allusions to animal sacrifices, see Marinatos 1986, 30-31.
137 Wright 1995, 300. In order to reach further conclusions, the religious implications at the funeral should be closely examined. At the Archaic Manicalunga necropolis at Selinunt, pouring vessels make up 15.5 % of the ceramic containers used as grave gifts, while drinking vessels amount to 70 %. Wieland presents a range of the possible meanings of the vessels present in the tombs, for example, for a symposium, but she also raises the question whether these vessels should be interpreted as a representative of a funerary meal or a sacrifice. Wieland 1997, 8.
138 In a study of the iconography of the Late Minoan painted larnakes, V. Watrous has suggested that "cult images on larnakes…… in some cases have been viewed as symbolic replacements for sacrifice, as in Egyptian tomb painting." Watrous 1991, 305.
139 Betz 1987, 537; Marinatos 1993, 5-6.
140 Hägg 1990; Carstens 1998, 216.
141 Hägg 1990, 183.
142 Hägg 1990, 183; Carstens 1998, 216; Gillis 1990, 134 on the use of red ochre in liquid form poured into conical cups and placed in tombs.
143 Protonotariou-Deilaki 1990, 80-83; Antonaccio 1995, 14-15.
144 Blegen 1937, 237-238, 242; Antonaccio 1995, 63. More generally, drinking and pouring vessels appear frequently in the majority of Helladic tombs from Middle Helladic times onwards. Wright 1995, 296-300. The Hagia Triada sarcophagus, often referred to in dealing with the Minoan funerary cult, depicts scenes of festivities, including libations, at the tomb. Evidence of such ritual behaviour had already been found in the tombs of Mesara. Branigan 1970. More generally, drinking and pouring vessels appear frequently in the majority of Helladic tombs from Middle Helladic times onwards.
145 Antonaccio 1995, 245, rejects the evidence of on-going tomb cult in the Bronze Age.
146 Contributions to the study of exchange in the Bronze Age based on archaeological evidence have been carried out mainly as studies of trade and have thus concentrated on the exchange of material goods (Sherratt & Sherratt 1991; Knapp & Cherry 1994, chapter 4).
147 Bergquist 1993. T. Olsson, Lunds University, has suggested an interpretative model for the study of inter-rituality. Carstens 1997, 191-192; Burkert 1985, 24.
148 Recent studies suggest that a religious *koiné* also included Anatolia and Kizzuwatna. Carstens 1997.
149 For libation as an Indo-European religious custom of both the Greeks and the Hittites, see Hägg 1990, 184 and Carstens 1997, chapter 6.
150 Watrous 1991, 305. One may claim that the iconography may not have depicted real rituals but rather represented the ritual acts. If so that may denote another way of using abbreviation in the ritual language.
151 Excavation published in Boysal 1967a, 39-43. The pottery: Boysal 1969, 29-31.
152 Boysal 1967a, 41-42.
153 Boysal 1967a, 41.
154 Boysal 1967a, 42.
155 Boysal 1967a, 42-43. Tomb 5 was interpreted as a kind of hearth, mainly because the east side was open and inside blackened stones and ashes were found. In the brief report (Mellink 1969, 211-212) Boysal mentioned that some of the skeletons were very well preserved. This may indicate that more skeletal material was found than stated in 1967a, 39-43.
156 Mellink 1969, 211-12. The fibula was never published and I have not had the opportunity to look for it in the Bodrum Museum. In Caner's monograph on Anatolian fibulae he has included a bronze fibula type Ia, from the Bodrum Museum, and marked the provenience as "erworben in Çömlekçi." Caner's type Ia is typologically dated to the first half of the 11th c. BC. Caner 1983, 28-29.
157 Boysal 1967a, 42.
158 Boysal 1969, 29-31.
159 Boysal 1967a, 39.
160 Boysal 1969, 29-31. Özgünel 1996, 147-150.
161 For an overview of the later East Greek Karian pottery, Lenz 1997. Carstens 2002b.
162 Bean & Cook 1955, 116-118.
163 Newton 1862-1863, 583-591.
164 Kara Toprak, Newton 1862-1863, 580.
165 Ak-shalleh, Newton 1862-1863, 580.
166 Newton 1862-1863, 585-586. The first was described as descending the hill…, the second "lower down the hills", while the third was found on the way home. As they were going to Çıfıt Kalesi the latter may be located to the southeast of Assarlık.
167 Paton 1887.
168 Paton 1887, 65-66. Paton only quoted the passage

168 Newton 1862-1863, 583-588. Paton & Myres 1896, 203-204, described the location of the tombs examined by Newton as "in a valley on the northwest of the fortress, and a little to the west of the road from Termera to Myndos." Assarlık was identified as Termera by Paton & Myres 1896, 192-210.
169 Paton 1887, 67. Chifoot-Kale-si = Çıfıt Kalesi.
170 Bean & Cook 1955, 116-118. Aspat = Çıfıt Kalesi. I have visited Assarlık several times during my fieldwork on the Halikarnassos peninsula, but unfortunately I have not been able to locate any of the built tombs. However, J. Zahle, taking part in the Danish excavations of the Maussolleion in the 1970s, found some of the Assarlık chamber tombs, one of them depicted as Fig. 20.
171 Paton 1887, 68.
172 Paton 1887, 67.
173 Paton 1887, 69.
174 Paton 1887, 68.
175 Paton 1887, 73.
176 Paton 1887, 74.
177 Paton 1887, 75. Here referred to as: SW of A & B.
178 Paton & Myres 1896, 242-264.
179 Paton & Myres 1896, 243-244.
180 Paton & Myres 1896, 245.
181 Paton & Myres 1896, 245-246. Ghiuk Chalar = Gökçeler. The tombs at Gökçeler, see Radt 1970, 215-236, and below.
182 Paton & Myres 1896, 246.
183 Paton 1887, 68.
184 Paton 1887, 68.
185 Paton 1887, 70.
186 Paton 1887, 72.
187 Paton 1887, 73.
188 Paton 1887, 75.
189 Paton 1887, 77.
190 Paton & Myres 1896, 243.
191 The pottery: Forsdyke 1925; the bronzes: Walters 1899; the jewellery: Marshall 1911.
192 With the recent publication of the Knossos North Cemetery (Coldstream & Catling 1996) the number of early Iron Age weapons has increased. The material shows a striking homogeneity combined with an apparent conservatism. The changes in typology through time seem very limited. This combined with the very summary descriptions by Paton does not allow for any speculation regarding style or date on the basis of the weapon finds.
193 Walters 1899.
194 Caner 1983.
195 Inventory numbers are those of the British Museum, except fibulae that are numbered in parentheses according to the catalogue in Caner 1983.
196 Caner 1983, 28-29.
197 Caner 1983, 30.
198 Caner 1983, 44.
199 Walters 1899.
200 Higgins 1980, 119.
201 Higgins 1980, 93.
202 Higgins 1980, 118.
203 Desborough 1952, 218-221.
204 Forsdyke 1925.
205 Desborough could in 1952 only write: "The preliminary report on this site claims continuity of settlement from Mycenaean to Protogeometric. Until fuller publications one must defer judgement on the nature of this settlement." Desborough 1952, 221.
206 Desborough 1952, 220.
207 Desborough 1952, 220-22.
208 Snodgrass 1971, 67.
209 Snodgrass 1971, 328-329. He obviously found that the material from the tomb at Dirmil spoke in favour of this theory. Snodgrass 1971, 158.
210 Coldstream 1968, 268.
211 Coldstream 1968, 265.
212 Özgünel 1979, 76-78.
213 Paton & Myres 1896, 207. Bean & Cook 1955, 130.
214 Paton & Myres 1896, 208. Indeed, rock-cut tombs are generally richly represented on the northern part of the peninsula.
215 I visited Dirmil in 1996 and tried to find the chamber tomb. A close survey of the entire southern slope of the hill did not reveal the tomb.
216 Bass 1963, 357-361.
217 Boysal 1967a, 44-45. The investigations also included a small survey in the vicinity of the tomb. Özgünel (1976) published the results. Özgünel published pottery found during these investigations in his monograph on Carian Geometric Pottery. Özgünel 1979.
218 Boysal 1967a, 44, note 13: "The tomb was built by carving three meters into the rock."
219 Boysal 1967a, 44, note 13.
220 Boysal 1967a, 44, note 13.
221 Tunakan 1964.
222 This pit was never described in Boysal 1967a.
223 Bass 1963. Akurgal in Mellink 1964, 161. The fibula was to my knowledge not published, and was not included in Caner's corpus (Caner 1983).
224 Boysal 1969, 31-32. I have not seen the sarcophagus in the Bodrum Museum. It was not described in Boysal 1967a or in Boysal 1969.
225 Coldstream 1968, 265.

226 Bass apparently showed the pottery material to Desborough shortly after the finds were made. He quoted Desborough's impression that the pottery was: "much closer to the Attic series than those found in the cist tombs on Cos. Bass 1963, 361.
227 Özgünel 1979, 70.
228 Bass 1963, 359.
229 Özgünel 1979, 69.
230 Sørensen 1992, 29, 35.
231 Pelon 1976, 416-417, 419.
232 See for example Pelon 1976, 423.
233 Snodgrass 1971, Chapter 4, 140-197.
234 Snodgrass (1971, 158) presented the theory that the Dirmil tomb formed part of the "tradition" illustrated in material from Kolophon, of cremation burials under tumuli.
235 Levi 1969-1970, 462-475.
236 In at least one case, tomb XXVIII, a jug was placed outside. Levi 1969-1970, fig. 4.
237 Tomb I, II, VII, XXIX, XXVII and XXXIX. Levi 1969-1970, fig. 12-14.
238 Levi 1969-1970, 469-470. Özgünel 1979 does not include the Iasos material.
239 Levi 1969-1970, 471.
240 Caner 1983, 24 and cat. no: 44, 49,-54, 75, 114a+b, 117. When Caner studied these fibulae the inventories of the Izmir Museum were not available and he was not able to find the precise contexts for the fibulae.
241 Levi 1969-1970, 470.
242 Bury and Meiggs 1987, 53-57.
243 Boardman 1980, 26-33.
244 Hooker 1976, 213-222.
245 The situation may be compared to the Balkan war, where indeed historical arguments, true or false, are put forward in order to justify warfare and resistance.
246 Osborne 1996, 1-18.
247 Desborough 1964, 254.
248 Snodgrass 1971, 177.
249 Coldstream & Catling 1996, 651-653, 674.
250 Radt 1970, 215-236. A. Diler, Centre of Karian Studies at the University of Muğla, has conducted surveys on the Halikarnassos peninsula from 1999 onwards.
251 Paton & Myres 1896, 212, 247, 249-254. Bean & Cook 1955, 123-128, 131. Radt 1970, 215-217, note 6.
252 Radt 1970, 208.
253 Maiuri 1928, 124.
254 Bean & Cook 1955, 124.
255 Radt 1970, 218.
256 I visited the Gökçeler site in June 1996 together with Mr. Ali Uçarer from the Bodrum Museum. We found one of the tumuli southeast of the hill fort opened by a hole in the rubble tumulus.
257 For the Karian Geometric pottery chronology, Özgünel 1979, 99-104.
258 As this tomb was described in detail by Radt I will here only comment on the main points concerning the construction. Radt 1970, 219-223.
259 In some cases the roof of the dromos was flat. Radt 1970, 223.
260 An outer closing device of the dromos was not found in any of the tombs investigated by Radt, Radt 1970, 223.
261 Radt 1970, Abb. 12:2. For the temple, Radt 1970, 259-262.
262 Stephanus of Byzantium 582.5-7 described the native city of the eponymous King Kar: "Souangela, a polis in Karia, where the grave of Kar was, which the name shows. The Karians call a grave soua and king gela. The citizen is called a Souangeleus." Translation by Dr. Pernille Flensted-Jensen. Radt speculated whether the bigger tumulus might be this tomb of King Kar and the settlement therefore Souangela. Radt 1970, 224.
263 Radt 1970, 218. These different types of farmsteads, both the compound buildings and the more rectilinear buildings were dealt with in Chapter II of Radt's monograph. Radt 1970, 145-214.
264 Radt 1970, 195.
265 The dating was based on his typology of the farmsteads. Radt 1970, 145-214. A close connection between farmstead and tomb is generally found in rural settlements, for example both in the Attic countryside, and – closer to the Halikarnassos region – in the hinterland of Miletos and in inland Lykia. Lohmann 1993, 184-185; Voigtländer 1988, Abb. 1; Kolb 1995b, 209.
266 Voigtländer 1986, 1988, 1989. Subsequently the survey activities on the Milesian peninsula have been continued by the Chora von Milet survey conducted by H. Lohmann, which began in 1990. Lohmann 1995, 1997, 1999.
267 Radt 1970. I had the opportunity to visit some of the sites in question, at the Bay of Akbük in September 1997, where Dr. Hans Lohmann most kindly showed me examples of the Archaic and Classical building types.
268 The tombs were interpreted as heroons, while the settlements in the area were labelled "Dynastenstätte", and the oval houses were dealt with in an aristocratic tone: "ein Vergleich dieser imposanten Anlage, die wie ein kleines Schloss seine Umgebung beherrscht." These interpretations were nowhere discussed, merely presented as facts. Voigtländer 1988, 582, 576.
269 The drain channels were also interpreted by Voigtländer

270 Kolb has related these heroons to the so-called podium-tombs found in substantial numbers (as published in 1995 c. 12 examples), during the Kyaneai surveys. Kolb 1995b, 208-209.
271 Voigtländer 1988, 587-589.
272 In Heroon 12 were found fragments of Archaic pottery, and heroon 65 was described as one of "den typologisch frühen Gräbern vorpersischer Zeit." Voigtländer 1988, 592, 593.
273 Zahle 1975.
274 Zahle 1975, 86.
275 Zahle 1975, 85.
276 In a report published in 1995 (Kolb 1995a, 208) the number of registered tumuli exceeded 60, but it has increased considerably since then. See for example the distribution chart in the Kolb 1998, Faltplan 1.
277 Blinkenberg & Kinch 1903, 89. Maiuri 1923-1924, 458. Radt also supported an early date (5th c. BC) for the Lindos tomb. Radt 1970, 232. Maiuri 1923-1924, 458. In the 1960 publication of the Lindos Acropolis architecture (Dyggve 1960, 486-489) the tomb is regarded as a Hellenistic building.
278 Özgünel 1976.
279 Özgünel 1979, catalogue no: 8, 9, 10, 11, 28, 30, 31, 32. As Özgünel is the only researcher who has studied the early Karian pottery in detail I generally accept his conclusions regarding production centres and dating. Furthermore they seem to be supported by the generally accepted view of the development in the later Archaic pottery of Karia as considered by Cook 1999; Lenz 1997, with references; Carstens 2002b.
280 Özgünel 1979, 76.
281 Özgünel 1979, 76.
282 Özgünel 1979, 79. The Karian Archaic pottery: Lenz 1997; Carstens 2002b.
283 Özgünel 1979, 81-97.
284 Özgünel 1979, 84, 95.
285 Akarca 1971, 15-19. Apparently about five cist tombs were found in the vicinity of Beçin at this occasion.
286 It was believed by Özgünel that the Late and Subgeometric periods in the local pottery production were influenced by various other production centres, in respect to shape by both Dodekanese pottery but also Attic and Argolid. In respect to decoration a Boiotian influence might also be argued for. Özgünel 1979, 99-104.
287 Akarca 1971, 10-11.
288 It is of course highly questionable if it is at all relevant to count the grave goods like that. A vast number of explanations may be put forward, notably that the vessels only derived from the latest burial, or that vessels disappeared before the Museum was notified.
289 Bean & Cook 1957, 89-96.
290 Işık 1990, 18-20.
291 Işık 1990, 27, 19-23.
292 Özgünel 1979, 99-104. Lenz 1997 and Cook 1993 follow this view also.
293 On the north coast of the Halikarnassos peninsula we find rock-cut tombs, difficult to date, but perhaps reaching back in time to at least the mature Archaic period.
294 So presented by Radt 1970. Carstens & Flensted-Jensen 2004.
295 Radt 1992.
296 Radt 1970, 200-211, Abb. 17; Voigtländer 1988, Abb. 6 and 9; Radt 1992, 7-8.
297 Bryce 1986, 103.
298 Hornblower 1982, 10-11.

Appendix

The necropolis at Müsgebi – contextual catalogue

The following catalogue is based on the excavation reports and the catalogue, Boysal 1964, 1965, 1967a, 1967b, 1969. The dates are corresponded with Mee 1978, Mountjoy 1986, and Leonard 1994. Numbers in parentheses refer to plates in Boysal 1969.
Legend: Vase name ("stirrup jar"), inventory no. ("638"), reference to illustration in Boysal 1969 (VIII:3a-b). Height (16.8), diameter (13.8), Furumark shape (166), Furumark motive (19).[1] Date (LHIIIA2).

Tomb 1, area A

Architectural features: no information
Photo: Boysal 1967a, pl. XIII:17
Contents: no information

Tomb 2, area A

Architectural features: no information
Contents: no information
Pottery:
Piriform jar 680 (I:2)
H 40.5; Dm 26
FS 35; FM 57
Date: LHIIIA2
Piriform jar 646 (II:1)
H 41; Dm 33.5
FS 35; FM 44
Date: LHIIIA2
Stirrup jar 638 (VIII:3a-b)
H 16.8; Dm 13.8
FS 166; FM 19
Date: LHIIIA2
Stirrup jar 630 (XI:4)
H 11; Dm 11
FS 171; FM 64
Date: LHIIIA2
Stirrup jar 998 (XI:6)
H 11.2; Dm 11.5
FS 171; FM 43
Date: LHIIIA2
Stirrup jar 695 (XIII:2a-b)
H 8.4; Dm 9
FS 171; FM 51
Date: LHIIIA2
Stirrup jar 696 (XIII:3a-b)
H 10.3; Dm 10.2
FS 171; FM 64
Date: LHIIIA2
Stirrup jar 619 (XVI:1)
H 11.6; Dm 11.1
FS 171; FM 58
Date: LHIIIA2
Cup 710 (XXIII:7)
H 3.7; Dm lip 8
FS 230; dark grey clay, black slip. "Ton glimmerhaltig"
Date: LHIIIA2
Cup 622 (XXIV:1)
H 3.8; Dm lip 7.8
FS 230; dark grey clay and slip
Date: LHIIIA2
Cup 706 (XXIV:2)
H 4; Dm lip 11.5
FS 220; FM 77 (Mee) Boysal: reddish clay and slip, dark red "Firnis"
Date: LHIIIA2
Cup 707 (XXIV:3)
H 4.9; Dm lip 12.3
FS 220; FM 77
Date: LHIIIA2
Kylix 1862 (XXVII:5)
H ÷; Dm lip 13.1
FS 256; FM 49
Date: LHIIIA2
Kylix 625 (XXVII:6)
H 16.2; Dm lip 15
FS 266; rose to beige clay and slip
Date: LHIIIA2
Goblet 686 (XXVIII:4)
H 12.2; Dm lip 11.2
FS 269; sand clay, red "Firnis"
Date: LHIIIA2

Goblet/kylix 618 (XXIX:6)
H 8; Dm lip 11
FS 267; rose to beige clay and slip
Date: LHIIIA2
Flask 722 (XXXII:4)
H 11.5; Dm 10
FS 190; FM 45
Date: LHIIIA2
Basket vase 622 (XXXII:5)
H 21.6; Dm 13.6
FS 319; FM 42+58
Date: LHIIIA2
Flask 721 (XXXIII:1a-b)
H 14; Dm 10
FS 188; FM 27 (Mee: linear)
Date: LHIIIA2

Tomb 3, area A

Architectural features: no information
Photo: Boysal 1967a, pl. XII:16
Contents: Boysal 1967b, 79:" Eine Urne mit Asche"!
Pottery:
Stirrup jar 697 (XIV:2a-b)
H 9.8; Dm 10
FS 185; FM 64+71
Date: LHIIIA2-B1
Stirrup jar 691 (XIV:3a-b)
H 9.4; Dm 13.1
FS 180; linear
Date: LHIIIB
Jug 720 (XVII:4)
H 10.1; Dm 10.2
FS 114; FM 64
Date: LHIIIA2
Bowl 660 (XX:3)
H 13; Dm lip 18.5
FS 284B; FM 53
Date: LHIIIB
Kylix 626 (XXX:2)
H 11; Dm lip 11.7
FS 267; rose to beige clay and slip
Date: LHIIIA2-B

Tomb 4, area A

Architectural features: no information
Photo: Boysal 1967a, pl. XII:16
Contents: no information
Pottery:
Conical cup 666 (XX:5)
H 5.9; Dm lip 15
FS 204; tile red clay and slip
Date: LHIIIA2-B
Jug 621 (XVIII:1)
H 13.9; Dm 13.1
FS 114; tile red clay, dark grey slip
Date: LHIIIA2-B1

Tomb 5, area A

Architectural features:
Burial chamber: H 1,80; Dm floor 1,75
Sketch: ÷
Photo: Boysal 1967a, pl. XII:16
Contents:

Tomb 6, area B

Architectural features:
Dromos: no measurements – collapsed
Burial chamber: "along the line of orientation of the skeleton" 2.00 m; D 1.70 m (elliptical)
Sketch: ÷
Photo: Boysal 1967a, pl. VIII + XVI:22b
Contents:
One complete skeleton
Pottery:
Alabastron 700 (XXV:2)
H 7.5; Dm 11; Dm lip 6.6
FS 94; FM 64
Date: LHIIIA2

Tomb 7, area B

Architectural features: no information
Photo: Boysal 1967a, pl. XII:15

Contents: no information
Pottery:
Conical cup 664 (XX:6)
H 7.4; Dm lip 15
FS 204; reddish clay and slip
Date: LHIIIA2-B
Alabastron 643 (XXV:3)
H 9.6; Dm 12.3
FS 94; FM 60
Date: LHIIIA2-B

Tomb 8, area B

Architectural features: no information
Photo: Boysal 1967a, pl. XII:15 and pl. XIII:18
Contents: no information

Tomb 9, area B

Architectural features: no information
Photo: Boysal 1967a, pl.XIV:19a-b
Contents: no information
Pottery:
Jug 658 (XVIII:2)
H 12.5; Dm 12.7
FS 114; reddish clay, dark grey slip
Date: LHIIIA2-B

Tomb 10, area B

Architectural features: no information
Sketch: Boysal 1967a, pl. XVII:23
Contents: no information
Pottery:
Jug 725 (XVII:9)
H 9; Dm 8.3
FS 114; linear
Date: LHIIIA2-B

Tomb 11, area B

Architectural features: no information

Photo: Boysal 1967a, pl. IX:11 and pl. XV:20
Contents: no information
Pottery:
Piriform jar 679 (I:1)
H 37; Dm 32
FS 35; FM 62
Date: LHIIIA2
Piriform jar 655 (V:2)
H 14.5; Dm 12.1
FS 45; FM 64
Date LHIIIA2

Tomb 12, area B

Architectural features:
Burial chamber: H? (collapser); Floor 2,40 * 1,80
Sketch: ÷
Photo: ÷
Contents:
Pottery:
Jug 668 (XVIII:4)
H 11.3; Dm 9
FS 114; tile red clay; dark red slip
Date: LHIIIA2-B
Kylix 688 (XXIX:2)
H 17.8; Dm lip 15
FS 257; FM 23
Date: LHIIIA2
668 and 688 were found together

Tomb 13, area B

Architectural features: no information
Photo: Boysal 1967a, pl. IX:12
Contents: no information
Pottery:
Piriform jar 678 (II:4)
H ÷; Dm lip 13.5
FS 37; FM 51
Date: LHIIIB
Amphoriskos 681 (VI:4)
H 37; Dm 32
FS 58; FM 53
Date: LHIIIC1

Amphoriskos 659 (VII:1)
H 18.6; Dm lip 9.6; Dm 15.8
FS 59; FM 53
Date: LHIIIC1
Amphoriskos 657 (VII:3)
H 15.9; Dm lip 13.5; Dm 14
FS 59; FM 42
Date: LHIIICl
Stirrup jar 631 (XI:9)
H 9.3; Dm 12.4
FS 180; FM 19
Date: LHIIIB
Kylix 690 (XXVIII:5)
H ÷; Dm lip 16.8
FS 266; light tile red clay, light beige slip, red to brown "Firnis"
Date: LHIIIB
Kylix 687 (XXIX:1)
H 18.5; Dm lip 17
FS 258; FM 23
Date: LHIIIB
Spouted stemmed bowl 683 (XXX:5)
H 21.7; Dm lip 27
FS 304; tile red clay and slip
Date: LHIIIA2
Flask 682 (XXXIII:2a-b)
H 28.4; Dm 18 to 23 (from lip to lip?)
FS 186; FM 53 (Mee: Linear)
Date: LHIIIC1

Tomb 14, area B

Architectural features: no information
Contents: no information
Pottery:
Alabastron 1863 (XXV:8)
H 11.4; Dm 13.6
FS 94; FM 19 + 43
Date: LHIIIA2-B
Jug? 645 (XXX:6)
H 23; Dm 19.1
FS?; reddish clay, reddish to grey slip
Date:?
Conical bowl, spouted 656 (XXXI:5)
H 12; Dm lip 22

FS 300; FM 45
Date: LHIIIB

Tomb 15, area B

Architectural features:
Dromos: L 1.80; W 1.10 (0.15 wider upwards)
Entrance: "dromos...with a hole 1 m in diameter in front of the door. On the burial chamber side, the dromos wall is in the form of a rectangle with the entrance in the centre. The door is at a point 0.20 m below the surface of the ground and 0.20 m from the sides. Being 0.45 m in length, the level of the door is about 0.20 m below that of the dromos and at the same level as the floor of the burial chamber." (Boysal 1967a, 37)
Burial chamber: D 1.10 m?
Sketch: ÷
Photo: ÷
Contents:
W of the entrance: pottery, group A
E of the entrance: pottery, group B
In front of the entrance: half a skull. In an E-W line a pile of bones, some discoloured black, others carbonised. Next to the bones a gold ring. The bones were found ca 0.05 – 0.10 m below the pottery level?
Pottery, group A
Piriform jar 726 (III:4)
H 29.5; Dm 24.5
FS 37; FM 61
Date: LHIIIB
Stirrup jar 698 (VIII:2a-b)
H 19.5; Dm 15.3
FS 166; FM 43+24
Date: LHIIIA2
Jug 724 (XVII:5)
H 9; Dm 7.2
FS 114; linear decoration
Date: LHIIIA2
Jug 718 (XVIII:6)
H 12; Dm 10
FS 114; FM 43
Date: LHIIIA2
Cup 709 (XXIII:1)
H 3.5; Dm 9.7
FS 220; dark tile red clay and slip; dark brown "Firnis"

Date: LHIIIA2
Pottery, group B
Alabastron 615 (XXV:5)
H 9.4; Dm 12.4
FS 94, two handles; FM 64
Date: LHIIIA2

Tomb 16, area B

Architectural features:
Dromos: L 2.35 m; W 1.10 m; H at door 1.30 m (? do not correspond with the plan)
Burial chamber: (measured on the plan) D 1.30 m; max. H 1.05 m; W 175 m
Entrance: D 0.55 m; W 0.60 m; H 0.45 m
Sketch: Boysal 1967a, pl. V
Photo: ÷
Contents:
Pottery:
Conical cup 667 (XX:8)
H 6.2; Dm lip 13
FS 204; reddish clay and slip
Date: LHIIIA2-B
Goblet 684 (XXVII:2)
H 15.9; Dm lip 17.4
FS 264; rose to light beige clay, beige slip, black "Firnis", in some places damaged/worn off.
Date: LHIIIA2
Kylix 685 (XXIX:3)
H 11.2; Dm lip 12.6
FS 267 one handle; tile red clay and slip
Date: LHIIIA2-B

Tomb 17, area?

Architectural features: no information
Photo: Boysal 1967a, pl.VI:7
Contents: no information

Tomb 18, area B

Architectural features: no information
Photo: Boysal 1967a, pl. VI:6

Contents: no information
Pottery:
Jug 637 (XVII:3)
H 12; Dm 10.6
FS 114; FM 75
Date: LHIIIB-C1
Jug 727 (XIX:2)
H 30.8; Dm 25.8
FS 109; FM? tile red clay, reddish cream slip (Mee: linear)
Date:?
Goblet 617 (XXVII:1)
H 14; Dm lip 18
FS 264; tile red clay. darker slip
Date: LHIIIA2
Kylix 689 (XXIX:4)
H 18.5; Dm lip 16.6
FS 266; tile red clay and slip
Date: LHIIIA2-B
Kylix 624 (XXX:1)
H 9.4; Dm lip 9
FS 267; rose clay and slip
Date:?

Tomb 20, area B

Architectural features: no information
Contents: no information
Pottery:
Jug 633 (XIX:4)
H 20.8; Dm 18
FS 109; dark tile red clay; greenish beige slip
Date:?
Kylix 628 (XXVIII:1)
H 14.5; Dm lip 14.5
FS 264; beige clay and slip
Date: LHIIIA2

Tomb 21, area B

Architectural features: no information
Photo: Boysal 1967a, pl. XV:21
Contents: no information
Pottery:

Stirrup jar 693 (XIV:1a-b)
H 11.8; Dm 11
FS 171; FM 19
Date: LHIIIA2
Kylix 627 (XXVII:4)
H 14.2; Dm lip 14.2
FS 264; grey beige clay; black slip
Date: LHIIIA2
Kylix 1861 (XXVIII:6)
H ÷; Dm lip 16.8
FS 257; FM 23
Date: LHIIIA2

Tomb 22, area C

Architectural features:
Burial chamber: app. rectangular L 1.95 to 1.85
Sketch: ÷
Photo: Boysal 1967a, pl. VII:9
Contents:
Long-bones (?), teeth
Pottery:
Piriform jar 647 (I:3)
H 35; Dm 30
FS 35; FM 57
Date: LHIIIA2
Piriform jar 728 (II:2)
H 36.3; Dm 30.5
FS 35; FM 62
Date: LHIIIA2
Piriform jar 635 (V:1)
H 16.5; Dm lip 8.7-13.5
FS 45; FM 42
Date: LHIIIA2
Piriform jar 636 (V:3)
H 20; Dm lip 10.8-16.3
FS 45; FM 49
Date: LHIIIA2
Piriform jar 634 (V:4)
H 20.7; Dm lip 11-18
FS 45; FM 64
Date: LHIIIA2
Mug 702 (XXI:3)
H 4.9; Dm lip 5.1
FS 227; no description

Date: LHIIIA2
Mug 701 (XXI:4)
H 5.4; Dm lip 7
FS 227 (form 62); no description
Date: LHIIIA2
Mug 703 (XXI:6)
H 4.7; Dm lip 6.4
FS 227; linear, tile red clay, dark red slip
Date: LHIIIA2
Cup 708 (XXIII:6)
H 4.5; Dm lip 12.3
FS 220; FM 77 (Mee: monochrome)
Date: LHIIIA2
Brazier 704 (XXXI:2)
H 8.1; Dm 11.5
FS 316 (form 93); tile red to grey clay
Date: LHIIIA2
Flask 719 (XXXII:1+3)
H 8.3; Dm 5 (thickness)
FS?; FM 52 (Mee: linear)
Date: LHIIIA2

Tomb 23, area C

Architectural features: no information
Contents: no information
Pottery:
Stirrup jar 694 (XIII:1a-b)
H 10.6; Dm 10.4
FS 171; FM 64
Date: LHIIIA2
Jug 661 (XIX:6)
H 21; Dm 18.7
FS 109; tile red clay; darker slip
Date: LHIIIA2-B
Brazier 705 (XXXI:4)
H 7.12; DM lip 9; Dm 10.1
FS 316; tile red rough clay; grey surface
Date: LHIIIA2-B

Tomb 24, area C

Architectural features: no information
Contents: no information

Pottery:
Stirrup jar 692 (VIII:1a-b)
H 14.1; Dm 11.3
FS 166; FM 57
Date: LHIIIA2
Cup 1866 (XXIII:3)
H 4.7; Dm lip 12
FS 220; FM 49
Date: LHIIIA2
Alabastron 699 (XXIV:8)
H 10; Dm 15.3
FS 94; FM 45
Date: LHIIIA2
Alabastron 723 (XXIV:9)
H 5.7; Dm 8.2
FS 85; FM 32
Date: LHIIIA2
Flask 682 (XXXII:6)
H 10.5; Dm 8
FS 190; FM 64
Date: LHIIIA2

Tomb 26, area C

Architectural features: no information
Contents: no information
Pottery:
Alabastron 1009 (XXV:9)
H 8.5; Dm lip 7.2; Dm 11.5
FS 94; FM 64
Date: LHIIIA2

Tomb 27, area C

Architectural features: no information
Photo: Boysal 1967a, pl. VII:8
Contents: no information
Pottery:
Piriform jar 985 (II:3)
H ÷; Dm lip 13
FS 37; FM 18
Date: LHIIIB
Stirrup jar 987 (XVI:3)
H 41; Dm 36.8

FS 164; dark tile red clay; brown "Firnis" (Mee: linear)
Date: LHIIIA2-B
Jug 980 (XVII:2)
H 11; Dm 10
FS 114; tile red clay, lighter slip; dark brown "Firnis"; "Ton glimmerhaltig" (Mee: FM 32)
Date: LHIIIA2-B
Alabastron 1008 (XXIV:7)
H 8.9; Dm lip 7.8; Dm 12.2
FS 94; FM 64
Date: LHIIIA2
Alabastron 1003 (XXV:4)
H 9; Dm lip 6.8; Dm 11.6
FS 94; FM 64
Date: LHIIIA2

Tomb 28, area A

Architectural features: no information
Contents: no information
Pottery:
Stirrup jar 994 (XV:1a-b)
H 9; Dm 13.7
FS 180; linear
Date: LHIIIB
Stirrup jar 1030 (XV:2a-b)
H 10.5; Dm 10.5
FS 173; FM 18
Date: LHIIIA2-B1
Stirrup jar 995 (XV:3a-b)
H 8.6; Dm 11.9
FS 180; linear
Date: LHIIIB
Jug 976 (XVIII:7)
H 8.3; Dm 7.3
FS 114; tile red clay; cream slip, "Firnis und Überzug stark abgerieben"
Date: LHIIIB

Tomb 29, area C

Architectural features: no information
Contents: no information
Pottery:

Stirrup jar 1032 (XVI:2)
H 12.2; Dm 10.9
FS 171; FM 42
Date: LHIIIA2-B
Jug 977 (XVIII:9)
H 7.2; Dm 8.3
FS 114; reddish clay; light tile red slip
Date: LHIIIA2-B

Tomb 30, area A

Architectural features: no information
Contents: no information
Pottery:
Cup 1015 (XXIII:8)
H 6.1; Dm lip 9.3
FS 232; dark grey clay; dark grey to black slip
Date: LHIIIA2-B

Tomb 31, area A

Architectural features: no information
Contents: no information
Pottery:
Alabastron 1006 (XXIV:6)
H 9; Dm 12.5
FS 94; FM 64
Date: LHIIIA2

Tomb 32, area A

Architectural features: no information
Photo: Boysal 1967a, pl.X:13
Contents: no information
Pottery:
Piriform jar 1022 (IV:4)
H 16.8; Dm lip 11; Dm 14.5
FS 45; FM 64
Date: LHIIIA2
Stirrup jar 1001 (IX:1a-b)
H 18; Dm 13.4
FS 166; FM 25
Date: LHIIIA2

Stirrup jar 999 (IX:2a-b)
H 12.8; Dm 10.3
FS 166; FM 45
Date: LHIIIA2
Stirrup jar 996 (IX:3a-b)
H 18.7; Dm 14
FS 166; FM 19
Date: LHIIIA2
Stirrup jar 1028 (XI:1)
H 12.6; Dm 9.7
FS 166; FM 76
Date: LHIIIA2
Stirrup jar 1000 (XII, 2a-b)
H 14.7; Dm 15.3
FS 171; FM 43
Date: LHIIIA2
Stirrup jar 997 (XII:3a-b)
H 10.4; Dm 10.2
FS 171; FM 58+64
Date: LHIIIA2
Jug 993 (XIX:1)
H 26; Dm 22.7
FS 145; linear
Date: LHIIIA2
Cup 973 (XX:4)
H 5.4; Dm lip 15.1
FS 204; reddish clay; tile red slip; brown "Firnis"
Date: LHIIIA2
Cup 974 (XX:7)
H 4.1; Dm lip 9.7
FS 204; reddish clay, lighter slip
Date: LHIIIA2
Mug 971 (XXI:5)
H 10.8; Dm lip 15.8
FS 227; tile red clay and slip; red "Firnis"
Date: LHIIIA2
Cup 1016 (XXIII:2)
H 3; DM lip 9.5
FS 220; black clay and slip
Date: LHIIIA2
Cup 1014 (XXIII:4)
H 2.8; Dm lip 9
FS 220; dark grey clay; black slip
Date: LHIIIA2
Cup 1013 (XXIII:5)
H 3.3; Dm lip 8.9

FS 220; black clay and slip
Date: LHIIIA2
Cup 1012 (XXIII:9?)
H 4.4; Dm lip 9.8
FS 230; FM 11
Date: LHIIIA2
Alabastron 1007 (XXV:6)
H 9.4; Dm lip 7.6; Dm 12.8
FS 94; FM 64
Date: LHIIIA2
Brazier 1020 (XXXI:1)
H 9.3; Dm 8.5
FS 316; tile red clay
Date: LHIIIA2
Brazier 1002 (XXXI:3)
H 7.7 (without foot); Dm 10
FS 316; tile red clay
Date: LHIIIA2
Askos 1017 (XXXII:2)
H 5.8; L 11.2
FS 194; FM 53
Date: LHIIIA2

Tomb 33, area A

Architectural features: no information
Contents: no information
Pottery:
Piriform jar 989 (IV:2)
H 41; Dm 32
FS 37; FM 61
Date: LHIIIB
Jug 1024 (XVIII:3)
H 13.7; Dm 12.6
FS 114; reddish clay; red slip; sandy clay
Date: LHIIIA2-B
Jug 975 (XVIII:5)
H 9.7; Dm 9.2
FS 114; light tile red clay; dark grey slip
Date: LHIIIA2-B
Cup 983 (XXII:1)
H 4.7; Dm lip 7.5
FS 231; FM 53
Date: LHIIIB
Cup 1011 (XXII:2)

H 5.1; Dm lip 11.1
FS 231; FM 19
Date: LHIIIB
Cup 984 (XXII:4)
H 3.5; DM lip 8.4
FS 220; FM 53
Date: LHIIIB
Alabastron 1004 (XXIV:4)
H 10.3; Dm lip 8.8; Dm 15
FS 94; FM 57
Date: LHIIIA2-B
Jug 972 (XXX:3)
H 11.8; Dm lip 8.4
FS 161; tile red clay and slip
Date: LHIIIA2-B

Tomb 34, area A

Architectural features: no information
Photo: Boysal 1967a, pl. XI:14
Contents: no information
Pottery:
Piriform jar 970 (IV:3)
H 13.8; DM 12.6
FS 45; FM 64
Date: LHIIIA2
Stirrup jar 1031 (XI:3)
H 10.5; Dm 10.7
FS 171; FM 45
Date: LHIIIA2
Stirrup jar 1033 (XI:7)
H 11.2; Dm 11.6
FS 171; FM?
Date: LHIIIA2-B1
Goblet 992 (XXVI:3)
H 16; Dm lip 18.3
FS 264; tile red clay; darker slip
Date: LHIIIA2

Tomb 35, area A

Architectural features: no information
Contents: no information
Pottery:

Piriform jar 990 (III:3)
H 36.7; Dm 31.6
FS 35; FM 44
Date: IIIA2
Stirrup jar 986 (XVI:4)
H 23; Dm 20.8
FS?; FM?
Date:?
Cup 1010 (XXII:7)
H 6.7; Dm lip 12.2
FS 214; FM 64
Date: LHIIIA2
Alabastron 1005 (XXVI:2)
H 16; Dm lip 12; Dm 18.5
FS 94; FM 58
Date: LHIIIA2
Goblet 991 (XXVI:6)
H 9.4; Dm lip 10.6
FS 264; light beige clay and slip; light brown "Firnis"
Date: LHIIIA2

Tomb 36. area A

Architectural features: no information
Contents: no information
Pottery:
Piriform jar 988 (I:4)
H 35; Dm 29.5
FS 35; FM 70
Date: LHIIIA2
Stirrup jar 1029 (X:3a-b)
H 19.2; Dm 14.3
FS 166; FM 19+43
Date: LHIIIA2
Jug 1025 (XVIII:8)
H 8.7; Dm 8.3
FS 114; grey clay; cream to beige slip; dark brown "Firnis"
Date: LHIIIA2
Cup 696 (XXII:9)
H 11.6; Dm lip 17.2
FS 283; FM 53
Date: LHIIIA2-B

Tomb 37, area A

Architectural features: no information
Contents: no information
Pottery:
Alabastron 1012 (XXV:1)
H 7.9; Dm 10.7
FS 94; FM 61+64
Date: LHIIIA2-B

Tomb 38, area C

Architectural features:
Burial chamber: H? (collapsed) + 2.50; Dm floor c. 3.40
Sketch: ÷
Photo: ÷
Contents:
Pottery:
Stirrup jar 2309 (XI:2)
H 8.9; Dm 8.6
FS 171; FM 25
Date: LHIIIA2-B

Tomb 39, area A

Architectural features:
Dromos: L 2.05 m; W 1.53 m; H at door 3.30 m
Burial chamber: H 2.50 m; sides of floor E 2.30 m; W 2.60 m; N 2.47 m;
S 3.00 m (trapezoid)
Sketch: ÷
Photo: ÷
Contents:
Skeletons of two persons: one on the NW side – burnt; one on the S side, near the edge(?) – unburnt (description Boysal 1967a – the informations are given without a sketch plan or indication of the facing of the tomb).
Pottery:
Piriform jar 2310 (III:2)
H 32.8; Dm 25.5
FS 37; FM 57
Date: LHIIIB
Stirrup jar 2312 (XI:5)
H 10.1; Dm 10

FS 171; FM 18
Date: LHIIIA2
Jug 2307 (XIX:3)
H 32.7; Dm 22
FS 133; FM 67
Date: LHIIIA2
Goblet 2320 (XXVI:4)
H 13; Dm lip 14.7
FS 264; creme to light beige clay, dark brown "Firnis"
Date: LHIIIA2
Goblet 2313 (XXVI:5)
H 13.5; Dm lip 14.3
FS 264; dark tile red clay, dark grey to dark brown slip.
Date: LHIIIA2

Tomb 40, area A

Architectural features: no information
Contents: no information
Pottery:
Jug 2318 (XIX:5)
H 15.4; Dm 13.3
FS 109; FM 41
Date: LHIIIA2-B

Tomb 41, area A

Architectural features: no information
Contents: no information
Pottery:
Piriform jar 2316 (VI:2)
H 11.7; Dm 10.5
FS 45; FM 76
Date: LHIIIA2-B
Cup 2308 (XXII:5)
H 3.1; Dm lip 11.5
FS 220; grey clay and slip
Date: LHIIIA2-B

Tomb 42, area?

Architectural features: no information
Contents: no information

Pottery:
Jug 2315 (XVII:6)
H 7.9; Dm 7.7
FS 114; linear
Date:?
Kylix 2311 (XXIX:5)
H ÷; Dm 14.5
FS 274; FM 61
Date: LHIIIC1

Tomb 43, area B

Architectural features:
Dromos: L 3.30; W 0.90; H at door 1.50
Burial chamber: H 1.25; Floor 1.30 · 1.40
Sketch: ÷
Photo: ÷
Contents: ÷

Tomb 44, area B

Architectural features:
Dromos: L 4.10; W 0.80; H at door 1.55
Sketch: ÷
Photo: ÷
Contents: ÷

Tomb 45, area B

Architectural features:
Dromos: L 3.55 (horizontally) – 3.70 (ground level)
Sides plastered; floor hard
Entrance: form dromos: W (lower) 0.65 (upper) 0.50; D 0.60; closed with wall in rubble masonry. Plastered.
Burial chamber: H 1.60; D 1.60; W 2.00. "There was an unfilled space at the top of the chamber of 0.80 m but the remainder of the tomb was filled with earth." (?!)
Contents:
Skeleton – from the middle of the left part of the tomb, c. 0.15 m above floor level. On the whole well preserved.
1 TC weight "and similar objects".
Pottery group A: 0.45 m above floor level.

Pottery group B: 0.25 m above floor level, in a series side by side tws the door.
Pottery group C: 0.30 m above floor level, in NE corner.
Pottery, group A:
Stirrup jar 2334 (X:1a-b)
H 20.4; Dm 15.9
FS 166; FM 45
Date: LHIIIA2
Pottery, group B:
Piriform jar 2331 (VI:1)
H 9; Dm 9
FS 45; FM 61
Date: LHIIIA2
Stirrup jar 2333 (XII:1a-b)
H 11; Dm 9.9
FS 171; FM 19
Date: LHIIIA2
Jug 2329 (XVII:7)
H 7.5; Dm 7.3
FS 114; FM 61
Date: LHIIIA2
Jug 2330 (XVII:8)
H 8.6; Dm 7.2
FS 114; FM 61
Date: LHIIIA2
Pottery, group C:
Mug 2332 (XXI:1)
H 6.5; Dm lip 8.2
FS 227; linear, reddish clay, cream slip, brown "Firnis"
Date: LHIIIA2

Tomb 46, area B

Architectural features:
Burial chamber: H 0.85; Floor 0.75 · 0.65
Sketch: ÷
Photo: ÷
Contents:
Pottery:
Jug 2336 (XX:1)
H 8.1; Dm 8.2
FS 114; linear decoration, "Ton glimmerhaltig"
Date: LHIIIA2-B
Cup 2335 (XXII:6)
H 3.6; Dm lip 8.5

FS 230; grey clay
Date: LHIIIA2-B

Tomb 47, area B

Architectural features: no information
Contents: no information
Pottery:
Stirrup jar 2339 (X:2a-b)
H 17.8; Dm 13.8
FS 166; FM 51
Date: LHIIIA2
Alabastron 2338 (XXIV:5)
H 9.3; Dm lip 7.8; Dm 13.6
FS 94; FM 57
Date: LHIIIA2

Pottery without context:
Piriform jar 48 (III:1)
H 33; Dm 24
FS 35; FM 11
Date: LHIIIA2-B

Piriform jar 2131 (IV:1)
H 37.8; Dm 30.2
FS 37; FM 46
Date: LHIIIB

Piriform jar 60 (VI:3)
H 9.7; Dm 8.9
FS 45; FM 61
Date: LHIIIA2-B

Stirrup jar 57 (VII:4)
H 13.5; Dm 11.2
FS 167; FM 18
Date: LHIIIB

Stirrup jar 1865 (XI:8)
H 9; Dm 11.3
FS 178; linear
Date: LHIIIA2

Jug 59 (XVII:1)
H 11; Dm 10.4

FS 114; reddish clay; brown slip
Date: LHIIIA2-B

Bowl 55 (XX:2)
H 10.2; Dm lip 15.1
FS 284; FM 64
Date: LHIIIB-C1

Mug 436 (XXI:2)
H 5.5; Dm lip 8.6
FS 231; FM 53
Date: LHIIIB

Cup 51 (XXII:3)
H 3.7; Dm lip 9.3
FS 230; linear; reddish clay; lighter slip; red "Firnis"
Date: LHIIIA2-B

Cup 1018 (XXII:8)
H 6.4; Dm lip 10
FS 230; FM 19
Date: LHIIIA2

Alabastron 56 (XXV:7)
H 12.7; Dm 15.6
FS 94; FM 57
Date: LHIIIA2-B

Alabastron 1864 (XXVI:1)
H 8; Dm 11.2
FS 94; FM 57
Date: LHIIIA2-B

Kylix 616 (XXVII:3)
H ÷; Dm ÷
FS 264; tile red clay; grey slip
Date: LHIIIA2

Kylix 58 (XXVIII:2)
H 12; Dm lip 12.3
FS 264; reddish clay; grey slip
Date: LHIIIA2

Kylix 52 (XXVIII:3)
H 14; Dm lip 14
FS 264; tile red clay; darker slip

Date: LHIIIA2

Stemmed bowl 2253 (XXX:4)
H 11; Dm lip 11
FS 305; reddish clay and slip (?)
Date: LHIIIB-C1

Jug 49 (XXXI:6)
H 21.5; Dm 18.5
FS 102; FM 49
Date: LHIIIA2

Notes

1 Furumark 1941.

Bibliography

Akarca 1971: A. Akarca, Beçin, *Belleten* 35, 1971, 3-37.
Akurgal 1978: E. Akurgal (ed.), *Proceedings of the Xth International Congress of Classical Archaeology, Ankara 1970*, Ankara 1978.
Antonaccio 1995: C.M. Antonaccio, *An Archaeology of Ancestors: Greek Tomb and Hero Cult,* Maryland 1995.
Barber 1987: R.L.N. Barber, *The Cyclades in the Bronze Age,* London 1987.
Bass 1963: G.F. Bass, Mycenean and Protogeometric Tombs in the Halicarnassus Peninsula, *AJA* 67, 1963, 353-361.
Bean & Cook 1955: G.E. Bean and J.M. Cook, The Halicarnassus Peninsula, *BSA* 50, 1955, 85-171.
Bean & Cook 1957: G.E. Bean and J.M. Cook, The Carian Coast III, *BSA* 52, 1957, 117-138.
Bean & Fraser 1954: G.E. Bean and P.M. Fraser, *The Rhodian Peraea and Islands*, London 1954.
Bell 1979-1980: M.R. Bell, Preliminary reports on the Mycenean pottery from Dier-El-Medina, *ASAE* 68, 1979-1980, 143-163.
Bent 1888: T. Bent, Discoveries in Asia Minor, *JHS* 9, 1888, 82-87.
Benzi 1992: M. Benzi, *Rodi e la Civiltà Micenea*, Roma 1992.
Bergquist 1993: B. Bergquist, Bronze Age sacrificial *koine* in the Eastern Mediterranean?, in *Ritual and sacrifice in the*

ancient Near East. Proceedings of the International Conference organized by the Katholieke Universiteit Leuven from the 17*th* to the 20*th* of April 1991, ed. E. Quaegebeur, (Orientalia Lovaniensia Analecta 55), Leuven 1993, 11-43.

Berthold 1984: R.M. Berthold, *Rhodes in the Hellenistic Age*, London 1984.

Betz 1987: H.D. Betz, Libation, in Eliade 1987, 537-539.

Bittel 1976: K. Bittel, *Die Hethiter*, München 1976.

Bittel et al. 1958: K. Bittel, W. Herre, H. Otten, M. Röhrs, and J. Schauble, *Die Hethitischen Grabfunde von Osmankayası*, Berlin 1958.

Blegen 1937: C. Blegen, *Prosymna. The Helladic settlement preceding the Argive Heraeum*, Cambridge 1937.

Blinkenberg & Kinch 1903: C. Blinkenberg and K.-F. Kinch, *Exploration Archéologique de Rhodes*, København 1903.

Blümel 1998: W. Blümel, Karien, die Karer und ihre Nachbarn, *Kadmos* 37, 163-173.

Boardman 1980: J. Boardman, *The Greeks Overseas*, London 1980.

Bouzek 1985: J. Bouzek, *The Aegean, Anatolia and Europe: Cultural interrelations in the second millennium B.C.*, SIMA 29, Göteborg 1985.

Boysal 1964: Y. Boysal, Milli Egitim Bakanliği Müsgebi Kısısı 1963 Yili Kısa Raporu, *TürkAD* 13:2, 1964, 81-85.

Boysal 1965: Y. Boysal, 1964 Müskebi Kazıları Hakkında Kısa Rapor, *TürkAD* 14, 1965, 123-126.

Boysal 1967a: Y. Boysal, New Excavations in Caria, *Anadolu* 11, 1967, 31-56.

Boysal 1967b: Y. Boysal, Müskebi Kazısı 1963 Kısa Raporu / Vorläufiger Bericht über die Grabungen 1963 in Müskebi, *Belleten* 31, 1967, 67-83.

Boysal 1969: Y. Boysal, *Katalog der Vasen im Museum in Bodrum. I. Mykenisch-Protogeometrisch*, Ankara 1969.

Branigan 1970: K. Branigan, *The Tombs of Mesara*, London 1970.

Branigan 1981: K. Branigan, Minoan Colonialism, *BSA* 76, 1981, 23-33.

Briese et al. 2002: M.B. Briese, A.M. Carstens, and P. Pedersen, Surveys and excavations in Halicarnassus, 1995-2001, *Acta Hyberborea* 9, 2002, 266-270

Bryce 1986: T.R. Bryce, *The Lycians in Literary and Epigraphic Sources*, København 1986.

Bryce 1989a: T.R. Bryce, The nature of Mycenean involvement in western Anatolia, *Historia* 38, 1989, 1-21.

Bryce 1989b: T.R. Bryce, Ahhiyawans and Myceneans – an Anatolian viewpoint, *OxfJA* 8, 1989, 297-310.

Burkert 1985: W. Burkert, *Greek Religion*, Cambridge, Massachusetts 1985.

Bury & Meiggs 1987: J.B. Bury and R. Meiggs, *A History of Greece*, (4th ed.) London 1987.

Caner 1983: E. Caner, *Fibeln in Anatolien*, (Prähistorische Bronzefunde, Abt. 14;8.), München 1983.

Carstens 1999: A.M. Carstens, *Death Matters. Funerary Architecture on the Halikarnassos peninsula*, Ph.d.-dissertation, University of Copenhagen 1999.

Carstens 2001: A.M. Carstens, Drinking vessels in tombs – a cultic connection?, in *Ceramics in context. Proceedings of the Internordic Colloquium on Ancient Pottery held at Stockholm, 13-15 June 1997*, ed. C. Scheffer, (Acta Universitatis Stockholmiensis 12), Stockholm 2001, 89-102.

Carstens 2002a: A.M. Carstens, Tomb cult on the Halikarnassos peninsula, *AJA* 106:3, 2002, 391-409.

Carstens 2002b: A.M. Carstens, Archaic Karian pottery – investigating culture?, in *Pots for the Living, Pots for the Dead*, eds. A. Rathje, M. Nielsen and B. Bundgaard Rasmussen, (*Acta Hyberborea* 9), København 2002, 127-143.

Carstens 1997: P. Carstens, *Drikoffer og Libation i Tempel og på Alter*, Ph.d.-dissertation, Aarhus University 1997.

Carstens 1998: P. Carstens, Why Does the God Have a Cup in His Hand?, *Scandinavian Journal of the Old Testament* 12, 1998, 214-232.

Carstens & Flensted-Jensen 2004: A.M. Carstens and P. Flensted-Jensen, Halikarnassos and the Lelegians, in *The Salmakis Inscription and Hellenistic* Halikarnassos, eds. S. Isager and P. Pedersen 2004, (*Halicarnassian Studies* IV), Odense 2004, 109-123.

Çiner 1964: R. Çiner, Bodrum – Müskebi Kazısı Iskelet Kalıntılarının Tetkiki, *Antropoloji* I:2, 1964, 56-79

Coldstream 1968: J.N. Coldstream, *Greek Geometric Pottery*, London 1968.

Coldstream & Catling 1996: J.N. Coldstream and H.W. Catling, (eds.), *Knossos North Cemetery: early Greek tombs*, Athens 1996.

Cook 1980: R.M. Cook, Antecedents of Fikellura, *Anadolu* 21, 1980, 71-74.

Cook 1993: R.M. Cook, A Carian Wild Goat Workshop, *OxfJA* 12, 1993, 109-115.

Cook 1999: R.M. Cook, A List of Carian Orientalizing Pottery, *OxfJA* 18, 1999, 79-93.

Dalton 1751-1752: R. Dalton, *A Series of Engravings Representing View of Places, Buildings, Antiquities, etc. in Sicily, Greece, Asia Minor, and Egypt*, London 1751-1752.

Desborough 1952: V.R.d'A. Desborough, *Protogeometric Pottery*, Oxford 1952.

Desborough 1964: V.R.d'A. Desborough, *The Last Mycenaeans and their successors. An archaeological survey c. 1200-c. 1000 BC*, Oxford 1964

Dickinson 1994: O. Dickinson, *The Aegean Bronze Age*, Cambridge 1994.

Doumas 1977: C. Doumas, *Early Bronze Age Burial Habits in the Cyclades,* SIMA 48, Göteborg 1977.

Dyggve 1960: E. Dyggve, *Lindos: Fouilles de l'Acropole 1902-1914 et 1952,* Berlin 1960.

Eliade 1987: M. Eliade (ed.), *The Encyclopedia of Religion,* Basingstoke 1987.

Emre 1978: K. Emre, *Afyon Yöresinde bir Hitit Mezarlığı / A Hittite Cemetery near Afyon,* Ankara 1978.

Erkanal 1987: A. Erkanal, Panaztepe Kazısının 1985 Yılı Sonuçları, *VIII Kazı Sonuçları Toplantısı 1986,* Ankara, 253-259.

Erkanal 1996: H. Erkanal, 1994 Panaztepe Kazıları Sonuçları, *XVII Kazı Sonuçları Toplantısı 1995,* Ankara, 329-335.

Flensted-Jensen 2004: P. Flensted-Jensen, Karia, in *An inventory of archaic and classical poleis: an investigation conducted by the Copenhagen Polis Centre for the Danish National Research Foundation*, eds. M. Herman Hansen & T. Heine Nielsen, Oxford 2004, 1108-1137.

Forsdyke 1925: E.J. Forsdyke, *Catalogue of the Greek and Etruscan Vases in the British Museum. Part I. Prehistoric Aegean Pottery,* London 1925.

Forrer 1924: E. Forrer, Vorhomerische Griechen in den Keilschrifttexten von Boghazköy, *MDOG* 63, 1924, 1-22.

Foxhall & Davies 1984: L. Foxhall and J.K. Davies (eds.), *The Trojan War, its Historicity and Context,* Bristol 1984.

Furumark 1941: A. Furumark, *Mycenaean Pottery,* Stockholm 1941.

Gabrielsen 1997: V. Gabrielsen, *The Naval Aristocracy of Hellenistic Rhodes,* København 1997.

Geiger 1993: A. Geiger, Ein Schwertheft aus dem Tempelviertel der Oberstadt von Boğazköy-Hattuša, *IstMitt* 43, 1993, 213-217.

Gejvall 1960: N.-G. Gejvall, *Westerhus Medieval populations and church in the light of skeletal remains,* Lund 1960.

Gillis 1990: C. Gillis, *Minoan Conical Cups: form, function and significance,* SIMA 89, Göteborg 1990.

Gödecken 1988: K.B. Gödecken, A Contribution to the Early History of Miletus. The Settlement in Mycenaean Times and its Connections Overseas, in *Problems in Greek Prehistory: papers presented at the centenary conference of the British School of Archaeology at Athens, Manchester April 1986,* eds. E. French and K. Wardle, Bristol 1988, 307-318.

Guidi 1921-1922: G. Guidi, Viaggio de Esplorazione in Caria, *ASAtene* 4-5, 1921-1922, 345-396.

Guldager Bilde 1995: P. Guldager Bilde, Gazetteer of Danish Classical Archaeological Fieldwork 1993-1994, *Acta Hyberborea* 6, 1995, 303-316.

Güterbock et al. 1983: H.G. Güterbock, M.J. Mellink, and E.T. Vermeule, The Hittites and the Aegean World, *AJA* 87, 1983, 133-143.

Hamilton 1842: W.J. Hamilton, *Researches in Asia Minor, Pontus and Armenia: with some account on their antiquities and geology,* London 1842.

Hägg, Marinatos & Nordquist 1988: R. Hägg, N. Marinatos, and C.G. Nordquist (eds.), *Early Greek Cult Practice,* Stockholm 1988.

Hägg 1990: R. Hägg, The Role of Libations in Mycenaean Ceremony and Cult, in *Celebrations of Death and Divinity in the Bronze Age Argolid,* eds. R. Hägg & G.C. Nordquist, Stockholm 1990, 177-184.

Herrmann 1990: B. Herrmann, *Prähistorische Anthropologie,* Berlin 1990.

Higgins 1980: R. Higgins, *Greek and Roman Jewellery,* 2nd ed., London 1980

Hood 1981-1982: S. Hood, *Prehistoric Emporia and Ayio Gala,* BSA Suppl. 15-16, Oxford 1981-1982.

Hooker 1976: J.T. Hooker, *Mycenean Greece,* London 1976.

Hornblower 1982: S. Hornblower, *Mausolus,* London 1982.

Hout 1994: Th.P.J. van den Hout, Death as a Privilege. The Hittite Royal Funerary Ritual, in *Hidden Futures: death and immortality in ancient Egypt, Anatolia, the classical, biblical and Arabic-Islamic world,* eds. J.M. Bremer, Th.P.J. van den Hout, and R. Peters, Amsterdam 1994, 37-75.

Iakovides 1970: S. Iakovides, *Perati,* Athens 1970.

Işık 1980: F. Işık, *Die Koroplastik von Theangela in Karien und ihre Beziehungen zu Ostionien zwischen 560 und 270 v.Chr., IstMitt Beih.* 21, 1980.

Işık 1990: F. Işık, Frühe Funde aus Theangela und die Gründung der Stadt, *IstMitt* 40, 1990, 17-36.

Jeppesen 2000: K. Jeppesen, *The Maussolleion at Halikarnassos. Reports of the Danish Archaeological Expedition to Bodrum, 4: The Quadrangle. The Foundations of the Maussolleion and its Sepulchral compartments,* Højbjerg 2000.

Jeppesen 2002: K. Jeppesen, *The Maussolleion at Halikarnassos. Reports of the Danish Archaeological Expedition to Bodrum, 5: The Superstructure,* Højbjerg 2002.

Knapp & Cherry 1994: A.B. Knapp and J.F. Cherry, *Provenience studies and Bronze Age Cyprus. Production, exchange and politico-economic change,* Wisconsin 1994.

Kolb 1995a: F. Kolb (ed.), *Lykische Studien 2. Forschungen auf dem Gebiet der Polis Kyaneai in Zentrallykien.(Asia Minor Studien* 18), Bonn 1995.

Kolb 1995b: F. Kolb, Neue Erkentnisse zu Gräbern im Antiken Lykien, *Eski Yakın Doğu Kültürleri Üzerine İncelemeler,* 207-211, Istanbul 1995.

Kolb 1998: F. Kolb (ed.), *Lykische Studien 4. Feld-forschungen auf dem gebiet von Kyaneai (Yavu-Bergland).* (*Asia Minor Studien* 29), Bonn 1998.

Korfmann & Kossatz 1988: M. Korfmann and A.-U. Kossatz, Beşik-Tepe. Vorbereicht über die Ergebnisse der Grabungen von 1985 und 1986, *AA* 1988, 391-404.

Kull 1988: B. Kull, *Demircihüyük V. Die Mittelbronze-zeitliche Siedlung,* Mainz 1988.

Küpper 1996: M. Küpper, *Mykenische Architektur. Material, Bearbeitungstechnik, Konstruktion und Erscheinungsbild,* Espelkamp 1996.

Laffineur 1986: R. Laffineur, Weitere Beiträge zur Symbolik im mykenischen Bestattungsritual, in *Kolloquium zur ägäischen Vorgeschichte* (*Schriften des Deutschen Archäologen Verbandes* 9), Mannheim 1986.

Laviosa 1978: C. Laviosa, Les Fouilles de Iasos, in Akurgal 1978, 1093-1099.

Lenz 1997: D. Lenz, Karische Keramik im Martin von Wagner-Museum, Würzburg, *ÖJh* 66, 1997, 29-61.

Leonard 1994: A. Leonard, *An Index of the Late Bronze Age Aegean Pottery from Syria-Palestine* (SIMA 94), Jonsered 1994.

Levi 1969-1970: D. Levi, Iasos. Le Campagne di Scave 1969-1970, *ASAtene* 47-48 (N.S. 31-32), 1969-1970, 461-532.

Lloyd & Mellaart 1962-1972: S. Lloyd and J. Mellaart, *Beycesultan I-III,* London 1962-1972.

Lohmann 1993: H. Lohmann, *Atene. Forschungen zu Siedlungs- und Wirtschaftsstruktur des klassischen Attika,* Köln 1993.

Lohmann 1995: H. Lohmann, Survey in der Chora von Milet. Vorbericht über die Kampagen der Jahre 1990, 1992 und 1993, *AA* 1995, 293-329.

Lohmann 1997: H. Lohmann, Survey in der Chora von Milet. Vorbericht über die Kampagnen der Jahren 1994 und 1995, *AA* 1997, 285-311.

Lohmann 1999: H. Lohmann, Survey in der Chora von Milet. Vorbericht über die Kampagnen der Jahre 1996 und 1997, *AA* 1999, 349-473.

Macqueen 1986: J. Macqueen, *The Hittites and their Contemporaries in Asia Minor,* Revised edition, London 1986.

Maiuri 1921-1922: A. Maiuri, Viaggio di esplorazione in Caria (Parte I, II e III), *ASAtene* 4-5, 1921-1922, 345-488.

Maiuri 1923-1924: A. Maiuri, Jalisos – Scave della missione archeologica italiana a Rodi (parte I e II), *ASAtene* 6-7, 1923-1924, 83-341.

Maiuri 1928: A. Maiuri, *Clara Rhodos* I, Roma 1928.

Marinatos 1986: N. Marinatos, *Minoan Sacrificial Ritual,* Stockholm 1986.

Marinatos 1993: N. Marinatos, *Minoan Religion,* South Carolina 1993.

Marshall 1911: F.H. Marshall, *Catalogue of the Jewellery, Greek, Etruscan and Roman, in the Departments of Antiquities, British Museum,* London 1911.

Mee 1978: C. Mee, Aegean Trade and Settlement in Anatolia in the Second Millennium B.C., *AnaSt* 28, 1978, 121-155.

Mee 1982: C. Mee, *Rhodes in the Bronze Age. An Archaeological Survey,* Warminster 1982.

Mellaart 1968: J. Mellaart, Anatolian trade with Europe and Anatolian Geography and Culture Provinces in the late Bronze Age, *AnaSt* 18, 1968, 187-202.

Mellink 1956: M.J. Mellink, *A Hittite cemetery at Gordion,* Philadelphia 1956.

Mellink 1964: M.J. Mellink, Archaeology in Asia Minor, *AJA* 68, 1964, 149-166.

Mellink 1966: M.J. Mellink, Archaeology in Asia Minor, *AJA* 70, 1966, 139-159.

Mellink 1969: M.J. Mellink, Archaeology in Asia Minor, *AJA* 73, 1969, 203-227.

Metcalf & Huntington 1993: P. Metcalf and R. Huntington (eds.), *Celebrations of Death,* Cambridge 1993.

Mountjoy 1986: P.A. Mountjoy, *Mycenean Decorated Pottery: A Guide to Identification,* SIMA 73, Göteborg 1994.

Mountjoy 1997: P.A. Mountjoy, Local Mycenaean Pottery at Troia, *Studia Troica* 7, 1997, 259-267.

Naumann 1971: R. Naumann, *Architektur Kleinasiens,* Tübingen 1971.

Newton 1862-1863: C.T. Newton, *A History of Discoveries at Halicarnassus, Cnidus and Branchidae,* London 1862-1863.

Niemeier & Niemeier 1997: B. Niemeier and W.-D. Niemeier, Milet 1994-1995. Projekt "Minoisch-Mykenisches bis Protogeometrisches Milet." Zielsetzung und Grabungen auf dem Stadionhügel und am Athenatempel, *AA* 1997, 189-248.

Özgüç 1978: T. Özgüç, *Excavations at Maşat Höyük and Investigations in its Vicinity,* Ankara 1978.

Özgünel 1976: C. Özgünel, Dirmil'de (Gökçebel) Bulunmuş Geometrik Kaplar, *Belleten* 40, 1976, 49-53.

Özgünel 1979: C. Özgünel, *Karian Geometric Pottery,* Ankara 1979.

Özgünel 1987: C. Özgünel, Selçuk Arkeoloji Müzesinde Saklanan Miken Pyxisi ve Düşündürdükleri, *Belleten* 51, 1987, 535-547.

Özgünel 1996: C. Özgünel, *Mykenische Keramik in Anatolien,* (*Asia Minor Studien* 23), Bonn 1996.

Orthmann 1967: W. Orthmann, *Das Gräberfeld bei Ilica,* Wiesbaden 1967.

Osborne 1996: R. Osborne, *Greece in the Making,* London 1996.

Paidoussis & Sbarounis 1975: M. Paidoussis and Ch.N. Sbarounis, A Study of Cremated Bones from the Cemetery of Perati, *OpusAth* 11, 1975, 129-160.

Paton 1887: W.R. Paton, Excavations in Caria, *JHS* 8, 1887, 64-82.

Paton & Myres 1896: W.R. Paton and J.L. Myres, Karian Sites and Inscription, *JHS* 16, 1896, 188-271.

Paton & Myres 1897: W.R. Paton and J.L. Myres, Researches in Karia, *Geographical Journal* 9, 1897, 38-54.

Pecorella 1984: P.E. Pecorella, *La Cultura Preistorica di Iasos in Caria,* Roma 1984.

Pedersen 1992: P. Pedersen, Surveys and excavations in Halicarnassus (1978; 1986; 1988; 1990; 1991), *Acta Hyberborea* 4, 1992, 378-379.

Pedersen 1993: P. Pedersen, Surveys and excavations in Halicarnassus. *Acta Hyberborea* 5, 1993, 399-404.

Pedersen 1994: P. Pedersen, The Fortifications of Halikarnassos. *REA* 96, 1994, 215-235.

Pelon 1976: O. Pelon, *Tholoi, Tumuli et Cercles Funéraires,* Paris 1976.

Philippson 1915: A. Philippson, *Reisen und Forschungen im westlichen Kleinasien. V. 5: Karien südlich des Mæander und das westlische Lykien,* Gotha 1915.

Poulsen 1994: B. Poulsen, The new excavations in Halikarnassos, in *Hekatomnid Caria and the Ionian Renaissance,* ed. J. Isager, (*Halicarnassian Studies* I), Odense 1994, 115-133.

Protonotariou-Deilaki 1990: E. Protonotariou-Deilaki, Burial Customs and Funerary Rites in the Prehistoric Argolid, in Hägg & Nordquist 1990, 69-83.

Radt 1970: W. Radt, *Siedlungen und Bauten auf der Halbinsel von Halikarnassos unter besonderer Berücksichtigung der archaischen Epoche,* Tübingen 1970.

Radt 1992: W. Radt, Lelegische Compounds und heutige verwandte Anlagen, in *Studien zum antiken Kleinasien II, Asia Minor Studien* 8, ed. A. Schütte, Bonn 1992, 1-15.

Renfrew 1969: C. Renfrew, The Development and Chronology of Early cycladic Figurines, *AJA* 73, 1969, 1-32.

Renfrew 1972: C. Renfrew, *The Emergence of Civilisation,* London 1972.

Ross 1852: L. Ross, *Reisen nach Kos, Halikarnassos, Rhodos und der Insel Cypern,* Halle 1852.

Schlenter 1960: U. Schlenter, *Brandbestattung und Seelenglauben. Verbreitung und Ursachen der Leichenverbrennung bei aussereuropäischen Völkern*, Berlin 1960.

Seeher 1991: J. Seeher, Die Nekropole von Sarıket – Demircihüyük. 1. Bericht, *IstMitt* 41, 1991, 97-123.

Seeher 1992: J. Seeher, Die Nekropole von Demircihüyük – Sarıket. Grabungskampagne 1991, *IstMitt* 42, 1992, 5-19.

Seeher 1993: J. Seeher, Körperbestattung und Kremation – ein Gegensatz? *IstMitt* 43, 1993, 219-226.

Sherratt & Sherratt 1991: A. Sherratt and S. Sherratt, From Luxuries to Commodities: The Nature of Mediterranean Bronze Age Trading Systems, in *Bronze Age Trade in the Mediterranean: papers presented at the conference held at Rewley House, Oxford, in December 1989,* ed. N.H. Gale (*SIMA* 90), Göteborg 1991, 351-384.

Siebler 1994: M. Siebler, *Troia – Geschichte, Grabungen, Kontroversen,* Mainz 1994.

Snodgrass 1971: A. Snodgrass, *The Dark Age of Greece,* Edinburgh 1971.

Sørensen 1992: L.W. Sørensen, *Lindos IV.2. Excavations and Surveys in Southern Rhodes: Part 1. The Post-Mycenean Periods until Roman Times,* København 1992.

Tournavitou 1992: I. Tournavitou, Practical use and social function: a neglected aspect of Mycenean pottery, *BSA* 87, 1992, 181-210.

Tunukan 1964: S. Tunukan, Bodrum-Dirmil kazisi Iskeletleri, *Belleten* 28, 1964, 361-371.

Vermeule 1964: E. Vermeule, The Early Bronze Age in Caria, *Archaeology* 17, 1964, 244-249.

Voigtländer 1986: W. Voigtländer, Umrisse einer vor- und früh-geschichtlichen Zentrums an der karisch-ionischen Küste, *AA* 1986, 613-667.

Voigtländer 1988: W. Voigtländer, Akbük – Teichiussa. Zweiter Vorbericht – Survey 1985/86, *AA* 1988, 567-625.

Voigtländer 1989: W. Voigtländer, Vorläufer des Maussolleion in Halikarnassos, *Boreas* 17, 1989, Uppsala, 51-62.

Walters 1899: H.B. Walters, *Catalogue of the Bronzes, Greek, Roman, and Etruscan, in the Department of Greek and Roman Antiquities, British Museum,* London 1899.

Watrous 1991: L.V. Watrous, The Origin and Iconography of the Late Minoan Painted Larnax, *Hesperia* 60, 1991, 285-307.

Wheeler 1974: T.S. Wheeler, Early Bronze Age Burial Customs in Western Anatolia, *AJA* 78, 1974, 415-425.

Wieland 1997: D.L. Wieland, Beobachtungen und Gedanken zu Grabbeigaben. Importierte und lokale Keramik aus der Nekropole Manicalonga von Selinunt, *AntK* 40:2, 1997, 3-19.

Wright 1995: J.C. Wright, Empty Cups and Empty Jugs: The Social Role of Wine in Minoan and Mycenaean Societies, in McGovern et al. 1995, 287-309.

Zahle 1975: J. Zahle, Archaic Tumulus Tombs in Central Lykia (Phellos), *Acta Archaeologica* 46, 1975, 77-94.

Hellenistic Totenmahl reliefs from the Halikarnassos Peninsula[1]

Sisse Stine Hansen

In the Bodrum Museum of Underwater Archaeology there are four reliefs with Totenmahl motifs from the Halikarnassos area. A fifth, also originating from Bodrum, is now in the British Museum. This is a very common type of tomb marker in the Hellenistic period, known in large numbers at other sites. In this article the five Totenmahl reliefs presently known from the Halikarnassos area will be described and studied in a wider context.[2]

"Totenmahl" is a term that covers a group of reliefs in which the central figure is a man reclining on a couch, a *kline*.[3] The Totenmahl relief exists in varying places of the Greek world from Archaic until Roman times. The most characteristic feature of the motif is a man reclining on a kline, resting on his left elbow and holding a cup in his left hand. In most cases the man is accompanied by a woman either sitting on the kline or on a separate stool, a *diphros*, in the left side of the relief. A table with fruit and cake usually stands in front of the kline and a cupbearer and a female servant often accompany the couple. In some cases more men and women are added to the scene, and in theses cases attending servants are often present as well. In addition to these regular features the scene often depicts various other figures among which the most common are: a horse's head, a snake, weapon and other equipment, a cupboard, *kylikeion*, for fine tableware and finally various other vessels.

Scholars in general agree that the first known archaeological example of a banquet-scene is the so-called "garden feast" from Ninive, which is dated to about the middle of the 7th century BC.[4]

The relief depicts a scene that is iconographically very similar to the Totenmahl scenes and is therefore counted as their predecessor. Roughly speaking, the theme spreads geographically towards the west along with the practice of dining reclined on a couch, and gradually it becomes popular throughout the Greek world.

In Classical Athens the typology of the motive reaches a comparatively fixed scheme and is primarily used for votive reliefs erected in honour of various types of heroes. In the same period the banquet motive turns up in Asia Minor in different variations as decoration on the tomb-monuments of the aristocracy. The motive thus becomes a demonstration of wealth and a model for other members of the society with social ambitions.[5]

In Hellenistic times the iconographical tendencies from Attica and Asia Minor converge to form the Hellenistic Totenmahl which then includes both heroic and aristocratic connotations. In general, the Hellenistic Totenmahl reliefs show many iconographical varieties, and these are accentuated differently in the various production places. Yet, since the type is especially popular in Samos, Kyzikos and Byzantion,[6] and since there is a continuous production and a great number of Totenmahl reliefs from these places, it is possible both to define some criteria for dating and to deduce some iconographical and typological preferences characteristic for each of these major production places.[7] From the second century BC the Totenmahl relief becomes one of the most popular grave reliefs in Asia Minor, and from then on it is almost only used for this purpose.[8]

Until now only one Totenmahl relief from Halikarnassos has been published (i.e. British Museum inventory no. 725), but there are at least four other reliefs in the Bodrum Museum of Underwater Archaeology depicting the same scene. All come from Halikarnassos or the surrounding area.[9] In this article, I shall try to draw some conclusions pertaining to each of the five reliefs individually and to reflect on the picture which they present of this widespread Hellenistic type of monument in relation to Halikarnassos in general.

Catalogue[10]

Stele A

(Figs. 1, 2, 3 and 4)

Location:
Bodrum Museum of Underwater Archaeology. Inventory no. 3

Provenance:
Bodrum. Acquired by the museum in 1962.

Material:
Fine-grained, greyish-white marble.

Dimensions:
Max. width: 43,5 cm.
Max. height: 54 cm.
Max. depth: 13 cm. (by the horizontal cornice).
Max. relief depth (from the background to the right elbow of the woman): 3,5 cm.

State of preservation:
Only the left side of stele A, which was split obliquely by a slanting break, is preserved. Dirt has settled in many places on the surface leaving dark marks. In general the surface is slightly eroded, it has a few superficial chips in it and looks a little grainy.

The left side of the kylikeion has been cut away as an unexplainable but intentional secondary adaptation. At the upper right corner on the back there is another later adaptation that may have been a repair of the marble.

Fig. 1. Stele A. Front.

Fig. 2. Stele A. Detail of left side.

Hellenistic Totenmahl reliefs from the Halikarnassos Peninsula 121

Fig. 3. Stele A. Detail.

Fig. 4. Stele A. Back.

Description:
The architectural framing of the naiskos, which continues onto the short side of the stele, consists of a pilaster with the base and capital supporting an architrave with two fasciae, a horizontal cornice, a pediment and a slanting cornice.

From the top left the scene depicts: a horse's head in a frame and part of a round shield.

From the bottom left: a kylikeion containing an upright standing omphalos bowl on the lower shelf and a hemispherical (megarian?) bowl turned upside down on the upper shelf. The size of the cutting along the left side of the kylikeion allows one to assume that there may originally have been two vessels on each shelf. A krater is standing on top of the kylikeion. Further, there is a small cupbearer, standing next to the kylikeion wearing a short chiton and holding a cup in his left hand, and a kline covered by draped fabric which only allows the leg to show. A woman is sitting on the left part of the kline. She is wearing a himation over a chiton and rests her feet on a footstool. A fragment of the himation of a man lying on the kline is also seen. Finally, on the floor just before the end of the slanting break there is a lion's foot from what was presumably a round, three-legged table.

Fig. 5. Stele B. Front.

Fig. 6. Stele B. Detail of upper right corner. The curve of the shield is indicated by two traces just below the upper frame to the left. The rough surface to the right may indicate the location of the horse's head.

Stele B

(Figs. 5, 6, 7 and 8)

Location:
Bodrum Museum of Underwater Archaeology. Inventory no. 2003/5/A

Provenance:
Peksimet, a village on the western part of the Bodrum peninsula. Earlier, the stele was built into the wall of the local mosque until Imam Süleyman Bayram donated it to the museum after a renovation in 2003.

Material:
Medium-grained, slightly greyish, white marble.

Dimensions:
Max. width: 54 cm.

Fig. 7. Stele B. Left side.

Fig. 8. Stele B. Back with remains of recent lime-mortar.

Max. height: 42 cm.
Max. depth: 12,5 cm.
Max. relief depth (from the background to the object in the hands of the lying man): 2,5 cm.

State of preservation:
In general the surface of stele B is quite worn and chipped, and especially the upper half is in a bad shape. The frame does not seem to be intact anywhere, and there are also thin layers of mortar in several places. On the back a shallow, rectangular panel has been carved, maybe as a later addition.

Description:
The background of the relief is shaped in a horizontal, concave curve.

About ⅓ from the upper border of the relief there is a horizontal line indicating the top of a low wall.

Above the wall from the left, there is a kalathos, a helmet with a cheek-piece, a partly visible round shield and the faintly discernable outline of a badly eroded horse's head, (see detail on fig. 6).

Below the wall from the left, there is a small female servant wearing a long chiton and crossing her left leg in front of her right leg. Next to her a woman wearing a himation over a chiton is sitting on a diphros while resting her feet on a footstool. The woman holds some kind of food in her right hand to feed a snake that is climbing over the low wall. A man is reclining on the kline holding an object (a cup?) in his right hand in front of him. In front of the kline there is a three-legged table appearing as pi-shaped, because only two legs are visible. On the table five pieces of fruit and a cake are displayed. To the right of the kline a small boy wearing a short chiton is resting on his left leg and having his arms akimbo. Slightly behind and to the right of him a kylikeion is seen, which is decorated with small columns on the front and contains two hemispherical (megarian?) bowls turned upside down on the shelf. On top of the kylikeion there is a krater.

Fig. 9. Stele C. Front.

Stele C

(Figs. 9, 10, 11 and 12)

Location:
In the Bodrum Museum of Underwater Archaeology. Inventory number not known.

Provenance:
Unknown. According to director of the museum, Mr. Yaşar Yildiz, the stele is most likely from the Bodrum peninsula, since the museum would usually not have acquired a marble stele found in another area.

Material:
Fine-grained, greyish marble with flecks of white.

Dimensions:
Max. width: 76,5 cm.
Max. height: 56 cm.
Max. depth: 32 cm.

Fig. 10. Stele C. Detail of the right side of the front showing the snake.

Fig. 11. Stele C. Front and left side.

Fig. 12. Stele C. Right side.

Max. relief depth (from the background to the object in the hands of the small female servant): 4,5 cm.

State of preservation:
Stele C is mended from two pieces leaving a repair of white mortar from top to bottom. The stele has several chips and is partly covered with a thin yellowish layer of lime.

Description:
A large curtain draped in curves constitutes the background of the scene. In front of this, the scene depicts from the left a female servant standing in front of a very large volute krater. She is wearing a long chiton and holding a plate with three fruits in her left arm in front of her chest. In her right hand she has a small lekythos. To the right of her, a round shield is partly visible above the curtain in the background.

The woman sitting in the foot of the kline can be difficult to make out due to the vertical break and the modern repair running all the way through the stele. The knot at the back of her head, which is still preserved, shows that her head is turned in profile towards the man. On both sides of the modern repair the contours of her arms are still visible, which indicates that her chest is depicted frontally. Heavy folds from the fabric of her dress are hanging from the edge of the foot of the kline. Underneath these folds one foot is resting on the footstool and pointing away from the man.

To the left of the footstool there is the broken and damaged outline of a vessel; probably a calyx krater. There may also have been a small vessel under the footstool, but the indistinctive traces here could also be remains of lime.

Next to the woman on the covered kline, a man is reclining. He is only wearing a himation, which covers his lower body. In his right arm he raises a rhyton, and in his left arm he holds a vessel in front of his chest. In front of the kline is a relatively large, round table with three legs of animal form. It has 5 pieces of fruit and cake on top of it. Finally, to the very right a snake is winding its way from underneath the table and up the frame of the relief, (see detail on fig. 10).

126 *Hellenistic Totenmahl reliefs from the Halikarnassos Peninsula*

Fig. 13. Stele D. View of the front.

Fig. 14. Stele D. Detail of architrave with inscription.

Dimensions:
Max. width: 72 cm.
Max. height: 101 cm.
Max. depth: 31 cm.
Max. relief depth (from the background to the table top): 8,5 cm.

State of preservation:
Stele D is badly worn. The erosion of the surface has exposed the natural veins in the stone in such a way

Stele D

(Figs. 13, 14, 15 and 16)

Location:
In the Bodrum Museum of Underwater Archaeology. Inventory no. 1.2.92

Provenance:
Kadikalesi, a village on the western part of the Bodrum peninsula, south of Myndos. Acquired by the museum in 1989.

Material:
Fine-grained, white marble.

Fig. 15. Stele D. Detail of basis with traces of inscription.

Fig. 16. Stele D. Left side of the stele showing the carefully executed ante-pillar.

that it looks as if a layer of lime or something similar has been running down the stele. There are a few fresh breaks, which reveal the white colour of the marble below the surface patina. The stele has been assembled from at least 6 fragments, and the repairs are filled with a white mortar.

None of the heads of the depicted characters are preserved.

Inscription:[11]
(see details on figs. 14 and 15)
On the architrave, from the left:
ἸΜΒΡΙΑΔΗΣΘΕΟΔΩ

The 'I' to the very left of the architrave is the most uncertain letter. It seems likely, though, that it is a vowel since the following letters are 'M' and 'B'. Furthermore, the limited space at this point does not seem to leave room for any other vowel. After the Ω it is impossible to make out any letters.

Beneath the baseline of the figural scene is inscribed: ΗΡΩ

Description:
Stele D is a large naiskos with very detailed architectural features. The frame consists of a coarsely finished base with pilasters or *antae* at each side, which have ante-bases at the bottom and capitals at the top. They support the entablature consisting of an architrave, a metope/triglyph-frieze, and a horizontal cornice. The architectural features are continued on the short sides of the stele.

Between the anta-bases the ground of the figural scene protrudes slightly in a convex curve.

Across the background of the scene there is a large curtain elegantly draped in curves. To the left in front of the curtain, a woman sits on a kline that is draped in fabric. She is wearing a chiton under a himation and grabbing the fabric of the himation with her right hand at her left shoulder, while her left hand rests on her right knee. She is resting her feet on a footstool. Underneath the woman there is a very small female servant dressed in a long chiton, who is carrying an unidentifiable attribute in each hand. Next to the woman a man reclines on the kline. He is raising a rhyton in the shape of an animal with his right hand and presumably holding a round vessel in front of his chest with his left hand. This area is heavily damaged on the surface. The man is wearing a himation over a chiton.

Finally, a cupbearer wearing a short chiton is standing next to the kline to the right. He rests on his right leg and holds a cup in front of his body with his left hand. His right arm hangs along the body.

In front of the kline there is a three-legged table with legs of animal form. The table has 5 pieces of fruit on top of it; one of these might be a cake.

Fig. 17. Stele E. View of the front. © Copyright the Trustees of the British Museum.

Stele E

(Fig. 17)

Location:
The British Museum. Inventory no. 725.[12]

Provenance:
Halikarnassos

Material:
White, coarse-grained marble.[13]

Dimensions[14]:
Max. width: 61cm.
Max. height: 34 cm.
Max. depth: 12cm.

State of preservation:
An uneven break has split stele E across and only the lower part is preserved. The heads of the two servants are missing as well. A vertical break to the right makes it impossible to decide whether the scene originally continued a little further in this direction or whether the frame followed immediately to the right of the small male servant. Some white incrustations are visible on different parts of the relief. The frame has been repaired in both of the lower corners.

Description:
The scene in stele E depicts, (from the left): a female servant wearing a long chiton. She rests on her right leg and crosses her left leg in front of the right leg. Her left arm is placed across her stomach while she raises a leaf-shaped fan in her right hand.[15] Next to her a woman is sitting on a kline, which is apparently elevated in the foot and all covered by draped fabric. The woman, who rests her feet on a footstool, supports herself with her right arm on the seat and holds

her left arm towards her left shoulder. Her head is not preserved. A man is reclining on the kline to the right of the woman. He is only wearing a himation, which covers his lower body. A round hole at the spot where his left hand should have been suggests that a vessel was added here, possibly in a different material.[16] Beneath this, a hole in the fabric of the kline suggests that a table was added here in similar way.[17] To the right a servant is resting on his left leg and holding his hands in front of his body. He is wearing a short chiton.

Analysis and discussion of the five Halikarnassian Totenmahl reliefs

Stele A

Stele A is a fragment of a naiskos stele. Originally this piece must have been somewhat wider in order to accommodate the full figure of the reclining man and therefore slightly higher as well. Within the complete body of Totenmahl reliefs, a naiskos of this size is fairly uncommon. Even more unique for such a small naiskos are the detailed architectural features that are continued onto the short sides of the stele, and there are very few pilasters with indications of bases.[18]

A relatively small naiskos from Kyzikos[19] has a similar type of base, but, as is the case for the Kyzikan naiskoi in general, the entablature is not crowned with a pediment. Two of the small naiskoi from Samos have indications of a capital and entablature on the sides of the frame,[20] but none of the pilasters on the Samian examples have bases.

A considerable group of Totenmahl reliefs from Samos has been recognized by R. Horn as being from the same workshop, the so-called 'Samian workshop'.[21] Among other characteristics of this group, the clothes of the women sitting on the klines are generally draped in a way that bears a resemblance to the woman on stele A. For example, the fabric of the himation hangs below her right thigh in a winding fold, and the chiton fans out in heavy folds below the himation in a similar way. Unlike the women from 'the Samian workshop' who always hold on to the edge of their himation on their right shoulder with their left arm, the woman on stele A bends her left arm upwards and touches her chin with her index finger. I have not found this particular position of the left hand anywhere else. It is striking that the little cupbearer to the left in the picture seems to hold his right hand and index finger in the same position – although he is not touching his chin – and that this too is the only example. The pointing index finger might be a personal touch only understandable to the family of the departed person and the sculptor. Even though the posture is different, the cupbearer from stele A is comparable to the Samian cupbearers in size, and he is wearing a short chiton which is draped in the same V-shaped pattern both under the neck and below the waist as some Samian cupbearers.[22]

The kylikeion to the left in the picture has a very unusual shape. In the Byzantian group there are no kylikeia, and the example from stele A looks nothing like the typical Samian type of kylikeion, which has small columns on the front.[23] There are certain similarities with the composition of the Kyzikan type[24], but I have not seen any Kyzikan kylikeia supported by legs. The same type is represented in one Samian relief[25], but that example has no legs. On a Totenmahl relief from Kos, a simple kylikeion with legs is represented[26], but this Koan example, which has presumably had the pottery painted onto the shelves, has very high and thin legs compared to stele A, and none of the other elements make a good reference standard.

The fact that the sitting woman is turned in a strict profile almost parallel to the kline (except of course for her thighs which are slightly turned outwards to give her a natural position) is a good indication for a date in the period after the second half of the 2nd. century BC, according to S. Schmidt's comments on Samian Totenmahl representations.[27] Considering the similarities with the folds in the clothes of both the cupbearers and the women from 'the Samian workshop' it seems plausible that stele A dates from the same period as this group, that is app. 130 – 110 BC.[28]

Stele B

In general, stele B is comparable to the pieces from the 'Samian workshop' mentioned earlier, described by R. Horn.[29] In all the examples from this workshop in which a woman is present, she is positioned almost parallel to the kline, the himation always covers the back of her head, and she holds on to the edge of the fabric with her left hand, creating a sharp fold running from her head past her right shoulder and around her right forearm. This type of fold seems to be visible on stele B, but unfortunately the distinguishing details in this area are almost worn away. The fan-shaped chiton hanging underneath the himation is another recognizable characteristic.

Stele B also depicts the cupbearer in the right side of the scene resting on his left foot with his arms akimbo, the kylikeon with small columns on the front containing two inverted hemispherical cups and the higher piece of furniture behind this with the krater; all features that are to be expected in a Totenmahl scene from the Samian workshop. Furthermore, the scene usually contains a female servant, who often rests her left hand on the pillow on top of the diphros and in some cases crosses her left leg in front of her right leg, as is seen on stele B.

In all of the Totenmahl reliefs from this workshop, a snake is to be found somewhere in the scene. In many cases it is winding its way over a low wall that is always present in the background. Different symbolic objects are present in the zone above this wall. A horse's head to the right is an obligatory feature, although it varies in shape. There may also be a depiction of a round shield, a suit of armour and a helmet with cheek piece, but these items are not all necessarily present, and they occur at random. In most cases a kalathos is placed on the low wall, slightly to the left of the woman's head.

Above the low wall stele B clearly depicts (from the left): a kalathos and a helmet with cheek piece. At the very top of the scene in the area above the head of the cupbearer are the traces of two concentric semicircles, which I believe are the remains of the characteristic, partly visible round shield. The area at the right edge of the scene above the krater is largely destroyed, but the contour of the shallow rise in the surface indicates – in my opinion – that this is the remains of the obligatory horse's head.

The man lying on the kline holds an unidentifiable object in his hands. This is not the common posture for the men from the Samian workshop, but it does exist.[30]

The table on stele B is a three-legged pi-shaped table. This type of table appears in a longer variant that fits the scene with the two men lying on the kline in a Totenmahl relief from the Samian workshop. In another Samian Totenmahl representation[31] which, according to R. Horn, bears stylistic similarities to the pieces from the workshop,[32] the exact same type of table is represented. I also believe that the fruits and cake on the table are of the same shape and appear in the same order as on the Samian relief.

In general, stele B bears so close a resemblance to the Totenmahl reliefs from the Samian workshop that there can be no doubt that it must be counted as a member of this group. In particular there is a striking resemblance to one relief (inv. no. 236, Vathy Museum).[33] There is an overall consistency in the composition of the scenes and almost all of the elements are identical. Only the pi-shaped table, the position of the reclining man's arms and the helmet differ noticeably and there is a slight variation in the position of the cupbearer's right foot. Furthermore, the proportions never vary more than a few centimetres.[34] I am tempted to believe that these Totenmahl reliefs are not only from the same workshop, but also by the same sculptor. However, the poor condition of stele B makes it almost impossible to compare important details such as folds in the clothing, and as I have not had the possibility of examining the relief in the Vathy Museum myself, I can only suggest this theory as a vague possibility.

There can be no doubt that stele B dates to the same period as the Totenmahl reliefs from the Samian workshop, i.e. app. 130 – 110 BC.[35]

Stele C

The 180 degrees turn in the sitting woman's body indicates that stele C dates from somewhere in the third century BC according to Fabricius.³⁶ Generally speaking, she sits more often in this position at the beginning of the century and gradually turns her legs more towards the man, but there are examples of the 180 degrees turn even towards the end of the century.³⁷

The reclining man is raising a rhyton, which is an attribute that can be found on examples throughout the third century BC, but in general it becomes rarer towards the end of the century. On the other hand, the man seems to have short hair and to be beardless, which indicates a date at the end of the century.³⁸

A grave stele from Kyzikos depicts a sitting woman accompanied by a standing female servant.³⁹ From the appearance of the servant's clothing S. Schmidt dates this stele to the end of the third century BC.⁴⁰ The servant is resting on her left foot, but the folds are so heavy and stiff that it almost looks as if they are supporting her, though they still reveal her right leg clearly through the fabric. This looks very much like the lower part of the female servant's chiton and posture on stele C. Furthermore, there is a remarkable resemblance between the two in the way a thick fold is draped around the right ankle.

Stele C shows a great depth perspective in the relief. At the back a round shield is hanging, partly covered by the cloth. In front of this is the large krater, and after that the female attendant. On the same line as the female servant are the woman and the man on the kline. At the very front are the three-legged table and at least one vessel. The tendency to focus on depth in the picture occurs at the end of the third century BC and becomes more conspicuous in the beginning of the second century BC.⁴¹ An example of this is seen on a stele from Samos, which is also the only other Totenmahl relief that I know of, where the baseline of the relief-scene is indicated at different levels.⁴²

The table and the krater on stele C both seem to be unusually large, and I have found no examples comparable to the snake winding its way up the frame.

Stele C has turned out to be a very unusual example of a Totenmahl relief. Nevertheless, it depicts some comparable features, which all together makes it possible to suggest a date in the second half of the third century BC, and most likely towards the turn of the century.

Not many grave reliefs in general date from the third century BC and the provenances of these are often unclear. Because most reliefs from this period are unique examples, it is very difficult to show a continuous, typological development for any place of production in the Greek area. When archaeologists attempt to show general tendencies and to put forward certain dating criteria, these attempts are often based on individual and unique reliefs.⁴³ This makes dating difficult, and some uncertainties must be expected in this century.

Stele D

Stele D is a relatively large naiskos, which is higher than it is wide. The dimensions are quite extraordinary compared to other Totenmahl naiskoi.⁴⁴ All of the 40 Samian examples are somewhat smaller and almost never higher than they are wide. The 15 large naiskoi from Kyzikos are all wide-sized, but a few of the app. 20 large Byzantian naiskoi are actually higher than they are wide. Still, stele D is app. 16 cm. higher than the highest Byzantian naiskos.

Neither the rhyton, which is partly shaped as an animal, nor the curtain, which covers the background, can be connected to one particular production place, but none of these features occur in the Byzantian Totenmahls.⁴⁵ The round three-legged table is common everywhere.

The two attending servants in the scene are also somewhat unusual. In both Kyzikan and Byzantian Totenmahl reliefs it is common for a scene depicting only one reclining man and one sitting woman to have a male servant to the right and a female one to the left.⁴⁶ Both of these production places often have the very small female servant standing beneath the woman's legs, but never holding more than one attribute. The female servant on stele D is holding two; one in each hand.

The cupbearer on stele D rests on his right leg, has his left leg pulled slightly backwards and holds a cup in front of the body with one hand while the other hand hangs along the body. A cupbearer in this exact posture is found neither in Kyzikos nor in Byzantion. A small difference in height between the two is very common in both places, but I have not found any cases where the difference is so conspicuous.

The posture of the cupbearer exists on a Samian Totenmahl relief,[47] but none of the Samian female servants hold two attributes in their hands, and they are far from small enough to fit underneath a sitting woman's legs.[48]

On the vast majority of the Totenmahl reliefs, the woman is holding on to the fabric of the himation with her left hand by her left shoulder. The woman on stele D crosses her right arm in front of her chest to hold on to the fabric by her left shoulder and grasps the fabric above her right knee, thus creating a falling fold. This way of holding the arms and grabbing the fabric is often seen with standing persons of both sexes on reliefs in general, but very seldom with sitting women.[49] I know of no other Totenmahl scene with the woman in this exact position. Only one Totenmahl relief from Byzantion[50] and a few reliefs from Kyzikos[51] depict the woman with her right arm in this way, but none of these women create the falling fold with their left hand.

The Byzantian women, like the woman on stele D, usually sit on the kline and rest their feet on a footstool. Typically, these women wear their hair under the himation in a knot, which is positioned very high on the back of their head, and therefore gives them an almost egg-shaped head.[52] The woman on stele D is wearing her knot much lower.

Apart from a differing hairstyle and posture of the arms the woman on stele D is very similar to the women on the Byzantian Totenmahl reliefs that S. Schmidt dates to about 100 BC.[53] Firstly, there is a close resemblance in the way the fabric of the himation is depicted as being thin and light whereas the chiton seems thick and heavy; secondly, in the way the himation is draped in a pattern of folds running from the woman's left knee, past her right shin and under her right thigh; and thirdly, in the way the folds of the chiton leave the tip of her foot uncovered. The footstool in the slanting position, which adds some depth to the scene, is another characteristic of the Byzantian

Totenmahl reliefs from about 100 BC. Having taken these similarities into consideration, I believe that a plausible date for stele D would also be about 100 BC. Furthermore, the women on the Byzantian steles remain in a similar posture in the first half of the first century BC, but the tendency goes towards depicting the folds of the clothes as larger and smoother, and already from about 80 BC the women's left legs are usually hidden behind her right legs. Due to her very small size the female servant indicates that stele D is not earlier than about 100 BC.[54]

The Byzantian Totenmahl reliefs relatively often bear inscriptions. Usually they are placed above the scene on the architrave and depict the name of the departed in the nominative followed by a patronymic in the genitive. App. ¼ of the Samian reliefs has at least part of an inscription carved onto the background of the scene above the heads of the participants or below the baseline. To the name of the departed in nominative followed by the patronymic is often added a ΗΡΩΣ or rarely ΗΡΩΙΝΗ. The inscriptions from Kyzikos follow the same pattern, but a ΗΡΩΣ is only added on four occasions.[55] This outline supports an understanding of stele D's inscription on the architrave as the name of the departed man on the kline: ΙΜΒΡΙΑΔΗΣΘΕΟΔΩ[ΡΟΥ], (i.e.: the name Imbriades in the nominative followed by the patronymic Theodoros in the genitive).[56] It is impossible to decide whether the inscription continued after this. Unfortunately I have not found Imbriades Theodorou mentioned anywhere else, so the name does not provide evidence for a more certain date of Stele D.

The inscription ΗΡΩ below the baseline of the scene could be part of a hero epithet either belonging to the man or the woman. The area before and after these letters is so badly damaged that it is impossible to see if any other letters were originally inscribed here.

Stele E, (Brit.Mus. inv. no. 725)

The fact that this fragmented Totenmahl relief is either without a table, or has had a table in another material attached to it, makes it quite unique. The round hole in the kline cover might suggest that the later possibility is the most likely one, and the fact that the technique is known from other reliefs supports this as well.[57]

Of the reclining man only the lower body and part of his arms are preserved. At the spot where his left hand was supposed to be, there is another round whole that may have been used to attach a cup or another type of vessel.

The servant, who is resting on his left foot and holding his arms in front of his body, is in general often seen in this position. The female servant, on the other hand, who is crossing her left leg in front of the right one, is only common within the Samian production. I have not found any Totenmahl reliefs depicting the female attendant both crossing her legs and holding a leaf-fan, but the type exists on other reliefs.[58]

The sitting woman on stele E bears a very close resemblance to a woman on a Kyzikan Totenmahl relief.[59] The women on both reliefs support themselves with their right hands on the seat. Their left arms are bending towards their left shoulders. The draping of the chitons are almost identical as well. Several folds run in lines from the women's left shoulders towards their right hands, which are covered by the fabric. From the point between the women's right thighs and their seats the folds run in two directions. The upper folds form a wavy line across the knees, whereas the lower ones run in a curve across the shins and also stop at the left knee. This Kyzikan Totenmahl relief dates from the second half of the second century BC, and I agree with S. Schmidt when he dates stele E some decades earlier because of the position of the sitting woman, who is depicted more frontally than the woman from Kyzikos.[60]

Comparison between the 5 Totenmahl reliefs and final conclusions.

I have argued for a date of the 5 Totenmahl reliefs as follows: (in chronological order) Stele C in the middle of or late in the third century BC; stele E late in the first half of the second century BC; stele A and stele B in the last third of the second century BC, and finally stele D about 100 BC. This means that the 5 existing Totenmahl reliefs from the Bodrum peninsula are spread over a period of more than a hundred years. This fact alone indicates that it is not possible to speak of a properly continuous Halikarnassian production or type.

Stele B, which I have argued belongs to 'the Samian workshop', is the only one of the 5 reliefs that can be said with certainty to be imported. It is remarkable that until now only one other stele from this workshop is known to have been found outside of Samos.[61] The four remaining reliefs from the Halikarnassian area all have different features that make them more or less unique.

It is not too surprising that stele C has a composition that looks like no other Totenmahl relief, and at the same time depicts a snake in a very unusual place, since the Totenmahl reliefs from the third century are unique examples in many cases. Unfortunately, this makes it impossible to even guess whether stele C is imported or is a local production, and also whether there has been inspiration from any specific production place.

The woman on stele E bears close similarities to the Kyzikan tradition, but the other features are not found in any other Totenmahl in this combination, and there are no other Totenmahl reliefs that show the exact same type of female servant or have had the table added in a different material. This does not prove that stele E is a local production, but it also makes it very difficult to argue that it is imported from any other specific production place. I therefore suggest that stele E is a local production with at least some inspiration from Kyzikos. The unique features, which are either the result of the customer's specific wishes or the decision of a local or visiting sculptor, indicate that stele E is more likely to be a commissioned work as opposed to a mass produced piece.

Stele A is a very detailed and carefully made naiskos, whose combination of unique quality, shape and size is not found in any other Totenmahl relief. This fact in itself indicates that stele A is a commissioned work. The scene on the stele is clearly inspired from Samos, but also has the unique kylikeion, which I have not found anywhere else. Therefore I argue that stele A is either a local production with inspiration from Samos or is imported from Samos.

Stele D is most likely a commissioned work as well, because this too has a unique naiskos with architectonical details of a high quality. The scene is comparable to both the Kyzikan and Byzantian Totenmahl reliefs, which between them have many iconographical and typological similarities. The rhyton is wellknown in Kyzikos, but does not exist in Byzantion. It is possible, though, that it is a unique example from this production place. The fairly large male servant is not similar to any of the Kyzikan or Byzantian servants, but is very close to the Samian type in both posture and size. On the other hand, there are several examples of unique features and compositions on the large Totenmahl naiskoi, and his unusually large size could simply be the result of a wish to fill out the right side of the scene. I believe that stele D is most likely imported from either the Byzantian or the Kyzikan area, or that it is produced by a sculptor visiting from either of these areas. If the reading of the name in the inscription as a Karian name is correct, the latter suggestion is the most plausible one.

It is of course a possibility for any of the 5 Totenmahl reliefs as well that they might originate from another place than one of the large production places, or that they are from one of these and just do not follow the tendencies that are normally seen. As the precise circumstances for the finding of the 5 Totenmahl reliefs are unknown, it is of course another possibility that the reliefs were not even present on the Bodrum peninsula in their own time, but have been imported later as works of art or ballast in a merchant ship.

Neither in Ephesus nor in Miletus has evidence been found of a continuous Totenmahl tradition, and it is therefore presumed that other kinds of grave markers were preferred in these areas,[62] and it is obvious that the tendency on the Bodrum peninsula in Hellenistic time is the same. The large number of cylindrical altars found in the Halikarnassian area indicates that this was perhaps the preferred way of marking a grave for a beloved departed person.[63]

Bibliography

Berges 1986: D. Berges, *Hellenistische Rundaltäre Kleinasiens*. Freiburg 1986.

Berges 1996: D. Berges, *Rundaltäre aus Kos und Rhodos*. Berlin 1996.

Dentzer 1982: J.M. Dentzer, *Le motif du banquet couché dans le proche-orient et le monde grec du VIIe au IVe siècle avant J.C.* Rome 1982.

Fabricius 1999: J. Fabricius, *Die hellenistischen Totenmahlreliefs*. München 1999.

Gerhard 1827: E. Gerhard, *Antike Bildwerke zum ersten Male Bekannt gemacht*. Stuttgart 1827.

Horn 1972: R. Horn, *Hellenistische Bildwerke aus Samos*. Samos XII. Bonn 1972.

P.M.: E. Pfuhl und H. Möbius, *Die ostgriechischen Grabreliefs*. Textband 1-2, Tafelband 1-2. Mainz 1977-79.

Poulsen 2004: B. Poulsen, Sculpture and Altars fom Hellenistic Halikarnassos. In: S. Isager and P. Pedersen (eds), *The Salmakis Inscription and Hellenistic Halikarnassos. HalStud* IV 2004 191-203.

Schmidt 1991: S. Schmidt, *Hellenistische Grabreliefs. Typologische und chronologische Beobachtungen*. Köln 1991.

Smith 1892: A.H. Smith, *Catalogue of Sculpture in the Department of Greek and Roman Antiquities, British Museum*. London 1892.

Thönges-Stringaris 1965: R. Thönges-Stringaris, Das griechische Totenmahl, *AM* 80, 1965, 1 – 99.

Notes

1   The present article is based on my thesis from the University of Southern Denmark, Odense. The foundation for the thesis was made in the autumn of 2005, when I spent three weeks in Bodrum conducting the study of 4 marble reliefs in The Bodrum Museum of Underwater Archaeology. In that connection I would like to thank firstly Mr. Yaşar Yildiz, Director of the Museum, and his staff for giving permission for my studies, offering assistance whenever it was needed and always making me feel welcome at the museum. Secondly, my supervisor, associate professor at The University of Southern Denmark, Poul Pedersen, who established the contact to Mr. Yildiz, drew my attention to two of the reliefs in the museum and kindly provided me with some photographic material. Thirdly, Maj Rygaard, conservator at The Danish Halikarnassos Project, who assisted me

in taking photographs and in identifying material. And last but not least, Signe Isager, associate professor at The University of Southern Denmark, who assisted me in doing research on the inscriptions.

    Illustrations: Poul Pedersen: figs. 1, 2, 3, 4, 5, 7 and 8; Maj Rygaard and Sisse Hansen: figs. 6, 9, 10, 11, 12, 13, 14, 15 and 16. Fig. 17 © Copyright the Trustees of the British Museum.

2 A brief general overview of the Hellenistic sculpture of Halikarnassos including my "Stele E" is found in Poulsen 2004.

3 The term was introduced in 1827 by E. Gerhard, who interpreted the scene as a banquet in the hereafter (Gerhard 1827 315f.), and it is still commonly used even though many scholars disagree with this interpretation.

4 Dentzer 1982 Pl. 15 fig. 675 and p. 54ff.

5 See e.g. Fabricius 1999 31ff.

6 Fabricius also includes the Rhodian Totenmahl in her analysis of the specific production places. The Rhodian Totenmahl is especially characterized by its reclining women.

7 See especially Fabricius passim and Schmidt 1991 24ff.

8 Fabricius 1999 39.

9 I believe that there are at least one or two additional fragments of a Totenmahl relief in the museum depot, but I was unfortunately not able to investigate these further during my stay in Bodrum.

10 The steles are not arranged chronologically, but occur in the order in which they were studied during my stay in Bodrum.

11 I am grateful to Signe Isager for giving me her opinion on the inscription.

12 Smith 1892 no. 725. I do not know this relief from autopsy.

13 P.M. 1554.

14 P.M. 1554.

15 Smith places the leaf-fan in her left hand, but that is surely a mistake. Smith 1892 no. 725.

16 Smith 1892 no. 725 and P.M. 1554 both suggest this solution.

17 Smith 1892 no. 725 and P.M. 1554 both suggest this solution.

18 Fabricius 1999 112, 226f. and 279f. for the shape and size of the naiskoi from Samos, Kyzikos and Byzantion.

19 P.M. 1570.

20 P.M. 1581 and P.M. 1872.

21 E.g. P.M. 1593, 1526, 1581, 1639, 1717, 1872 and 1916. Also Horn 1972 60f. and 160ff.

22 E.g. P.M. 1639.

23 E.g. P.M. 1872.

24 E.g. P.M. 1961.

25 P.M. 1519.

26 P.M. 1515.

27 Schmidt 1991 103f.

28 Schmidt 1991 67ff.

29 E.g. P.M. 1593, 1526, 1581, 1639, 1717, 1872 and 1916. Also Horn 1972 60f. and 160ff.

30 E.g. P.M. 1872.

31 P.M. 1596.

32 Horn 1972 61.

33 P.M. 1593, Horn 1972 no. 144.

34 Measurements in cm. according to Horn 1972 no.144, followed by my measurements of stele B in brackets ().

    Inner picture frame: w. 37 x h. 29 (w. 40 x h. 30). Female slave: h. 17 (h. 17). Sitting Woman: h. 22 (h. 22). Reclining man h. 24 (h. 25). The size of the kylikeion is not mentioned by Horn, but it seems to be lower than the kylikeion on stele B. The background of the scene is shaped in a horizontal concave curve in both cases; the largest depth measured from the background to the centre of the front edge of the picture frame is: d. 3,9 (d. 3), but the front edge of stele B is somewhat worn and broken. The largest depth within the picture, measured from the background, is: d. 3,5 (d. 2,5), but this measurement on stele B occurs between the hands of the reclining man, where the surface is so broken that the object cannot be identified.

35 Pfuhl/Möbius dates inv. no. 236, Vathy Museum to the first half of the second century BC, but never argues for this date, no. 1593. Horn dates the group to the last third of the second century BC, p. 61. Schmidt compares the folds of the clothes and the postures of the sitting women to a group of reliefs from a workshop in Delos that has a continuous production and therefore offers a more reliable relative date. This leads to a plausible date between 130 – 110 BC for the reliefs from the Samian Workshop, p. 103f.

36 Fabricius 1999 23f.

37 E.g. P.M. 1859.

38 Thönges-Stringaris 1965 42f.

39 Schmidt 1991 fig. 9.

40 Schmidt 1991 57ff.

41 Schmidt 1991 59f.

42 P.M. 1863.

43 Schmidt 1991 59f.

44 Fabricius 1999 112, 226f. and 279f. for the size of the naiskoi from Samos, Kyzikos and Byzantion.

45 Fabricius 1999 235f.
46 Fabricius 1999 230f. and 288.
47 P.M. 1557.
48 Fabricius 1999 119.
49 P.M. p. 71.
50 P.M. 2035.
51 E.g. P.M. 1628.
52 E.g. P.M. 1570. Fabricius 1999 230.
53 E.g. P.M. 2037 and P.M. 2038. Schmidt 1991 105f. and Tabelle III.
54 Fabricius 1999 230f.
55 Fabricius 1999 255ff., 127ff. and 301f.
56 I have not found any precedent for the name Imbriades, but Imbros is the name of the island west of the Dardannelles and of an island, famous for the cult of the Karian Hermes Imbramos, and also the name of a mountain and a fortress in Karia. Many men's names are derived from Imbros. From Karia Imbarsis, or Imbrassis, is known, and from Lykia Imbres, Imbras, Imbraios and Imbrasidas. (See A. Laumonier, "Les cultes Indigenes en Carie", 1958. p.697 and note 8). The name Imbriades may derive from Imbros and be formed in the same way as the common Asklepiades, which derives from Asklepios.
57 E.g. P.M. 1555 that has had weapons or other attributes attached to the background in a similar way. Fabricius 1999 283.
58 E.g. P.M. 440 from Chios or P.M. 904 from Samos.
59 P.M. 1555.
60 Schmidt 1991 104f.
61 P.M. 1639. Horn 1972 60.
62 Schmidt 1991 21.
63 Poulsen 2004 195ff; Berges 1986; Berges 1996. For the number of cylindrical altars in Halikarnassos see Berges 1986 Beilage 2. For the function of the cylindrical altars see the discussion in Berges 1986 12ff.

The Stadion of Ancient Halikarnassos

Bahadir Berkaya, Signe Isager and Poul Pedersen[1]

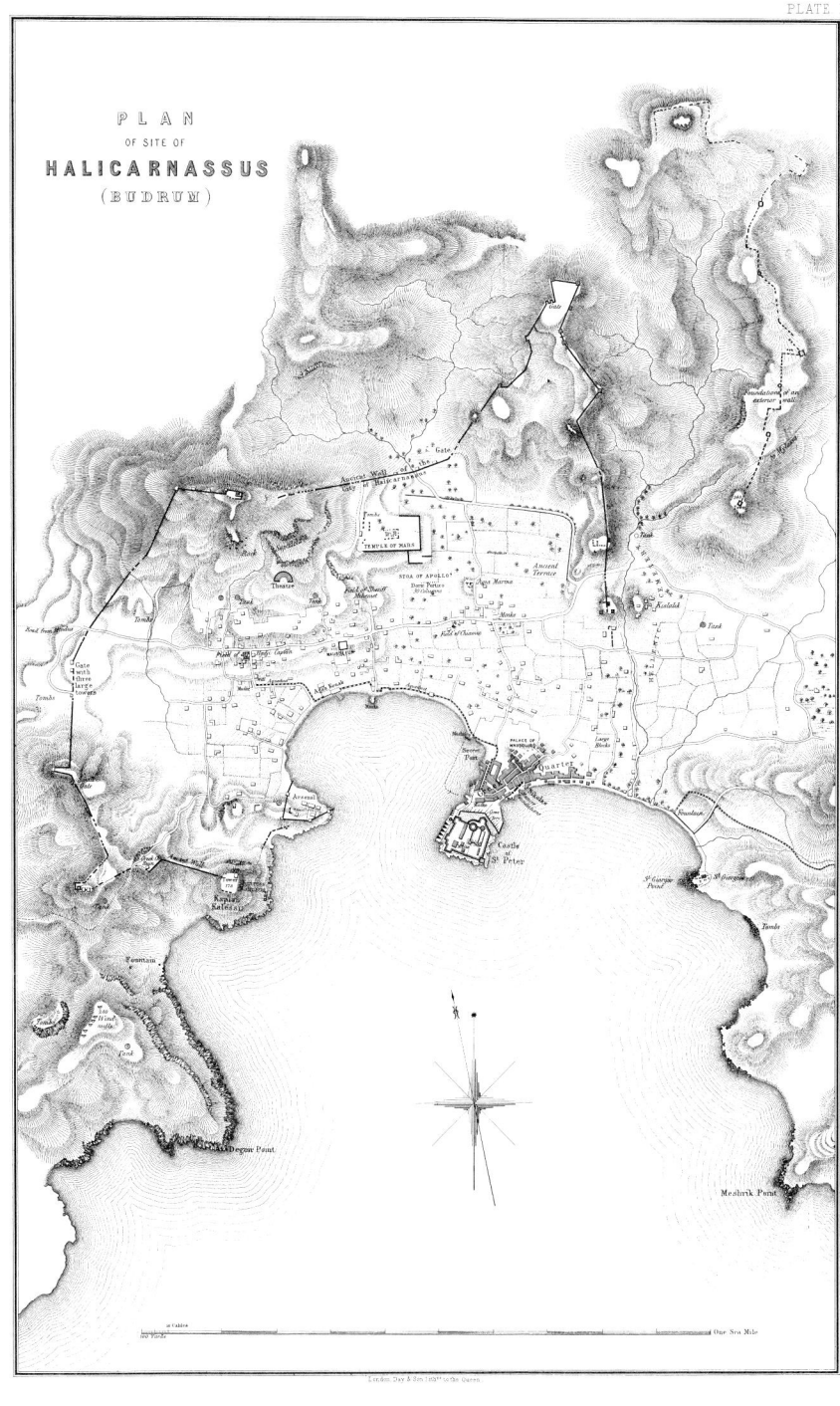

A very prominent feature on C.T. Newton's map of Halikarnassos from 1862[2] is a location designated "Ancient Terrace" (fig. 1). It is situated in the northeastern part of the ancient city, and is bordered to the north and east by a strong wall, on top of which there is a small road or lane. The higher ground outside the terrace continues for 50-100 m to the north before it meets the slopes of the hills in the northeast extension of the city. Immediately east of the terrace area is a hill, which carries the east wall of the city fortifications on its summit. The level area of the "Ancient Terrace" stretches almost 500 meters to the west, where it stops at the foot of the Terrace of the Sanctuary of Mars[3]. To the southwest it meets the "Doric Stoa" and the monastery and church of Hagia Marina at present day "Türkkuyusu". But broadly spoken, a large, continuous area runs from the "Ancient Terrace" all the way down to the harbour in a very gentle slope without any natural obstacles except for the small hill of Hagia Marina in Türkkuyusu. As Halikarnassos

Fig. 1. Newton's map of Halikarnassos from 1862.

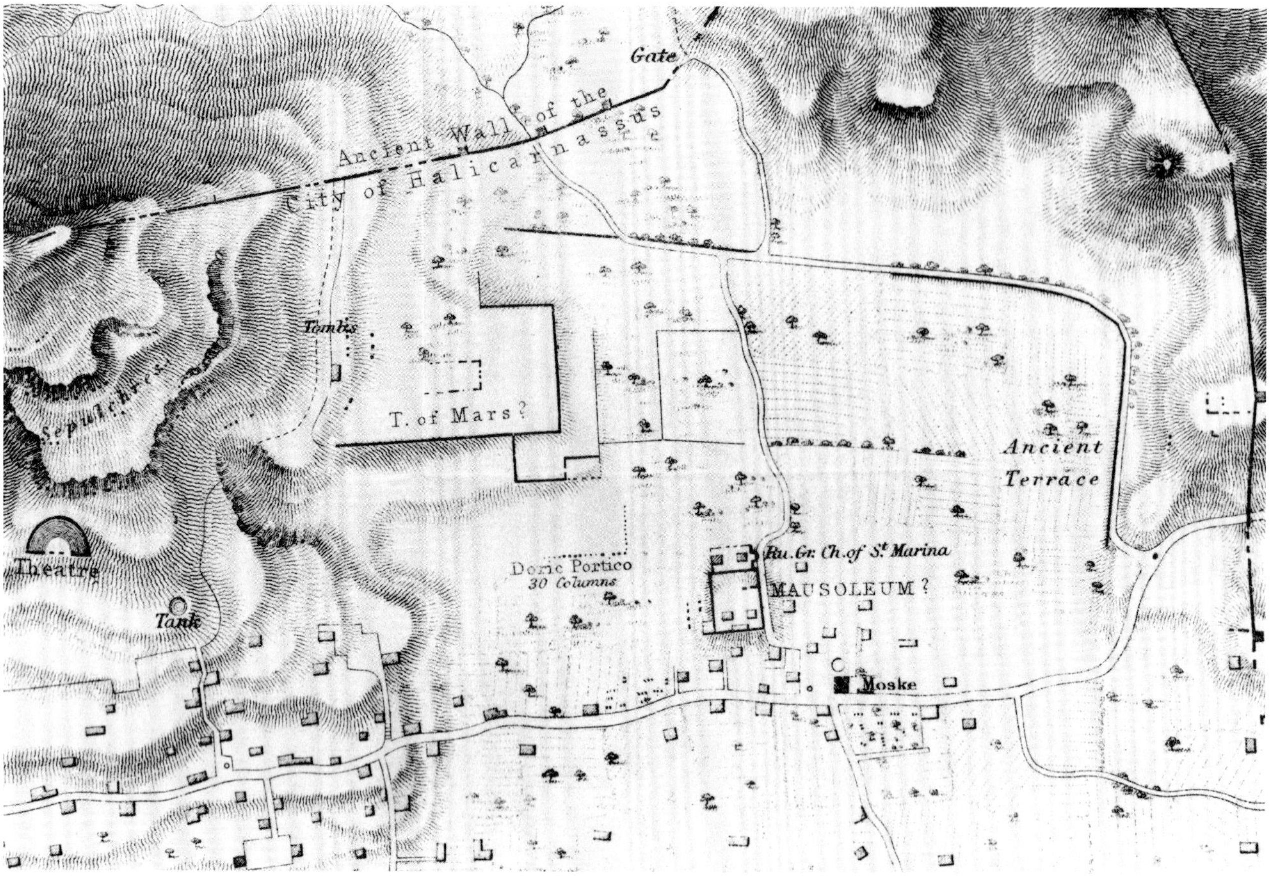

Fig. 2. Section of Spratt's map of Halikarnassos from 1856, showing the area from the theatre in the west to the eastern limits of the "Ancient Terrace" in the east.

Fig. 3. Inscribed base (upside down) in field on "Ancient Terrace" The Greek word "NIKH" can be discerned (1977).

is sometimes referred to as a double city, composed of Salmakis and Halikarnassos,[4] this area would probably constitute one part, while a similar but smaller area spreading out west of the harbour would constitute the other, Salmakis, the two being separated by the south slopes of the "Göktepe" hill and the Maussolleion terrace.

In the western half of the "Ancient Terrace", about a hundred meters east of the Terrace of Mars (fig. 2), the municipality of Bodrum excavated a large trench for a modern drainage some 15 years ago. The earth remaining on the surface afterwards contained Hellenistic pottery along with a few blocks of small-scale, decorative marble architecture, giving the impression that in Antiquity this western part of the area was mainly occupied by private houses. Remains of well-built foundations have been said to exist at a deep level southwest of the Doric Stoa, and this, in combination with the occasional discovery of architectural fragments in the area, suggests that important public buildings known from inscriptions may well have been

Fig. 4. Pile of architectural stones, including some seats lying on the south side of the embankment of the new highway (1977).

situated in the area adjoining the Doric Stoa. But all of this will be, of course, very uncertain until archaeological excavations have been carried out.[5]

In the 1970s, some round bases with remains of inscriptions could be seen in the eastern part of the "Ancient Terrace" area, approximately where the modern football-stadium is now situated, (fig. 3).

The large, strong wall which delimitates the "Ancient Terrace" to the north and east probably had as its main purpose the retention of the earth and soil of the higher ground to the north and east, preventing it from sliding down into the cultivated fields of the terrace. The wall is generally constructed with some use of mortar and contains many re-utilized ancient building stones, indicating its rather late date. The strong and solid nature of the wall might lead one to think that it could have had some fortificative function, but this can be ruled out when the general topography of the area is considered, with the ground rising on the outside of the wall to a level considerably above that of the "Ancient Terrace" itself.

If the wall did continue unbroken for several hundred meters, as it seems to have done, this is a comparatively comprehensive construction, which one would expect to have been erected in a period in which Halikarnassos flourished. This could very well be the 5th-6th century AD, which also saw the great Late-Roman Domus in Halikarnassos, and many other houses with mosaic-decorated floors, the rich early Christian religious complex at Torba and the monumental tomb-buildings of the necropolis southwest of the Myndos gate at Halikarnassos.

Today, modern road construction has obliterated most of the terrace wall (figs. 4, 5) except for a short stretch on the north side of the highway, opposite to the terrace of Mars, and a short line of the east wall

Fig. 5. Stone seat from the same place as fig. 4 (1977).

Fig. 6. "Karian" masonry style in the large retaining wall east of "Ancient Terrace" (1989).

close to the corner where the north wall meets the east wall. The corner can be studied below the junction of the large highway and the street running from here down towards the west side of the bus-station, more or less on the trace of the ancient lane east of the "Ancient Terrace". In this corner the wall changes its character. The part coming from the south is built in a dry-stone technique of fieldstones (fig. 6) neatly arranged and looking like the local "Karian" technique of all periods. Just before reaching the corner it changes, and from here onwards it contains many re-used ancient building stones, among which there are a number of stone-seats (figs. 7, 8).

Fig. 7. Stone-benches re-used as building stones in the north-east corner of the large retaining wall (1989).

Fig. 8. Detail of the same wall as fig. 7 (1989). Notice the anathyrosis on the short side of some seats reused as "headers". Of some seats, reused as "stretchers" in the wall, the projecting part of the front of the seat has been knocked off in order to give the wall a more flush facing.

Fig. 9. Farm house with drinking trough in the foreground to the right (1977).

Fig. 10. Drinking trough on fig. 9. Note the lion leg to the right (1977).

A few more stone-seats used to lie on the ground in this area, and in the 1970s one particularly interesting example could be seen in front of a house. It had secondarily been hollowed out for use as a drinking trough (figs. 9, 10, 11). A sculpted leg of a lion had been carved along one end of the seat, while the other end was plain and undecorated. We judged that the number of stone-benches found here was an indication that the structure to which they once belonged could not be far away. As this place is close to the city wall and far away from the town-centre, the building could hardly have been a bouleuterion or an odeion, and as the theatre had already been located and excavated in

Fig. 11. Detail of drinking trough (1977). The short side extending from the lion leg is only roughly worked and has no anathyrosis.

142 The Stadion of Ancient Halikarnassos

Fig. 12. Bodrum's new complex of industrial workshops ("sanayi") from the north, situated along the road leading to Bodrum city centre. The buildings have been erected on the area designated "Ancient Terrace" in Newton and Spratt's maps. The buildings' façades follow the east wing of the stadium's auditorium, as can be seen on the plan, fig. 14. The north-east corner of the large retaining wall is located just below the plastic in the foreground (1987).

Fig. 13. Part of the eastern auditorium during excavation, from the south. At a difficult early stage of the test excavation when the soil threatened to slide back down into the excavation (1987).

another part of Halikarnassos, we concluded at that time that the stone seats most probably came from the ancient stadion of Halikarnassos. In 1988 Bahadir Berkaya proved that this assumption was correct.

During the 1980s the appearance of the area altered completely. Because of the construction of the new highway, most of the northern terrace wall had been destroyed or buried in the embankment of the highway, as mentioned above. The terrace area itself had been used for the construction of a number of new houses and a modern football stadium. Most important, however, was the fact that the entire east part of the level area had been utilized for the construction of Bodrum's new, large "sanayi"-complex with garages and workshops (fig. 12).

In the winter of 1988 deep excavations were made for pipes related to the sanayi-buildings, and in the course of this work, stone seats suddenly turned up, and work was brought to a standstill. In the spring of 1988, Bodrum Museum, in collaboration with the city authorities and with the permission of the General Directorate of Antiquities and Museums, attempted to excavate a greater part of this place, which proved extremely difficult, however. The original rows of benches were encountered at great depth below the corner of the retaining wall described above. But the deep layers of soil contain much water at this time of the year, and they rapidly turned into mud, which consistently flowed down into the excavated area and made excavation almost impossible (figs. 13). The authorities refrained from a more comprehensive excavation because of the grave inconvenience this would have caused for traffic and the life of this busy part of the town. Therefore, as many observations as possible had to be carried out rather quickly. In order to have some idea of the extent of the ancient stadion, Bahadir Berkaya made several test trenches further south on behalf of Bodrum Museum (fig. 14).

In spite of the difficult conditions, a few simple facts are now known about the stadion of ancient Halikarnassos.

The eastern side of the auditorium runs along the east side of the "Ancient Terrace" mentioned on Newton's map from 1862 (fig. 1) and on Spratt's map from 1856 (fig. 2). The test trenches excavated by the museum demonstrated that remains of the long east side of the auditorium were preserved for more than 150 meters and were even, at least in some places, in good condition (fig. 15).

The orientation of the stadion differs from that of the ancient town plan. This is no doubt due to its location in the outskirts of the town-area proper, close to the city wall where a natural slope could be utilized as support for most of the east side of the auditorium. The northern limit of the east side of the auditorium was not located in the excavated area, and it is at present unknown if the auditorium turned to the west in a curve north of the excavated area, or if it was finished in some other way below the corner of the late-Antique retaining wall. Nor is it known

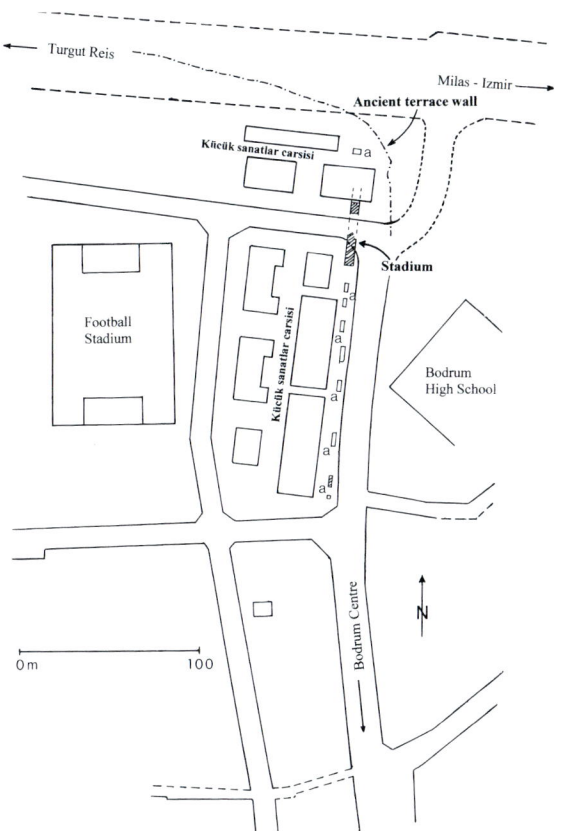

Fig. 14. Plan showing the position of the "Ancient Terrace" wall and of the main excavation field with rows of stone seats. The letter "a" indicates the location of other test trenches carried out by Bodrum Museum in 1987.

Fig. 15. Five rows of stone seats in situ during the test excavation in 1987. The seats to the left all have a sculpted, stylized lion leg or -paw to the left, which once flanked a stair connecting the upper tiers with the lower ones (1987).

Fig. 16. A standard stone seat from the stadium, now kept in Bodrum Museum (2005).

Fig. 17. Seat block no. 1. The front side.

whether the auditorium of the stadion had a complete west wing, which would of course have involved much more labour and expense, as no natural hill existed on this side to be used as support for the rows of benches. The west side of the cavea might have consisted of an earthen rampart as at Aphrodisias, but in that case one would have expected it to have left some trace in this area.[6] The stadion may well have been of U-shape and it would probably have had its entrance side towards the south. It must have reached almost as far south as the ancient main street of Halikarnassos, present day Turgut Reïs Caddesi. At this place there is still an old Turkish house largely constructed of extraordinary big ashlars of marble or limestone. These blocks must have been taken from some large public structure and it is an obvious guess that they come from the retaining walls or the entrance side of the stadion.

The auditorium comprised an unknown number of rows of seats. Below the lowest row of seats there was a narrow passage, and then a drop down to the floor of the stadion, which, however, was not reached during the excavations.

The seats were normally simple, with a cavetto profile in front, ending in a flat profile, which met the surface of the seat at a right or slightly slanting angle (fig. 16). Letters were incised on the front of this vertical band (fig. 33), apparently indicating who had donated the seats (see the chapter on the inscriptions).

The material is limestone, varying in colour from dark blue to light, yellowish grey. The top side of the seats was made wider by means of stone slabs so as to make room for the feet of the spectators sitting on the next row of seats. Each step must have been 60 cm wide (or slightly more), but there does not seem to have been any depression in the surface for the feet of the spectators on the next seat as is often seen in theatres.

At certain intervals stairs led up through the auditorium, and in these places the seats were ornamented with sculptured lions' paws adjoining the steps of the staircase (fig. 15). The re-utilized bench noticed in 1977 (fig. 10) belongs to this category. The seats seem to have a comparatively close parallel in the stadion at Aphrodisias.[7]

The stadion seats in the Bodrum Museum of Underwater Archaeology

Seven seat blocks in Bodrum Museum are believed to come from the stadion. Three of these (nos. 1-3) are presently placed in the entrance yard in front of the ticket office, two seat blocks with lion paws on their right side (nos. 4-5) are kept in the west moat of the Castle, where the cafeteria is, and the last two blocks (nos. 6-7) are situated in the lower yard in the castle in front of the amphora exhibition stoa.

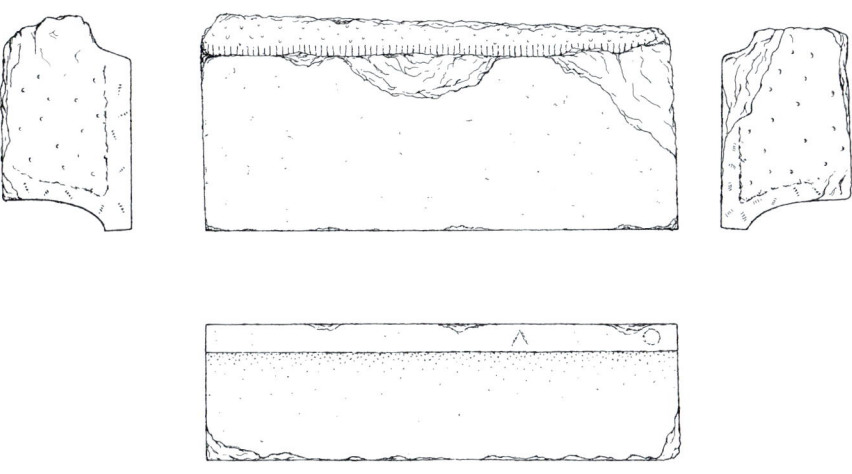

Fig. 18. Seat block no. 1. Drawing.

Seat block no.1. (figs. 17, 18, 19, 20).
This seat is preserved in its full length and has anathyrosis preserved on both shorter ends. The length of the block is 128.2 cm and the height 36.5 cm. The width is 46 cm from the front of the seat to the beginning of the recess. The frame of the anathyrosis has been treated with claw-chisel, while the centre has been worked roughly with a point or a pickaxe, which is quite normal. The right side of the block is not precisely at a right angle to the surface of the block, nor is it at an exact right angle to the front of the block. The upper side and the front of the seat have been finely worked with a point chisel. A narrow, almost vertical band about 7 cm in height runs along the upper edge of the front. Is has remains of an inscription. The back of the block is mostly hammer-dressed, but it has a neatly cut recess running along the entire length of the block. As seen on figs. 13 and 15, the purpose of the recess was no doubt to make room for stone slabs that formed an extension of the surface of the seat and constituted the foundation for the next row of seats. The limestone of seat block no. 1 has a light pink-grey tint similar to that of seat block no. 2, and it also seems very similar to block no. 4.

Fig. 19. Seat block no. 1. Back showing recess for neighbouring slab.

Fig. 20. Seat block no. 1. Short side with typical anathyrosis.

Fig. 21. Seat block no. 2. The front side.

Seat block no. 2. (fig. 21).
The maximum length is about 131.5 cm, but the left side is broken. The height is ca. 36 cm. The right short side is probably original, but has no remains of the anathyrosis and seems only to have been rather crudely worked with a pickaxe or something similar. Material and workmanship is otherwise very similar to seat block no. 1, and like this it has a recess along the back side. The width of the surface (excl. the recess) is 45-46 cm. The straight band along the front of the seat is ca. 7 cm in height and is not vertical but slopes inwards towards its upper edge, as do some of the others. It has remains of letters.

Fig. 22. Seat block no. 3. The front side.

Fig. 24. Seat block no. 3. Top side and back.

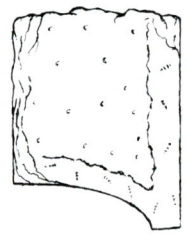

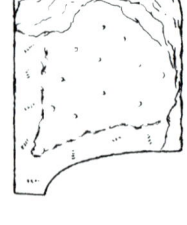
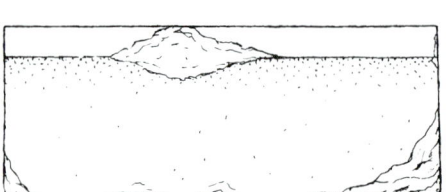

Fig. 23. Seat block no. 3. Drawing.

Fig. 21. Seat block no. 2. The front side.

Seat block no. 2. (fig. 21).
The maximum length is about 131.5 cm, but the left side is broken. The height is ca. 36 cm. The right short side is probably original, but has no remains of the anathyrosis and seems only to have been rather crudely worked with a pickaxe or something similar. Material and workmanship is otherwise very similar to seat block no. 1, and like this it has a recess along the back side. The width of the surface (excl. the recess) is 45-46 cm. The straight band along the front of the seat is ca. 7 cm in height and is not vertical but slopes inwards towards its upper edge, as do some of the others. It has remains of letters.

Fig. 22. Seat block no. 3. The front side.

Fig. 24. Seat block no. 3. Top side and back.

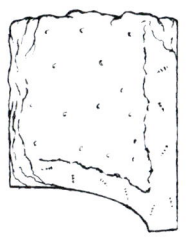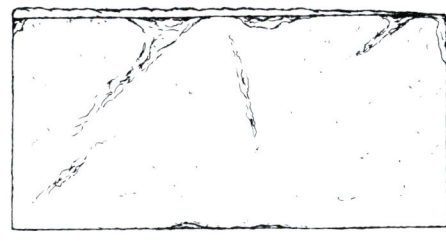

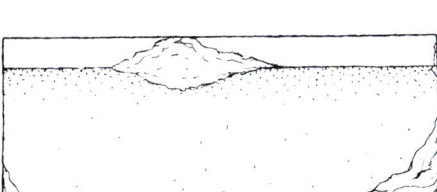

Fig. 23. Seat block no. 3. Drawing.

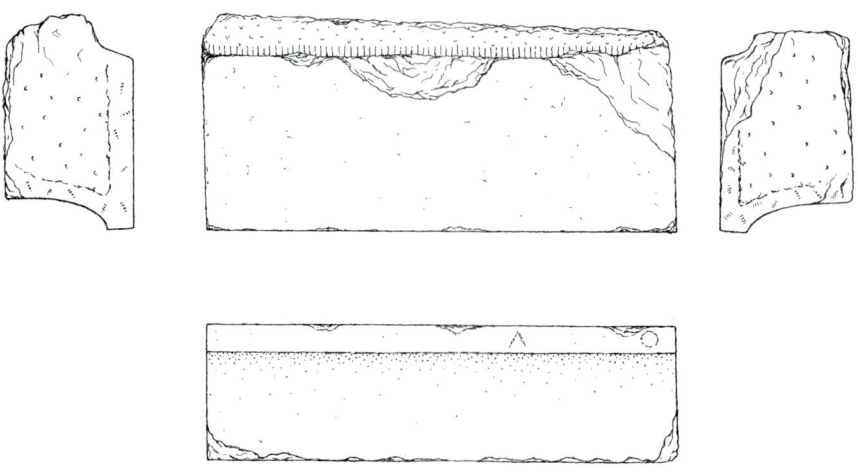

Fig. 18. Seat block no. 1. Drawing.

Seat block no.1. (figs. 17, 18, 19, 20).
This seat is preserved in its full length and has anathyrosis preserved on both shorter ends. The length of the block is 128.2 cm and the height 36.5 cm. The width is 46 cm from the front of the seat to the beginning of the recess. The frame of the anathyrosis has been treated with claw-chisel, while the centre has been worked roughly with a point or a pickaxe, which is quite normal. The right side of the block is not precisely at a right angle to the surface of the block, nor is it at an exact right angle to the front of the block. The upper side and the front of the seat have been finely worked with a point chisel. A narrow, almost vertical band about 7 cm in height runs along the upper edge of the front. Is has remains of an inscription. The back of the block is mostly hammer-dressed, but it has a neatly cut recess running along the entire length of the block. As seen on figs. 13 and 15, the purpose of the recess was no doubt to make room for stone slabs that formed an extension of the surface of the seat and constituted the foundation for the next row of seats. The limestone of seat block no. 1 has a light pink-grey tint similar to that of seat block no. 2, and it also seems very similar to block no. 4.

Fig. 19. Seat block no. 1. Back showing recess for neighbouring slab.

Fig. 20. Seat block no. 1. Short side with typical anathyrosis.

8   I am grateful to prof. Kristian Jeppesen for making a new sketch drawing of this stone, after my own drawing was lost. The drawing presented here was based on Jeppesens drawing and my own notes and photos.
9   The dimensions of seat block nos. 6 and 7 were kindly taken by Sisse Hansen and Helle Strehle.
10 *Teatri Classici in Asia Minore*. Vol. 4. *Deduzioni e proposte*. Roma 1974, pp. 106 ff.
11 Welch 1998 554f.
12 On the stadia in Asia Minor in general and with references, see Welch 1998 547-569.
13 Or we may have an abbreviation (*ipp.*?) followed by *anetheken*?
14 *SEG* 50, no. 428. Themelis 2000, 65. No photo nor drawing. Themelis tentatively identifies the dedicator with the person of the same name who together with his wife raised dedicated a statue of his daughter to Artemis, *SEG* 31, 221.
15 Petrakos 1997 nr. 439.
16 Haussoullier, *BCH* 4, 1880, 404, no. 16, McCabe Halikarnassos nr. 51. No doubt the present Türkkuyusu quarter of Bodrum.

None of the other names on the list can be identified as yet. The name Theudobidas is seemingly a *hapax*.

The Philokles mentioned in the list as father of Apollodoros might be the Philokles on the seats of the stadion.

Bibliography

Bean and Cook 1955: G.E. Bean and J.M. Cook, The Halicarnassus Peninsula. *ABSA* 50, 1955, 85-169.

Haussoullier 1880: B. Haussoullier, Inscriptions d'Halicarnasse (1), *BCH* 4, 1880, 395-408.

Isager 2004: S. Isager, Halikarnassos and the Ptolemies I – Inscriptions on public buildings. In: *HalStud* IV, 2004, 133-144.

McCabe 1996: D. McCabe, Bibliography and texts of the inscriptions of Karia, accessible via *Packard Humanities Institute Greek Documentary Texts*, CD Rom 7, 1996.

Newton 1862: C.T. Newton, *A History of Discoveries at Halicarnassus, Cnidus and Branchidae*, London 1862.

Pedersen 1988: P. Pedersen, Two Ionic buildings in Halikarnassos. *Araştirma Sonuçlari Toplantisi* V, 359-368, Ankara 1988.

Pedersen 2004: P. Pedersen, Halikarnassos and the Ptolemies II. The Architecture of Hellenistic Halikarnassos, In: *HalStud* IV 2004, 145-164.

Petrakos 1997: B.Ch. Petrakos, Οἱ ἐπιγραφὲς τοῦ Ὠρωποῦ, Athens 1997.

Spratt 1856: T. Spratt, On Halicarnassus. In: *Transactions of the Royal Society of Literature* V, 1856, 1-23.

Themelis 2001: P. Themelis, *EAH* 2000, 58-70.

Welch 1998: K. Welch, The Stadium at Aphrodisias. In: *AJA* 102, 1998, 547-569.

Notes

1. The first observations in 1977 and 1978 were made by Poul Pedersen together with Ali Uçarer, who was later employed at Bodrum Museum. The excavations of 1987 were directed by Bahadir Berkaya from Bodrum Museum of Underwater Archaeology. The excavations were visited by Poul Pedersen and by Frederick van Doorninck, who made squeezes of some of the inscriptions on the seats of the stadion at that time. Prof. van Doorninck's squeezes have been fundamental for Signe Isager's work on the inscriptions in the stadion.

   Of the illustrations, fig. 1 is from Newton 1862 Pl. I. Fig. 2 is from Spratt 1856. Figs. 3-13 and 17, 19-22, 24, 25, 28, 29 and 33 are by P. Pedersen. Fig. 14 is redrawn by P. Pedersen after the original plan by B. Berkaya. Fig. 15 and 32 are by B. Berkaya, and 16, 30 and 31 are by H. Strehle. Figs. 18, 23, 26, 27 are by P. Pedersen. We are grateful to Kristian and Lotte Jeppesen for doing a measured sketch drawing of block no. 4 and for making additional squeezes of no 6 and 7. We thank Sisse Hansen and Helle Strehle for additional descriptions and measurements of the stadium seats, which are now in Bodrum Museum in the Castle.

2. Newton, 1862 Pl. I. Also to be seen on the map in Spratt 1856, of which a section is illustrated on our fig. 2. Spratt's map of Halikarnassos was made before Newton had determined the location of the Maussolleion, and Spratt thought it should be placed in the Türkkuyusu quarter as indicated on his map. He also indicates the entire outline of the large church of Hagia Marina, of which the apse and a few more traces may be still be seen in situ today.

3. For the Sanctuary of Mars: Newton 1862 265 ff. P. Pedersen, "Two Ionic Buildings in Halikarnassos" in: Arastirma Sonuclari Toplantisi. Ankara 1988 359-368.

4. Discussion by Bean and Cook 1955 89f and 93f.

5. A discussion relating to the buildings in this area can be found in S. Isager, Halikarnassos and the Ptolemies I – Inscriptions on public buildings. In: *HalStud* IV 2004 133-144 and P. Pedersen, Halikarnassos and the Ptolemies II. The Architecture of Hellenistic Halikarnassos, In: *HalStud* IV 2004 145-164.

6. Welch 1998 551ff.

7. Welch 1998 547-569. For the details on the dimensions and shape of the seats we will have to await the final publication, but according to Figs. 5 and 12, the seats seem to be very similar to those from the Halikarnassos stadion.

The interval between letters, measured from middle to middle of the letters, is 17 cm.

Text:

N K A I

]N καὶ

Apart from the word-division there is little to say. The last three letters may be a word in itself or it may be the beginning of a longer word which continues on the following block.

No. 7

The left part of the face of the stone is totally ruined, but the right half has three letters, the space between them being 15,5 cm, measured from middle to middle of the letters. There are probably traces of another letter 15,5 cm after the last sigma, but it is not possible to guess its identity.

Text:

]Σ Ι Σ [.

Dedicatory inscriptions?

The inscriptions on 1 and 8-13 clearly belong to one series, the same inscription repeated on each of three rows, probably placed one above the other. As to the rest of the inscriptions, we do not know if they belong to the same series.

If so, nos. 4 and 5 would form the (identical) end of two of the inscriptions, the lion's paw marking the end of a row, and the inscriptions might be considered dedicatory. No. 3 might fit in the text. I have found no obvious suggestions for the restoration of nos. 2, 6, and 7, which may or may not belong to the same series.

A plausible suggestion seems to be that a gift is recorded as being addressed to the people of Halikarnassos (probably preceded by one or more gods).

It may have been something like this:

Φιλοκλῆς Ἀπολλοδώρου γυμνασιαρχήσας Ἑρμεῖ καὶ Ἡρακλεῖ καὶ τῶ Δήμωι

A parallel might be the newly announced dedicatory inscription found in the stadion of Messene:

Θιώτας Φιλίνου γυμνασιαρχήσας θεοῖς πᾶσι καὶ τᾶι πόλει

The Messenian inscription was cut in large letters into the narrow front face of the blocks that crown the lower diazoma of the stadion. The inscription is dated to the first century BC.[14]

What would the dedication by Philokles consist of? It may have been all the seats of the stadion, or a part of them, perhaps the seats covered by the inscriptions. For a parallel to a repeating of the same dedicatory text, compare the seats in the theatre of the Amphiareion at Oropos, also dated to the first century BC.[15]

Philokles, son of Apollodoros

Philokles, son of Apollodoros, is not known for certain in other connections, but we do have an Apollodoros, son of Philokles on the fragment of a Halikarnassian, undated, list of names, copied by Haussoullier in the house of Kaiali Achmet, behind the Turkish mosche Turk Kouou si.[16]

[-]Α[-]Ο[-]
[Με]νεκράτης Μενεκράτου
[Ἀπο]λλόδωρος Φιλοκλέους
[Ἀρτε]μίδωρος Θευδωβίδα
[-]δωρος Βασιλείδου

We have not seen the stone or any copy of it. As far as can be judged from the printed letters in *BCH*, there need not be a chronological gap between our texts. Unfortunately, no *pi* occurs in the preserved part of the list.

```
| 8   | 9         | 10                |
| Ι Λ | Ο Κ Λ Η Σ Α | Π Ο Λ Λ Ο Δ Ω Ρ Ο Υ |
```
```
            | 1                |
            | Σ Α Π Ο Λ Λ Ο    |
```
```
| 11    | 12        | 13              |
| Φ Ι Λ | Ο Κ Λ Η Σ Α | Π Ο Λ Λ Ο Δ Ω Ρ |
```

Nos. 8-10   Φ]ιλοκλῆς Ἀπολλοδώρου

No. 1   Φιλοκλῆ]ς Ἀπολλο[δώρου

Nos. 11-13   Φιλοκλῆς Ἀπολλοδώρ[ου

No. 2

It is natural to suppose that the inscription on block no. 2 should be part of a continuation of one of the above inscriptions. Unfortunately, the inscribed surface is effaced to a great extent.

Text:

.]Π Π Α Ν[

It is not obvious how the text fits in. Many personal names, both male and female, end in –ippa, (e.g. Agrippa, Philippa), but we may also have the genitive of a personal name ending in -ppas. *Ny* may be the first letter in the next word.[13]

No. 3

The front of the block is partly damaged, and the remaining letters are only just discernable

Text:

Α [- -] Α Κ

The whole text of the block may have read, e.g.:

Α [Ι Η Ρ] Α Κ
κ]α[ὶ Ἡρ]ακ[λεῖ

No. 4

This is a short block ending in a lion's paw. There are only two letters on the stone.

Text:

Ω Ι

A comparison with the inscription on block 5 makes it likely that the inscription is dedicatory and that the foregoing block ended in ΔΗΜ.

δήμ]ωι

No. 5

The stone has a lion's paw at one end and in general it is heavily battered. Especially the top is badly preserved, partly because the block has been reworked sometime to function as a drinking trough for animals.

Intervals between letters, measured from middle to middle of the letters, read from left to right: 20 cm, 15½ cm, 17 cm, 17 cm. All letters are discernable. I found no trace of an iota after the first omega.

Text:

Ω Δ Η Μ Ω Ι

τ]ῶ δήμωι

No. 6

While the narrow strip preserved on the left part of the stone has no trace of letters, the right half of the face is not too damaged, and four letters are discernable.

Alpha: The crossbar is broken.
Eta and *my*: The verticals are slightly curved.
Pi: The left vertical curves slightly; the right vertical does not reach the bottom of the letter space. It is difficult from the stones to judge if the horizontal extends beyond the verticals or just forms a continuation of the initial vertical. The squeezed *pi*'s of no. 9 and no. 13, on the other hand, show the initial vertical extending slightly beyond the horizontal in one case only, while the horizontal in both cases extends beyond the second vertical and ends in a rather sharp, downward bend.
Omega: The rounded part is circular, but not quite closed. It has deep cut but not very long seriphs.

Seat block no. 1
Intervals between letters, measured from middle to middle of the letters and read from left to right: 19 cm, 17½ cm, 19 cm, 17½ cm, 17½ cm, 17½ cm.

Text:

Σ Α Π Ο Λ Λ Ο

The text obviously started on the blocks of seats to the left of this block and continued on the seat to the right. It seemed a priori likely that we have here a donor's name or rather the name of a donor's father. A comparison with the inscriptions on seat blocks nos. 8-13 makes it possible to supplement the text on seat block no. 1.

Prof. van Doorninck made squeezes of each letter separately on these blocks and secured the correct sequence by numbering each squeeze. The squeezes of blocks nos. 8 – 13, thus show the following distribution of letters.

No. 8
Ι Λ

No. 9
Ο Κ Λ Η Σ Α Π

Fig. 33. Omega and iota on seat block no. 4.

No. 10
Ο Λ Λ Ο Δ Ω Ρ Ο Υ

No. 11
Φ Ι Λ

No. 12
Ο Κ Λ Η Σ Α

No. 13
Π Ο Λ Λ Ο Δ Ω Ρ

Van Doorninck's careful registration indicates that the inscriptions he squeezed ran as a one-line inscription on each of two rows of seats. The squeezes make clear that each inscription began with the name Philokles. Without hesitation, we can supplement that for inscription nr. 1. But neither the stone nor the squeezes allow us to determine how long each inscription was and how it ended. Inscription no. 1 was probably placed on another row of seats, and the distribution might have been, but need not, of course, have been as illustrated below:

Fig. 32. Seats of the stadion photographed in 1987. This is presumably the section from which the squeezes discussed in the article were taken.

sector in the theatron was finished with lion paws as was also the case in the stadion at Halikarnassos. There are numerous examples of this in Western Asia Minor, but often the construction phases in which these were introduced are not precisely dated. The stadion at Aphrodisias seems to have many similarities with the stadion at Halikarnassos. Based on stylistic and historical criteria K. Welch has recently dated the Aphrodisias stadion to the first century AD.[11] While the inscriptions on the seats in Aphrodisias are believed to be secondary, – mostly of High Imperial times or even Late Antiquity – the inscriptions in Halikarnassos are probably from the time of construction as they seem to give the name of the donors.

In the opinion of S. Isager the letter forms would not contradict a dating early in this period, while the general impression of the rough workmanship and not very precise technical finish is not what one usually associates with the Julio-Claudian period, but rather with a later part of this period.[12] So until more secure evidence turns up one might venture to suggest late first or early second century AD for the Stadion at Halikarnassos.

It may be regretted that the stadion of Halikarnassos has been found and is probably in a reasonably good condition, but cannot be excavated and exhibited to visitors and the citizens of Bodrum. However, it may be some comfort to know that the ruins of the stadion remain well-protected in their present state. It will then be up to future citizens of Bodrum to decide when to unveil this large monument.

Modern Bodrum is in many ways connected to its past. The main thoroughfare, Turgut Reis Caddesi, runs precisely above the main street of ancient Halikarnassos. Now we also know that by a strange coincidence the modern football stadium has been placed just next to the ancient stadion where the Halikarnassians enthusiastically watched sporting events two millennia ago.

Inscriptions on the seats of the stadion at Halikarnassos

The seven blocks of seats (nos. 1-7, described above) that formed part of the stadion and are now on exhibition in the Castle of Bodrum all have a one-line inscription running as a band on the narrow face of the seat proper, the inscription thus facing the stadion.

To this material in stone we are fortunately able to add the text of the inscriptions on six other blocks of seats (nos. 8-13), now covered by modern structures placed over the ancient stadion (fig. 32). Professor Frederick van Doorninck Jr. has kindly entrusted to us the squeezes which he made of those inscriptions before the blocks of seats were overbuilt.

Letters

It is not given a priori that the seats were all inscribed at the same time. On the other hand, the letters have some common features, such as height and, to some extent, distance between the letters, and they will be described together.
The letter height is about 5cm.
The letters are generally worn and not easily discernable. Only the *omega*s are so deep-cut that they still stand out clearly (fig. 33). The squeezes of nos. 8-13 help to determine some questions of doubt.

band above the cavetto profile of the front is presently 6 – 6.2 cm high and has traces of inscribed letters. The transition from the band to the cavetto profile is less distinct than in the other seats, and therefore the entire profile of the front of the seat appears almost like a cymation profile. The lion paw on the right side of the front is very similar to that of seat no. 4 and the right hand side of the stone shows the same very rough workmanship as no. 4, so in spite of the differences in dimensions there is no reason to doubt that the provenience is the stadion. The left side of the stone is flat and although it does not have a distinct anathyrosis, it was clearly prepared to meet a neighbouring seat block on this side. The back of the stone, however, is only roughly hammer-dressed and was not prepared to join another block. The material from which seat no. 5 was made is a dark bluish limestone, very much like that of seat no. 3. As the measurements also correspond quite well to those of no. 3, it may be assumed that no. 3 and no. 5 belong to another building phase or another section of the stadion than do the other 5 stone seats in the Castle.

The top side has a large, secondary, rectangular cutting that forms a basin of ca. 48 x 91 x 52 x 92 cm. From the bottom of the basin there is an outlet carried through to the front side of the stone where it is provided with a small iron pipe.

Seat block no. 6 (fig. 30).[9]
Block no. 6 and 7 are very similar in material and dimension to nos. 1, 2 and 4. The length of no. 6 is ca. 112 cm and the height 36 cm. The height of the band above the cavetto profile on the front is 7 cm. It slopes slightly inwards and has remains of letters. On the back it has a recess like seat no. 1 to secure a tight joint to an additional slab behind the seat, and the back is roughly worked below this. The width of the top of the seat exclusive of the recess was measured to ca. 51.5 cm.

Seat block no 7 (fig. 31).
The width of this seat, which is very similar to no. 6, is ca. 86.5 cm. Its height was measured to ca. 37 cm, and the width of the top of the seat exclusive of the recess on the back is ca. 45 cm. The narrow band on the front slopes inwards towards the top as in seat no. 6 and is likewise 7 cm in height and has remains of letters.

No finds have been made that can suggest an exact date for the construction of the stone auditorium of the Halikarnassos stadion. The dating must therefore depend on a comparison with other and more precisely dated stadia. However, for such a procedure the evidence from Halikarnassos is still insufficient, and a tentative dating must at present rest on a general evaluation of the type of seats, the workmanship, and the inscriptions. In "Teatri Classici in Asia Minore" it is assumed that the seats of the theatron receive a more elegant form in the so-called period of transition more or less corresponding to the first century BC and the first century AD.[10] In this period monolithic seat blocks became normal, and the outermost seat of each

Fig. 30. Seat block no. 6.

Fig. 31. Seat block no. 7.

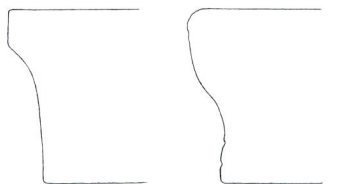

Fig. 27. Seat block no. 4. Section showing normal profile and profile through lion paw.

Fig. 28. Seat block no. 4. Right hand side, originally flanking a flight of stairs.

along a flight of stairs. As can be seen on fig. 15, blocks of very large dimensions were regularly chosen for the seats along the stairs, probably to secure a greater stability in the structure. The left side of the block has a well-preserved anathyrosis band along the top (4 cm wide) and front (ca. 7 cm wide). The right side (fig. 28), however, is very roughly dressed except for a smooth area on its right part, perhaps for a step of the stair or some other additional stone. As this side was exposed to full view for people walking on the staircase, it may surprise that it was so roughly worked, but this seems to have been the case for all seats flanking the staircases, as could be seen on seats preserved in situ.

The front of the seat has the usual cavetto profile finished upwards by a smooth band ca 7.4 cm in height. On the band two letters have been engraved, and they are very well preserved. The right side of the front has a sculptural rendering of a slightly protruding lion leg or lion paw. It is stylized and quite roughly executed. The good state of preservation of the surface shows that it was crudely carved probably with a blunt point chisel or even with a pickaxe without any use of finer tools. The upper right side of the lion paw is broken, but when viewed from the right side (fig. 28) it can be seen that the paw simply disappeared into the roughly worked side of the stone without much subtlety.

The top of seat block no. 4 is a regular, slightly worn surface, which was originally worked with a point chisel. There are no traces of a setting line or erosion line which could indicate where the seat block on top of this one was placed.

The back of the block is irregular and has only been roughly hammer-dressed. There is no anathyrosis on this side, which is probably an indication that no additional stones followed behind this one, and that the fill of the auditorium consisted of earth and rubble.

Seat block no. 5. (figs. 29, 10, 11).
Like no. 4 this block also has a lion paw on the right side of the front and therefore must have been placed against a flight of stairs in the stadion. It is clearly identical with the block that was photographed by Pedersen in 1977 and 1978 in front of a farm house (figs. 9, 10, 11). This block is heavily battered and worn from the time when it was reused as a drinking trough for animals, and it is difficult to determine its exact dimensions. The front is approximately 116 cm and the depth on the right side ca. 77.8 cm and on the left ca. 77 cm. The height was measured to just 35.2 cm, but it may have been slightly higher originally, as the upper side of the block is heavily worn. The

Fig. 29. Seat block no. 5.

Fig. 25. Seat block no. 4.

Seat block no. 3. (figs. 22, 23, 24).
The block is preserved in its full length of 92 cm and has anathyrosis preserved on both short sides. The band of the anathyrosis is only carefully executed along the top and the front of the stone as would be expected and as in all other seats that have remains of anathyrosis preserved. The short sides are not at exact right angles to the surface of the stone. The stone is different in several aspects from no. 1 and no. 2. It is only 35.5 cm high, and the surface is only 43.5 cm wide. It has no real recess on the back, but it does have a smooth band along the upper edge to secure a fine joint to a neighbouring slab on the back side. The narrow band along the upper edge of the front is only 6.2 – 6.4 cm in height and slopes a little inwards and upwards. It has faint traces of inscribed letters. The limestone of this seat is dark blue-grey like that of seat no. 5.

Seat block no. 4. (figs. 25, 26, 27, 28).
This is the best preserved block of all of the stadion blocks in the Castle.[8] All sides are preserved. The seat is ca. 71 cm long and 92.5 cm deep. The height is about 36.5 cm. The exceptional depth of this stone is no doubt to be explained by the fact that it was placed

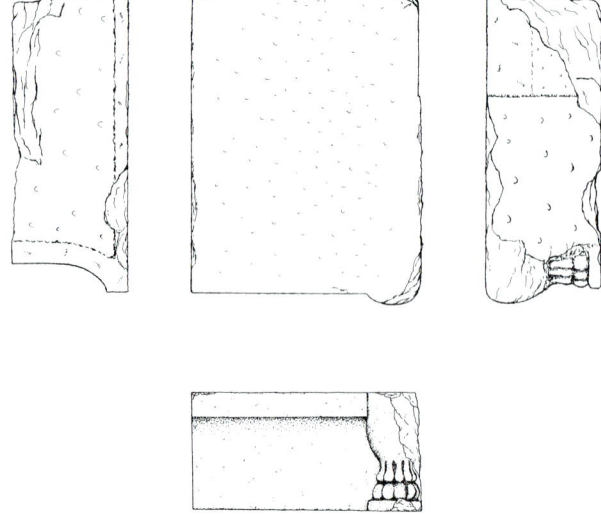

Fig. 26. Seat block no. 4. Drawing.